'With Gaza in ruins and its people bombed, starved, and displaced, accounting for Israel's genocidal campaign and its impact on Palestinians is an urgent necessity. In this accessible analytical narrative, Anne Irfan convincingly shows how the destruction condenses the confrontation between the long-term Israeli ambition to deport Gaza's Palestinian inhabitants – mostly descended from Nakba refugees – and their obdurate determination to remain in their homeland. *A Short History of the Gaza Strip* is a much-needed historical contextualisation.'

A. Dirk Moses, author of *The Problems of Genocide*

'An incredible, informative and powerful book. It tells us that you can't understand the current destruction of Gaza without going back to the beginning and then does exactly that, in such a readable and devastating way.'

Rachel Shabi, author of *Off-White: The Truth About Antisemitism*

A Short History
of the Gaza Strip

A Short History of the Gaza Strip

Anne Irfan

With a foreword by
Muhammad Shehada

**SIMON &
SCHUSTER**

London · New York · Amsterdam/Antwerp · Sydney/Melbourne · Toronto · New Delhi

First published in Great Britain by Simon & Schuster UK Ltd, 2025

1 3 5 7 9 10 8 6 4 2

Simon & Schuster UK Ltd
1st Floor
222 Gray's Inn Road
London WC1X 8HB

www.simonandschuster.co.uk
www.simonandschuster.com.au
www.simonandschuster.co.in

Simon & Schuster Australia, Sydney
Simon & Schuster India, New Delhi

The authorised representative in the EEA is Simon & Schuster
Netherlands BV, Herculesplein 96, 3584 AA Utrecht, Netherlands.
info@simonandschuster.nl

A CIP catalogue record for this book is available from the British Library

Hardback ISBN: 978-1-3985-3619-7
Trade Paperback ISBN: 978-1-3985-5290-6
eBook ISBN: 978-1-3985-3620-3

Typeset in Bembo Std by
Palimpsest Book Production Limited, Falkirk, Stirlingshire

Printed and Bound in India by Thomson Press India Ltd.

MIX
Paper | Supporting
responsible forestry
FSC
www.fsc.org
FSC® C010615

Contents

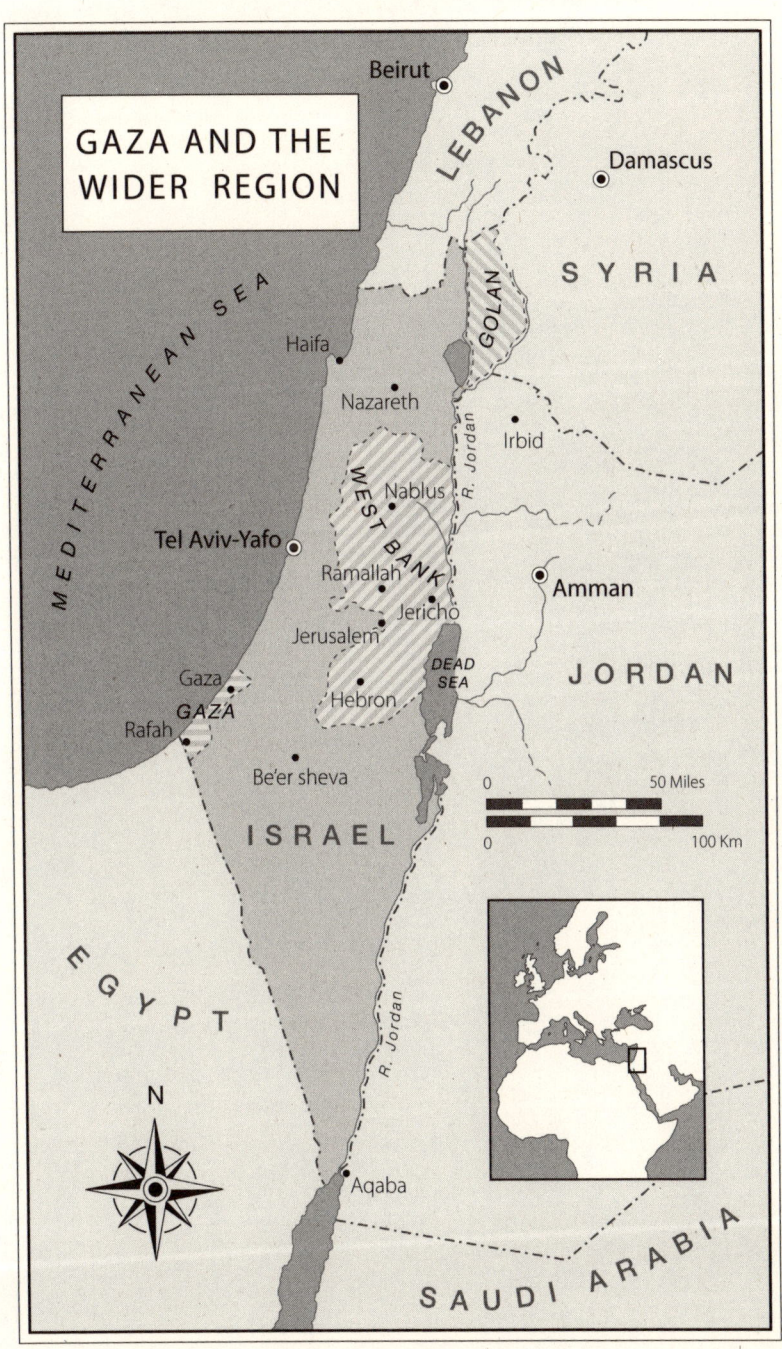

GAZA AND THE WIDER REGION

MEDITERRANEAN SEA

Beirut

LEBANON

Damascus

SYRIA

GOLAN

Haifa

Nazareth

R. Jordan

Irbid

WEST BANK

Nablus

Tel Aviv-Yafo

Ramallah

Amman

Jericho

Jerusalem

JORDAN

Gaza

DEAD SEA

GAZA

Rafah

Hebron

Be'er sheva

0   50 Miles

0   100 Km

ISRAEL

EGYPT

R. Jordan

N

Aqaba

SAUDI ARABIA

FOREWORD: GAZA'S HISTORY

by Muhammad Shehada

My first memory of Gaza is an airstrike. My second is an Israeli checkpoint. My third is of frequent demonstrations. And my fourth is of my overcrowded UNRWA school for Palestinian refugees. Gaza is a giant refugee camp; a 'huge concentration camp' as Israel's (then) national security chief, Giora Eiland, called it back in 2004. At the same time, it's a unique place of vivid culture, rich diversity and huge yet unattainable potentials – all reminders that its bleak present is purely man-made and was completely preventable. It's also an unbreakable fortress of rebellion, resistance and insurgency. And it is a place of many contradictions and paradoxes.

Growing up in Gaza, I lived through three wars, ten major Israeli military operations and two full ground invasions, all within less than two decades. But none of them came anywhere near the genocide of 2023–25 in terms of magnitude, severity and sheer brutality. 'There is a thick stench of death, of rotting corpses and gunpowder, enveloping all of Gaza,' a friend who visited the besieged enclave in February 2025 told me. 'It's everywhere. It's all over.' He compared it directly to the 2003 Darfur genocide, which he had also experienced.

There are two questions Gazans have usually asked each other since the start of this campaign of unrelenting and systematic

1

destruction, starvation, displacement and mass killing. The first is, 'How many family members have you lost?' The answer is always in the dozens, no matter who you ask. I personally stopped counting by February 2024. I couldn't bear it after Israel killed thirty-four of my relatives. But every time I opened my social media apps, there were new pictures of relatives, colleagues, loved ones, neighbours and friends in grey, relegated to the past tense from 'is' to 'was'.

The second question is, 'Is your home still standing?' Virtually every single person I know has had their home bombed, burned down, bulldozed or damaged to the point of becoming un-inhabitable. Israel wiped out entire cities with nothing left but an abundance of rubble mixed with thousands of corpses stuck underneath. Watching from outside Gaza, I stood paralysed and powerless the entire time the genocide was unfolding. I didn't dare tell any loved ones to 'stay safe', because I couldn't provide any advice whatsoever on what they could do to increase their chances of survival. 'Seek shelter at a UN school', 'go to a hospital', 'stay near journalists', 'stay near international organisa-tions' . . . any advice that would have previously been helpful now became a trap as Israel went on to destroy the vast majority of UN schools and hospitals and directly slaughter the highest number of journalists and humanitarian workers ever recorded within such a short space of time.

Even in our darkest imaginations, no one could have conceived of Gaza's streets littered with the decomposing bodies and skele-tal remains of our loved ones; that stray dogs and cats would be filmed feasting on those bodies; that Israeli soldiers would confess to driving their tanks over hundreds of living and dead humans and crushing them into mush; that parents would scour the streets looking for hacked pieces of human flesh to put randomly in plastic bags and consider each 10–20 kilos a child;

that thousands of kidnapped Palestinians in Israeli 'torture camps' would be systematically and routinely beaten, raped, forced to perform sexual acts on each other, forced to drink from toilets, starved to near death, blindfolded and chained 24/7 in crowded cages whose air is filled with the 'putrid stench' of 'neglected wounds left to rot' and amputated limbs, that the perpetrators would document and brag about their atrocities every minute of the day; and that the world would watch all this livestreamed and yet allow it to continue unconstrained.

How, then, is one to understand this total war? How far back into history does one need to go to judge these actions? Is it sufficient to look at the atrocities committed on 7 October 2023? What led to that fateful day unfolding? Does one need to go back to 2007, when Israel officially imposed its siege on Gaza? Or to Hamas' violent takeover of Gaza right before that? What about the group winning a democratic election in 2006? Israel's 2005 unilateral 'disengagement' from Gaza? The second intifada? The 1993 Oslo 'peace process'? Israel's closure and separation policy in Gaza since 1991? The first intifada? The 1973 war? The 1967 war? The 1956 war? The 1948 Nakba? The 1947 partition plan? The 1917 Balfour Declaration? Or even further? And why does virtually every Palestinian have those dates memorised by heart? What terrible significance do they hold?

In *A Short History of the Gaza Strip*, Anne Irfan answers these questions brilliantly, compellingly and succinctly. Drawing on more than a decade of academic research, as well as her rich personal heritage and wide network of expert friends and colleagues in Palestine, Israel and the wider Middle East, she takes the reader on a vital journey through six critical episodes in the history of the Gaza Strip. By learning this history, the reader can acquire sufficient knowledge and intellectual self-defence to make up their mind and educate others about this incredibly sensitive topic, which is so often clouded by a swamp of propaganda and bad faith arguments.

Irfan eloquently presents a damning and timely analysis of Israel's consistent view of Gaza as a demographic threat to be settled – a point of crucial importance at this moment when much of the enclave has been annihilated and Israel and the US are openly pushing to 'empty it out' completely. This book shows how such ideas are nothing new, but rather go back to at least the 1950s, having been repeated scores of times over the years. Irfan does a remarkable job of presenting a historical arc that connects the dots between seemingly discrete events. Even as a Gazan myself, and having spent my entire career documenting life and death in Gaza as a journalist and researcher, this book helped me put some things into perspective and make sense of my own past and present.

More than that, Irfan's book personalises Gaza's dense history through the stories of several protagonists whose lives epitomise the modern experience of this small, defiant piece of land. In these stories, we see another important theme: that Gaza has not only been a place of war, violence and destruction, but also of culture, creativity and hope. As the history shows us, it is a site of the contradictions that characterise the human experience.

Growing up, my parents never needed to explain the occupation to me. In fact, they actively tried to hide it from me, to shield me from its toxicity, to give me a sense of normal life. They told me it was thunder the first time I heard an airstrike. The strewn rubble and burned furniture I saw all over the street the next morning were self-explanatory.

I became politically aware at a very early age as we travelled back and forth between Gaza and Egypt. My late father tried to maintain that routine to renew our Egyptian residency permits annually out of fear Israel would expel us from our home again one day. In the original Nakba of 1948, they had forcibly uprooted his father from the land he had just bought a couple of miles to the east of the Gaza Strip, and wiped out his entire village.

In Gaza's Shati refugee camp, my grandfather built a modest shack, brick by brick, on the spot where his tent was erected. He planted a fig tree to remind him of his hometown. UNRWA's schooling system crucially contributed to my father becoming a genius doctor whose memory instills pride in me, after Israel made him a barefoot child refugee running around a camp in worn-out rags.

But just as my father and his family tried to breathe a sigh of relief and rebuild a fraction of their ruptured lives, Israel kicked them out again in 1967, this time to Egypt. They were allowed back in 1994 with the Oslo Accords – but the 1990s 'peace process' didn't assuage my father's fear of another expulsion. 'They will do it to us again one day,' my dad often said. And he was right. That's why I remember those dates, and why every Palestinian does as well. They are not just national milestones, but as Irfan elaborates, they are intimately personal and traumatic to each of us.

In 1995, the *New York Times* reported that Palestinians in Gaza were calling the Strip an 'open-air prison'. Every time we tried to travel, we had to sign up months in advance. Israel opened and closed Gaza's borders with Egypt arbitrarily and without warning. We would only learn about our time of departure the night before, rushing to pack then squeezing into an overcrowded car the next day. Sand dunes, ruined streets marked by the tracks of IDF tanks, destruction, bullets . . . a vivid picture was forming in my head of the stark difference between the openness of a cosmopolitan Cairo and the militarisation and entrapment of an isolated Gaza.

Sometimes, we'd reach the Rafah crossing only to find out Israel had shut it again at the last minute, as collective punishment for something Hamas had done elsewhere or for pure political pressure. Sometimes, we'd stay with relatives in Rafah because we didn't want to risk crossing the checkpoint back into Gaza City and having to wait for days there again. Other times it was clear that it would take a while for the crossing to reopen and we'd go back home and wait for a phone call.

Up until 2005, the crossing was divided into three areas: a Palestinian room, an Israeli hall and an Egyptian hall. To get from the Palestinian building to the Israeli building, we had to cram into an orange taxi that carried us the few dozen metres between them (because Israel dictated we could not walk). Many times, we'd sit in that taxi for hours waiting for Israel to let us in. Once on the Israeli side, we were ordered not to open the windows and to leave the car only through the right-hand doors.

One of the first Israeli soldiers I remember encountering was a soldier at the Abu Holi checkpoint set up in 2001 as punishment for the second intifada. It was named after the owner of the farmland Israel had confiscated to build the barrier on. I never saw the soldier's face, because he sat in a watchtower manning the checkpoint that Israel arbitrarily closed most of the time. I couldn't see the whole watchtower either; I glimpsed parts of it as we sat in the car in an endless queue of vehicles under the boiling sun for hours, waiting to make a journey that would otherwise have taken thirty minutes. No one, not even animals, were allowed to cross on foot. Donkeys were stuffed in cars' back seats. 'Don't open any doors or windows,' my mother would say, as we suffocated in the heat, afraid that the soldier would shoot us, as happened to many.

At Rafah, we were herded like cattle through crammed corridors at the Israeli-controlled side of the border. There, I could see clearly what the soldiers looked like. Their smirks, their sunglasses, hostile demeanour and the big rifles they pointed at us have been etched in my mind ever since, along with the piercing noise of them yelling and cursing condescendingly in broken Arabic. So has the panicked and powerless look in my parents' eyes as soldiers seized my eldest brother from the queue and sent him back to Gaza only because he had turned sixteen. It taught me a lot.

Yet I learned more in 2007. We were stuck in Egypt on a medical trip when Hamas took over Gaza and Israel shut down all the enclave's borders. After Egyptian intervention, a rare exception was made, and we and other stuck Gazans were allowed to return through a different and unusual route: the al-Ouga commercial crossing (Nitzana) between Israel and Egypt. It was instantly clear that the young Israeli soldiers there had never met a Palestinian or been to the occupied territory. They were different from their peers at Rafah; relatively polite, calmer, they brought us food and water, and provided a wheel-chair for an old woman who travelled with us in the shuttle bus. The occupation, this wretched apartheid system, dehuman-ises us both; it corrupts the souls of the oppressors as much as it ruins the lives of the oppressed.

After that, aside from one short medical trip in 2010, we couldn't travel to Egypt for a decade; Israel's siege was tightened, and we were locked up in a permanent state of non-life. Israel was at best allowing the luckiest of us to keep our 'heads above the water, but nothing more than that' as their defence minister put it in 2018.

In his last days, my dying father longed for figs and other fruit, but thyme and duqqa were the only foods available in abundance under siege. For 'security reasons', Israel had even banned the import of pasta, as Irfan describes later in the book.

I went door to door searching for fruit but found nothing. Defeated, I could not bear to bring myself back home that night until I was sure my father was asleep.

New phrases were added to my dictionary. 'Hot Winter', 'Cast Lead', 'Pillar of Defence', 'Protective Edge', 'Closed Garden', 'Black Belt', 'Guardians of the Walls', 'Breaking Dawn' . . . Those were the names of Israeli 'military operations' that punctuated the endless suffocation imposed on us. They were periodic massacres and killing sprees that Israel would describe as 'mowing the lawn'. The average young Gazan measures his age by how many of those wars we survived.

The term 'slow death', however, was the most chronic. I heard it every single day. It resonated even more deeply as I took my first steps into adulthood and found that most people around me had no hope of any meaningful future. Most Gazans who had come of age or graduated from university in 2006 when Israel's blockade was imposed were in 2023 reaching the second half of their thirties without ever having had a job, despite their impressive educational achievements. They couldn't afford to fall in love and start a family, because they couldn't afford to put food on the table or move out of their parents' homes.

Ali, my childhood friend, was one of the smartest people I've ever known. You could have a conversation with him about any topic at all and be impressed by his deep knowledge: EU migration policies, Russia–Ukraine, China–Taiwan, domestic US politics, economic history, climate change, Noam Chomsky, Jordan Peterson . . . We used to talk almost every day; even when I was outside Gaza, I'd call him when his electricity was on.

We would fume, laugh, discuss life, memories, movies, sports and politics. Every time Ali and I talked over the phone, I could always hear a buzzing noise lurking in the background throughout our conversations. It came from the Israeli predator and surveillance drones that have hovered above Gazans' heads 24/7 since the start of the siege. They are equipped with rockets to shoot to kill at any second. Their noise got loudest at night when the city became quiet.

Ali studied hard, applied for countless jobs and scholarships for a decade, freelanced intermittently, volunteered . . . but he never got a break. Despite his brilliance and intellect, he was prevented from having a full life by being born on the wrong side of Israel's separation fence. There wasn't much for him to do in Gaza except count days, months and years.

Every day brought Ali shame and burning rage: when he crawled out of bed and left his room to eat a breakfast meal with his family that he didn't contribute to; when he asked for pocket money from his parents to buy snacks, clothes or get a haircut; when he went for a walk in the neighbourhood with his head bowed in embarrassment and devastation. He hated his birthdays, because each one reminded him that his life was wasting before his eyes.

Ali was killed by Israel in January 2024 at the gate of al-Aqsa hospital in Deir al-Balah, and my world has been in ruins since. I have had no one to mourn him with, because he never had the chance to be known – to work with colleagues or make new friends, to gain a name for himself as a journalist or leave any kind of footprint outside of his immediate family. The toughest thing about his death is that, like most young Gazans, Ali never got the opportunity to experience living, despite how hard he tried every single day.

March 2025

Author's Note

This book tells the history of the Gaza Strip from 1948 to the 2020s, based on my time researching and teaching Palestinian history over the last decade. It does not seek to speak for Palestinians in and from Gaza, whose own accounts provide insights and perspectives that an outsider could never convey. Many Palestinians in and from Gaza have published memoirs and testimonies about their lives in the Strip, some of which are listed at the end of this book (page 208) and all of which I encourage you to read.

NOTE ON TERMINOLOGY

In geographical terms, 'Gaza' can have two meanings. Gaza City is an ancient coastal city on the eastern Mediterranean, which also gave its name to a large geographical district in the British Mandate of Palestine. In 1948, the state of Israel was established by military force on 78 per cent of Mandate Palestine. It claimed the majority of the Gaza district, leaving just 141 square miles as the newly formed Gaza Strip, whose boundaries were determined by an armistice agreement between Israel and Egypt. In this book, which focuses on post-1948 history, I generally use the term 'Gaza' to refer to the Strip.

The majority of Palestinians living in Gaza today are refugees who were expelled and displaced across the country in 1948. As such, they are Palestinians from Gaza, but not Gazan in terms of their heritage. In view of this, I only use the term 'Gazan' in this book to refer to geographical sites, or to people living in Gaza before 1948. Otherwise, I speak of Palestinians in Gaza.

Introduction

Why Gaza Matters

On Saturday 5 December 1998, forty-eight passengers boarded a plane at the newly built international airport in the Gaza Strip. As the first commercial flight to take off from the airport, it was loaded with symbolism. Captain Jamal al-How, a Palestinian from Jabalia refugee camp in Gaza, proclaimed it a 'historic moment' as he piloted the Palestinian Airlines plane to Queen Alia International Airport in Amman, Jordan. Less than a fortnight later, US President Bill Clinton and First Lady Hillary Clinton flew into Gaza to formally inaugurate the new airport alongside Palestinian President Yasser Arafat and his wife Suha.

Over the following year, around 100,000 Palestinians passed through the gleaming terminal of Gaza's new airport, boarding flights operated by Palestinian Airlines, EgyptAir, Royal Jordanian and Royal Air Maroc. Among them was Sahbaa al-Barbari, a lifelong Palestinian activist who had been born in Gaza in 1932. Describing her trip, she remarked, 'I travelled with Palestinian Airlines in a Palestinian plane flown by a Palestinian pilot with a Palestinian ticket to the United Arab Emirates! It was the happiest trip of my life. It was a wonderful feeling.'[1] Like many, she hoped that the airport would signal a new era of Palestinian freedom, directly connecting Palestine to the wider world and enabling its people to leave and return freely.

Such hopes proved short-lived. Throughout its operations, Gaza International Airport remained under Israeli control. Palestinians were required to report all take-offs and landings to Israeli officials, who also oversaw passport control, security and flight routes. Then, in October 2000, Israel shut down the airport as part of its suppression of the second *intifada* (Palestinian uprising). In December 2001 – three years after Jamal al-How had piloted that first commercial flight – Israel bombed the airport, making it inoperable. Since then, there have been no more commercial flights in or out of Gaza. Further bombardments between 2006 and 2014 left the airport in ruins.

Accounts of flying directly into Gaza on commercial planes are a far cry from today's reality. In recent years, Gaza has become synonymous with isolation and inaccessibility, not to mention intensive violence and suffering. Since October 2023, the Palestinians of Gaza have endured one of the most brutal military onslaughts in modern history, launched in response to the Hamas-led attacks of 7 October that killed nearly 1,200 Israelis, wounded more than 5,400 and took 251 captive.[2] By the time a short-lived ceasefire came into force in January 2025, Israeli forces had killed more than 47,000 Palestinians in Gaza; scientific researchers argue that the true figure may be in excess of 186,000 if adjusted to include indirect deaths from war-induced malnutrition and disease.[3] Just two months later, Israel broke the ceasefire and resumed its intensive bombing of Gaza, meaning that at the time of writing in late March 2025 the death toll is again rising rapidly.

Israel's onslaught on Gaza has left much of the Strip unfit for human life. By the time of the January 2025 ceasefire, 92 per cent of homes in Gaza had been damaged or destroyed, and nearly the entire population had been displaced, many multiple times.[4] More than 1.8 million people faced extreme hunger, with repeated warnings of imminent famine from aid agencies present on the ground.[5] The life expectancy of Palestinians in Gaza almost halved between October 2023 and September 2024.[6]

The totalising nature of the Israeli attack led many Palestinians to describe it as genocidal from early on. As the months passed, an increasing number of international human rights organisations and legal experts agreed, arguing that Israel was deliberately inflicting conditions of life designed to bring about the Palestinians' physical destruction in Gaza. They pointed to the indiscriminate nature of Israeli violence, including the flattening of entire towns in the northern Strip; the destruction of more than 70 per cent of Gaza's infrastructure; the total siege and intentional deprivation of water and aid from more than two million Palestinians; the systematic destruction of Gaza's healthcare sector, including military attacks on hospitals and clinics; and the repeated displacements of civilians to areas that Israel then bombed.[7] The case was underpinned by repeated claims from Israeli politicians that there are 'no innocents in Gaza'.[8] In January 2024 – a full twelve months before the short-term ceasefire – the International Court of Justice (ICJ) ruled that there was a risk of genocide in Gaza, and that Israel should immediately act to prevent genocidal acts.[9]

Even prior to October 2023, Gaza had long been in a state of crisis. For seventy-five years, the Palestinian people had endured dispossession, displacement, occupation, impoverishment, collective punishment and ethnic cleansing – with those in Gaza often bearing the brunt of it. After Hamas took power in 2007, Israel imposed a total blockade on the Gaza Strip that made it near-impossible for anyone to get in or out. As a result, many from Gaza's younger generations have never left its 141 square miles.

Seen through this contemporary lens, the fact that Gaza once hosted an international airport with direct commercial flights may seem astonishing – as Atef Alshaer, a Palestinian writer from

Gaza, puts it, 'Rub your eyes, but Bill Clinton once landed in Gaza.'[10] Yet seen through a long historical lens, the idea of an international airport in Gaza is entirely unsurprising. For much of its history, Gaza wasn't just open to the wider world but actually functioned as a hub for travellers. As a port city on the eastern Mediterranean, in close proximity to north Africa, the Middle East and southeastern Europe, it was both a target for expansionist empires and an important site for traders. When the British army conquered Palestine at the end of the First World War, they entered the country by invading Gaza.

In fact, the history of Gaza stretches back into ancient times. Mentioned in the very first book of the Old Testament,[11] Gaza has found itself in the thick of power struggles over the millennia between an array of empires and forces including the Egyptians, Persians, Greeks, Romans, Byzantines, Arabs, Fatimids, Crusaders, Ayyubids, Mongols, Mamluks, Ottomans, French and British.[12] Traders, warriors, explorers and refugees passed through the seaport. Even well into the twentieth century, Gaza hosted visits by high-profile international figures from political, cultural and intellectual spheres. In the 1950s and 1960s, visitors to Gaza included the French feminist writer Simone de Beauvoir, African-American political activist Malcolm X and Indian Prime Minister Jawaharlal Nehru. Such luminaries expressed their solidarity with Palestinians in Gaza not only remotely, but in person.

Despite the blockade from 2007, Gaza and Palestine as a whole remain central to many international conversations in the twenty-first century. From October 2023, Israel's war on Gaza became a subject of deep contention around the world, with few places escaping the resultant spikes in antisemitism, Islamophobia and anti-Arab racism. In the US, it sparked the biggest student protests since the Vietnam War. Elections in the UK, US and France in 2024 all saw some voter realignment over the issue. And the ICJ ruling mentioned above resulted from a case brought by South Africa, further highlighting Gaza's international salience.

In the Middle East, the war has never been limited to Gaza and Israel. At the same time as declaring war on Gaza after 7 October, Israel closed off the West Bank – the other Palestinian territory that it has illegally occupied since 1967 – and imposed further restrictions on a population who have already endured limited freedom of movement for decades. Since October 2023, Israel has launched intensive raids across the West Bank, causing further displacement of Palestinians, with the national security minister openly arming vigilante settlers – Israeli citizens living illegally on occupied Palestinian land, in breach of international law. With settler and military violence against Palestinians reaching unprecedented heights, children are being killed in greater numbers than at any time since the Israeli occupation of the West Bank began in 1967.

The war has also heightened longstanding hostilities between the two axes of power in the region, as the US has provided advanced weaponry to Israel while Iran and its Lebanese proxy Hizbollah have supported Hamas. As a result, the violence has not only engulfed Palestine and Israel but also spilled over into Yemen, Syria, Iran and Lebanon. At the time of writing, the latter was the most seriously affected, as intensifying clashes on the Israeli–Lebanese border erupted into a full-scale Israeli ground invasion of Lebanon in September 2024. By the time a ceasefire was finally brokered in November 2024, thirteen months of hostilities between Hizbollah and Israel had killed 3,544 people in Lebanon and 72 in Israel, while displacing more than 1.2 million people in Lebanon and 68,000 in northern Israel.[13]

The war on Gaza, then, isn't confined to Gaza, or even to Palestine and Israel. But the question remains as to why this tiny strip of land – just 141 square miles, less than a quarter the size of London – has such an outsized significance across the region and the rest of the world.

On the surface, there is no obvious explanation for the Gaza Strip's huge importance. Unlike the West Bank, it isn't home to a wealth of religious sites. Nor is it geo-strategically significant or rich in natural resources. Instead, Gaza's particular importance has come about due to historical conditions that can be traced back to the events of 1948. In other words, we can understand Gaza's significance by looking not to theology, geography or ecology, but only to history.

In this book, I identify six key junctures in the Gaza Strip's modern history, each of which proved pivotal in its evolution and each of which shows the tiny territory's long-running importance in Palestinian, Israeli and Middle Eastern history. When the state of Israel was created in 1948, expelling and displacing the majority of the Palestinian population, Gaza absorbed more Palestinian refugees per head than anywhere else. Eight years later, it was the site of the newly established Israeli state's first temporary military occupation. After the regional war of 1967, Gaza was where Israel sought to carry out further expulsions of the Palestinian population. In 1987, the first Palestinian intifada began in Gaza. In 1994, the Palestinian Authority (PA) established its first headquarters in the territory. In 2005, it was the site where Israel carried out its first – and to date, only – evacuation of settlers from Palestinian land. And two years later, it was where Hamas established its first government.

Collectively, these six episodes can help explain how we arrived at the catastrophe of the 2020s. They also show that the genocidal violence unleashed in Gaza since October 2023 comes on the back of long-running structural themes: expulsion, isolation, even annihilation. To quote an apocryphal saying attributed to the American writer Mark Twain, 'history doesn't repeat itself, but it often rhymes'. This is certainly the case for Gaza, and indeed for the whole of Palestine.

Since October 2023, it has become increasingly controversial to talk about the importance of historical context in Palestine and Israel. Anyone who does so risks being accused of justifying either the Hamas-led war crimes of 7 October or Israel's subsequent genocidal war on Gaza. And yet this history remains crucial if we want to truly understand what's happening today. To understand is not to justify; to explain is not to excuse. Instead, historical context can bring clarity. It can also complicate the overly simplistic depictions that often dominate media reports, where Gaza is reduced to violence and poverty, and its people are stripped of their multidimensional humanity.

Finally, Gaza's history not only helps to explain its present but can also point to a different future. With the story of Gaza International Airport, we see how an alternative reality was once possible – and the entirely unnecessary and man-made nature of the catastrophe engulfing the Strip today.

1

CATASTROPHE CREATES THE STRIP

The Gaza Strip's modern history, like that of Palestine as a whole, was forged in the catastrophic dispossession of 1948. The establishment of the state of Israel that year turned the Palestinians into a stateless people and marked the beginning of their continuing displacement and dispersal. The same war that created Israel also produced the modern-day Gaza Strip, with its contemporary territorial boundaries.

Since 1948, the Gaza Strip has been central to Palestinian and Israeli politics. It absorbed more refugees per head than anywhere else in the region that year, a demographic shift that would form the core of its identity and make it the cradle of Palestinian nationalist activism. Its politics and demographics were a major factor in the state of Israel's early decision-making, as successive governments and the military sought to suppress any potential uprisings from the Strip. Almost entirely closed in by Israel and at a huge disadvantage militarily, financially, politically and diplomatically, the Gaza Strip has constantly struggled to survive under the impact, if not the direct control, of its enemy neighbour.

The Gaza Strip and the state of Israel were born together in 1948. Their fates have remained entwined ever since. Yet to fully understand the events of that year, we must first look to the

Palestinians' struggle for statehood in the preceding decades, alongside the simultaneous rise of Zionism.

GAZA UNDER THE BRITISH

At the dawn of the twentieth century, Palestine had been under Ottoman rule for nearly 400 years. But the Ottomans were now facing threats to their long-held power and Arab nationalist ideas were gathering steam in the Middle East, including in Palestine. Seismic changes were about to take place.

When the First World War swept through the Middle East, it put an end to the Ottoman Empire, after more than six centuries. The close proximity of Gaza City to the Egyptian border situated it on the front line of hostilities between the British, who had occupied Egypt since 1882, and the German-allied Ottomans. Heavy British shelling caused widespread death and destruction as the two empires fought intensively across Sinai and southern Palestine.[1]

By late 1917, the British had gained the upper hand and on 9 November, General Allenby, the commander of Britain's Egyptian Expeditionary Force, entered Gaza with his troops. They found a shattered and deserted city, its inhabitants having fled to escape the bombs.[2] In the months after the British victory, Gaza's displaced population tentatively started returning to their homes and British troops set about constructing two military cemeteries to bury thousands of their soldiers who had died in Palestine. Both cemeteries remained in Gaza into the twenty-first century, tended by a local Palestinian family.[3]

Gaza would act as a gateway to Palestine for the British. In December 1917, the British army took the capital city of Jerusalem. By the end of 1918, with the Ottoman Empire collapsing, the British had occupied the entire country. For the next three decades, a succession of British high commissioners governed Palestine from Jerusalem, relying on heavily centralised military power to maintain the regime. In 1922, their authority gained a veneer of international legitimacy when the newly established League of Nations granted the British Mandate of Palestine, formalising Britain's control over the country.[4] A creation of the post-war era, the mandate system was especially prominent in the Middle East, where Britain and France had wasted no time in dividing the spoils of the fallen Ottoman Empire between them. The League of Nations, created in 1919, appointed Britain as the mandate power in Palestine, Transjordan* and Iraq, while France took the equivalent role in Syria and Lebanon.

The mandate system ushered in a new phase in the long-running European domination over the Global South. In theory, it 'provisionally recognised' the independence of the countries involved, 'subject to the rendering of administrative advice and assistance by a Mandatory [Power] until such time as they are able to stand alone'.[5] In practice, though, mandate governance was simply colonialism by another name.[6]

The League of Nations' supposed 'internationalism' was also somewhat farcical. The League may have portrayed itself as a global body, but in reality it was dominated by the European powers, particularly Britain and France. Most of the global population were still under colonial rule and therefore without their own representation. As mandate powers, Britain and France were required to submit annual reports to the League's council detailing their progress in preparing the territories for self-rule – but they sat on the council themselves as two of its four permanent members. They were, to some degree, policing themselves.

---

* Transjordan was officially renamed Jordan in 1949, three years after independence.

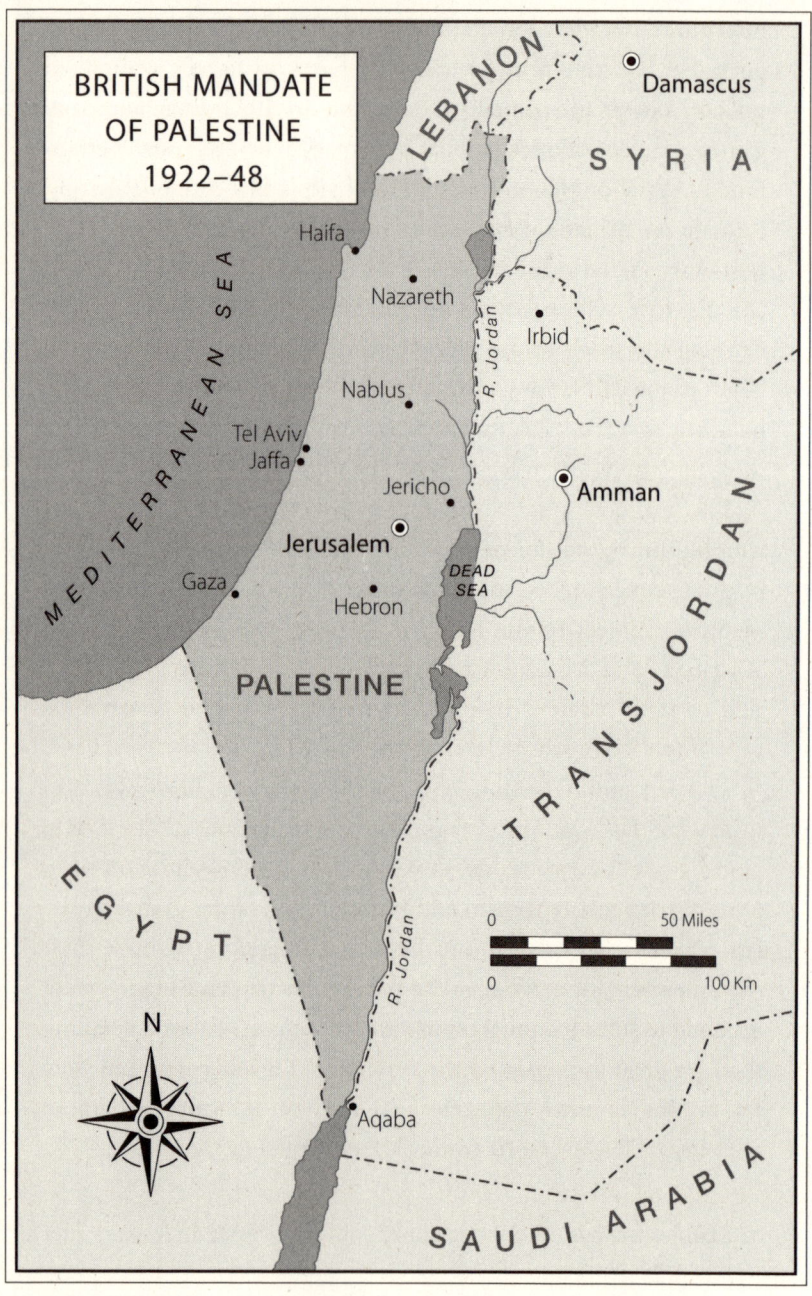

BRITISH MANDATE
OF PALESTINE
1922–48

LEBANON

Damascus

SYRIA

Haifa

Nazareth

Irbid

R. Jordan

MEDITERRANEAN SEA

Nablus

Tel Aviv
Jaffa

Jericho

Amman

Jerusalem

DEAD
SEA

Gaza

Hebron

PALESTINE

TRANSJORDAN

EGYPT

0   50 Miles

0   100 Km

R. Jordan

N

Aqaba

SAUDI ARABIA

THE STRUGGLE FOR PALESTINE

In the case of Palestine, there was an added complication in any discussion about self-rule. Like their Arab neighbours across the region, the Palestinians had found their political aspirations for independence frustrated when one imperial regime (the Ottomans) was replaced by another (the British) at the end of the First World War. Yet Palestinian nationalists also faced an additional challenge from the Zionist movement, whose activists were seeking to establish their own Jewish state in the country.

Modern political Zionism had emerged in nineteenth-century Europe as a reaction to the horrific and often violent antisemitism that had long dogged the continent. Observing the rising power of nation-states, Viennese journalist Theodor Herzl concluded that the best way to guarantee Jewish safety and security would be for the Jewish people to have their own state, where they could form a majority and enjoy all the power, trappings and respect of independent statehood.[7] The Zionist movement quickly came to focus its attentions on Palestine, in view of the country's ancient religious significance to the Jewish people. The problem for the Zionists, of course, was that Palestine was already home to a national population: the Palestinians. At this time, there were a small number of Jewish communities in Palestine, whose presence there pre-dated the Zionist movement.[8] With a notable presence in Jerusalem, Jaffa and Hebron, these Jewish Palestinian communities spoke Arabic and were often culturally indistinguishable from their Muslim and Christian neighbours.[9]

Herzl and his supporters were prolific in working to garner support for Zionism, but in the early twentieth century the movement still held only minority support among most Jewish communities.[10] In 1917, it got a major boost in the form of support from the British government – head of the most powerful empire in the world and the incoming ruler of Palestine itself. On the very same day that British troops entered Gaza, the government published a letter from Foreign Secretary Arthur Balfour to the prominent British Zionist Lord Rothschild. In it, Balfour declared British support for 'the establishment in Palestine of a national home for the Jewish people'.[11]

The British government had various motives in aligning itself with Zionism at this point. For one thing, it calculated that doing so would enable it to keep Palestine in its long-term sphere of interest, which was critical given the country's proximity to the Suez Canal, a key trading route for the British Empire. It also judged that a pro-Zionist position might rally Jewish support for the Allies in the US and revolutionary Russia. On top of this, some members of the British government – including Prime Minister David Lloyd George – were ideologically committed Christian Zionists, believing that the Jewish people's return to the Holy Land would precipitate the Second Coming.

The Balfour Declaration, as it became known, failed to mention the Palestinian people at all, referring to them only as 'non-Jewish communities', and pledging to respect their 'civil and religious rights' with no mention of their national or political rights.[12] To make matters even worse in the eyes of many Palestinians, it also directly contradicted a pledge that the British had made to Arab nationalists less than two years earlier. In correspondence with leading Arab nationalist Sherif Hussein of Mecca,[13] the British high commissioner to Egypt had promised support for post-war Arab independence in the Middle East – including Palestine – in exchange for Hussein's forces fighting against the Ottomans.[14]

The Balfour Declaration was subsequently incorporated into the text of the 1922 Mandate, which explicitly spoke of the Jewish historical connection to Palestine and the imperative of facilitating Jewish immigration and land acquisition there, while staying silent on the rights of the Palestinian national community.[15] This meant that when the British authorities submitted their yearly reports to the League of Nations, they were also required to report on what progress was being made in establishing a Jewish national home. As legal scholar Noura Erakat argues, this created a funda-mental contradiction in the Mandate, which was simultaneously supposed to prepare Palestine for self-governance and deny self-determination to the majority of its people.[16]

From its outset, the Mandate authorities granted the *yishuv* (Jewish community in Palestine) autonomy under the officially recognised authority of the Jewish Agency (JA). The JA's sophis-ticated para-state infrastructure would eventually come to include thirty-seven departments, with financial and immigration programmes and control of its own education system. It was also allowed a paramilitary, known as Haganah ('Defence'), which the British did not formally recognise but sometimes co-operated with.[17] By contrast, Palestinian Arab institutions were given considerably less autonomy and there was no recognised Arab representative body in the Mandate.[18]

Under the Mandate, and in keeping with the pledges of the Balfour Declaration, Jewish immigration to Palestine increased significantly. In 1922, when the Mandate was officially declared, 13 per cent of Palestine's population had been Jewish. By 1946 – around a quarter of a century into the Mandate – the Jewish population of Palestine had shot up to just under a third of the total. This major demographic shift was made possible by the multiple waves of Jewish immigration, nearly all of which came from Europe. Some immigrants were motivated by Zionist ideological conviction, others came as refugees fleeing antisem-itism, and others still were driven by a combination of the two.

Unsurprisingly, Jewish immigration to Palestine spiked after Hitler came to power in Germany in 1933 and Europe's Jewish communities faced new levels of antisemitic violence, persecution and eventual genocide. Many Jewish refugees from the Third Reich looked to the US and UK as their sanctuaries of choice, but found that both states had mostly closed their doors – meaning large numbers ended up in Palestine instead. The number of Jewish immigrants to Palestine rose from just under 10,000 in 1932 to 30,327 in 1933, 42,359 in 1934 and a whopping 61,854 in 1935.[19] Palestinians, who had been struggling for independence since the late Ottoman era, were perturbed by what this influx meant for their national rights.

Where did Gaza fit into all this? Under the British administration, Gaza was designated a sub-district in southwestern Palestine, spanning the coastline from Rafah to Isdud. It was part of Palestine's large Southern District (which, confusingly, was sometimes also referred to as the Gaza District) and its predominantly Muslim population were largely rural and agricultural, in keeping with the typical lifestyle across much of the country.[20] The Gaza District's large geographical span was at odds with its lack of political power in the Mandate. With the British centralising their power in Jerusalem – far more so than the Ottomans had done – Gaza found itself pushed to the periphery in political as well as geographical terms.

While Gaza's port was a trading hotspot, the city was less politically and culturally prominent than Jerusalem, Haifa or Jaffa, so it was relatively unaffected by the major waves of Jewish immigration in this period – at least in comparison to other parts of Palestine.[21] Its dearth of Jewish holy sites, along with its positioning in the southwestern corner of Palestine, meant it wasn't a priority for the Zionist movement. The older, pre-Zionist Palestinian Jewish community in Gaza City was tiny, numbering fewer than 100 people in the 1920s.[22] The wider sub-district had a few small communities but they still totalled less than 0.5 per cent of the entire population.[23]

Despite its relative demographic homogeneity, Gaza wasn't spared when inter-communal riots broke out in cities across Palestine in 1929, beginning over tensions around religious sites in Jerusalem and spreading to the mixed cities of Hebron, Safad and Haifa. The death toll eventually numbered 133 Jews, killed mainly by Arab rioters, and 116 non-Jewish Arabs, killed mostly by British forces.[24] When the riots reached Gaza City, neighbours stood in solidarity with the small Jewish community there, and former mayor Said Shawwa intervened to protect them. As a result, there were no fatalities in Gaza – but the city's Jewish residents were so petrified by the attacks that they chose to leave Gaza afterwards, seeking the security of larger Jewish communities elsewhere in Palestine.[25]

With Zionist activity intensifying across the country as Jewish immigration reached new levels in the 1930s, and the JA receiving direct support from the Mandate authorities, Palestinians saw their nationalist goals and right to self-determination further and further suppressed. In November 1935, tensions escalated when British police killed the preacher and Arab nationalist Sheikh Izzeldin al-Qassam after he declared and led an armed struggle against British colonialism.[26] His death would precipitate the biggest nationalist uprising in Palestinian history.

In May 1936, the newly formed Arab Higher Committee – a Palestinian organisation made up of political parties and notables under the leadership of the Grand Mufti of Jerusalem – responded to the mounting crisis by calling for a general strike in Palestine. Heeding the call, Gazans joined their compatriots across the country in withdrawing their labour for six months and taking to the streets to demonstrate against British rule and Zionism.[27]

The British brutally suppressed the revolt, working with the Haganah to quash Palestinian uprisings across the country. Many nationalist leaders from Gaza and elsewhere were arrested and exiled; by the time the revolt finally ended in 1939, an estimated one in ten Palestinian men had been executed, wounded, imprisoned or expelled. As a consequence, the Palestinian national community was left seriously weakened in the run-up to 1948.[28]

Yet Britain's brutality would not preserve its long-term power in Palestine. In 1944, a hardline Zionist militia called the Irgun Zvai Leumi declared open rebellion against the Mandate regime as part of its campaign to establish a Jewish state in Palestine. After years of indiscriminate attacks against not only the British authorities but also Palestinian civilians, the Irgun now joined with the extremist Lehi militia to escalate its assaults. In the Western imagination, this period of insurgency is most associated with the 1946 bombing of the King David Hotel in Jerusalem, which killed ninety-one people and was engineered under the leadership of Irgun commander Menachem Begin (later prime minister of Israel from 1977 to 1983).[29] Yet the violence also targeted the Palestinian population, with both the Irgun and Lehi regularly attacking Arab neighbourhoods, buses and marketplaces.

Gaza remained largely on the sidelines during this time and, compared to elsewhere in Palestine, it wasn't seriously affected by the Zionist insurgency. Nevertheless, Gazans increasingly felt the impact of Palestine's demographic shifts, as the district's Jewish population grew significantly over the 1940s. In 1946, the Jewish National Fund, a Zionist organisation seeking to settle Palestine, opened eleven *kibbutzim* – Zionist communal agricultural settlements – across the Gaza District. By that time, 2 per cent of its population was Jewish and 4 per cent of its land was Jewish-owned.[30]

In 1947, with Palestine swept up in increasing violence and instability, and Britain struggling with its post-war recovery at home, the Mandate regime announced plans to withdraw and referred the so-called 'Question of Palestine' to the United Nations. Created two years prior, the UN had superseded the now-disbanded League of Nations. In response to the British referral, the UN recommended that Palestine be partitioned into two states, one Jewish and one Arab. Gaza City, along with most – but not all – of its sub-district, was assigned to the would-be Arab state.[31]

The Partition Plan – which, it should be noted, was only ever a recommendation and not a binding resolution – never came to pass. Although it had the support and acceptance of mainstream Zionist leadership through the JA, it was rejected by the more hardline factions of the Zionist movement, as well as the Arab states and the Palestinian leadership, with the latter seeing it as another denial of their right to self-determination. Many pointed out the injustice of the partition plan, which gave 55 per cent of the land to the Jewish community, who then composed less than a third of the country's population.

Thereafter, Palestine descended into worsening violence. The British authorities withdrew – first unofficially, then formally on 15 May 1948. Meanwhile, Gaza's position as peripheral to national Palestinian politics was about to be upturned completely.

1948

The events of 1948 are among the most contested and controversial in modern history – so much so that no one can even agree on what to call them. For Israelis, 1948 was the War of Independence (Milhemet Ha'Atzmaout), which established the modern Jewish state after centuries of dispersal and persecution. Coming so soon after the devastating horrors of the Holocaust,

UN PARTITION PLAN
November 1947

Arab State
Jewish State
City of Jerusalem

many Jews around the world looked to the new Israeli state as a site of much-needed sanctuary. But for Palestinians, 1948 was the Nakba, an Arabic word meaning 'catastrophe', in which they were displaced and dispossessed, beginning what would become a decades-long exile.

For both peoples, the human cost was devastating. The Jewish-Israeli death toll was around 6,000; the Palestinian death toll was at least as high and may have even exceeded 13,000.[32] And by the end of 1948, more than 750,000 Palestinians – around two thirds of the population – had been forced to flee and become refugees.[33] More than 200,000 went to the territory of the Gaza Strip, joining the 80,000 Palestinians who already lived there.[34] The Strip's infamous population density in the twenty-first century can be directly traced to these events.

How did such a drastic transformation happen so quickly? The Partition Plan of November 1947 provided the immediate trigger for Palestine's descent into disorder. No community was untouched as Zionist and Palestinian fighters went to war. Determined to establish their new state, Zionist militias – including not only the Irgun and Lehi but also the Jewish Agency's Haganah – seized the opportunity to expel the Palestinian population and establish a Jewish majority, in a process of ethnic cleansing that involved large-scale raids, indiscriminate attacks, expulsions at gunpoint, rapes and massacres.

These crimes were not simply the result of war. In fact, the ethnic cleansing of Palestinians – referred to euphemistically as 'transfer' – had long been key to Zionist ideology.[35] Decades later, Israeli historian Benny Morris would reflect: 'Transfer was inevitable and inbuilt into Zionism – because [Zionism] sought to transform a land which was "Arab" into a "Jewish" state and a Jewish state could not have arisen without a major displacement of [the] Arab population.'[36]

31

The Nakba must be understood within this ideological context. Massacres included the indiscriminate killings in December 1947 of up to seventy Palestinians at the village of Balad al-Shaykh, twelve at the village of Khisas and thirteen at Al-Tira. These were followed in February 1948 by the massacre of up to seventy villagers at Sa'sa' in northern Palestine. The sheer brutality of such attacks ensured a total overhaul of Palestine's population, as the Palestinians were driven out of much of the country and became increasingly concentrated in smaller parts of it. In December 1947 alone, Zionist militias forced 75,000 Palestinians into exile.[37]

The violence intensified even further from March 1948, when the JA's Haganah launched its formal plan for territorial conquest and expulsion: Plan Dalet.[38] That same month, the Irgun and Lehi attacked the village of Deir Yassin, just outside Jerusalem. Disregarding the non-aggression pact that its Muslim residents had recently signed with their Jewish neighbours, the militias rampaged through the village and slaughtered its unarmed residents, including women, children and the elderly. The final death toll is unknown, with estimates ranging from 100 to 250 out of a population of around 600.[39] Survivors' testimonies speak to the horrific nature of the attack; Mohammad Jaber, who was a young boy at the time, later recounted how the attackers forced his whole family against the wall and shot them, including a woman carrying a three-month-old baby.[40]

The Deir Yassin massacre had a huge impact on the Palestinian psyche. As word spread of its horrors, Palestinians across the country were compelled to flee rather than risk being exposed to another attack. Reports of rapes were met with particular alarm, leading many men to conclude that protecting their female relatives should take priority over struggling to stay on the land.[41] Everyone fleeing expected their exile to be temporary and anticipated returning home once the fighting was over. With this in mind, many took their house keys with them.

Salah Khalaf, who was fourteen at the time, would recount years later how his family fled their home in Jaffa shortly after hearing of Deir Yassin. Along with many others, they boarded a makeshift boat to seek refuge with relatives in Gaza. His account of the journey expresses the panic and terror that characterised the mass flight:

> The boat had scarcely lifted anchor when a woman started shrieking. One of her four children wasn't on board . . . Some of us tried to calm her by saying that her young son would surely be picked up and later brought to Gaza. But in vain. Her nerves finally cracked and she straddled the rail, throwing herself into the sea. In an apparent effort to save her, her husband jumped in after her. It soon became clear that neither knew how to swim. The angry waves finally swallowed them up under our very eyes.[42]

The scenes were so chaotic that many families were torn apart. Like the Khalafs, the al-Naffars were forcibly expelled from Jaffa and compelled to seek safety elsewhere. With mass violence and ethnic cleansing across much of Palestine, the family was scattered north, east and south, their dispersal encapsulating the Palestinian people's new condition.[43]

As one of the few Arab strongholds, Gaza became an obvious destination for those seeking safety. In April and May 1948, the city received 10,000 refugees from Jaffa alone.[44] Among them was one branch of the al-Naffar family, who ended up boarding a boat to seek shelter in a camp there. Hekmat al-Taweel, a Gazan native, would later recall the influx:

I remember seeing streams of people, a continuous flow
that you could see the beginning of but not the end.
Women, children, men; people of all ages and from different
places in Palestine who didn't know where to go . . . They
were so tired, so they slept in the streets when the night
came and continued their journey the next day. Many of
them used their blankets or any cloth they had and put up
some sort of tent. Gaza at that time was full of tents . . .
Some people were even looking in the garbage and at
nearby fields to find sticks, some wood, or anything to
make fire and make bread and feed their families.[45]

The refugee movement into Gaza continued for many months.[46]
Not everyone survived the journey, which often required walking
for weeks on end in extreme heat without adequate food, water
or shelter. Children and the elderly were especially vulnerable,
and some women had to give birth on the side of the road
during the trek. Some survivors later recalled having nothing to
eat but grass.[47]

On 14 May 1948, JA Chair David Ben-Gurion declared the
establishment of the new state of Israel.[48] His declaration came
as British forces formally withdrew from Palestine, handing
over control of much of the infrastructure directly to the JA.[49]
By this time, between 250,000 and 375,000 Palestinians had
already been expelled and displaced.[50] The Haganah now formed
the basis of the official Israeli army: the Israel Defense Forces
(IDF).

The day after Ben-Gurion's declaration, the neighbouring
Arab states – Jordan, Egypt, Syria, Iraq and Lebanon – declared
war on Israel, acting on their opposition to the Partition Plan
and aiming both to stem the flow of refugees and to push back
on Zionist-Israeli gains.[51] In at least one case, there were other

aims at play too; decades later, historians would discover that Jordan's Abdullah I had previously held secret talks with the JA, agreeing to carve up Palestine between them. Accordingly, he directed his troops not to extend too far in their fight with Israeli forces, which he conducted largely to keep up appearances in the Arab world.[52]

The Israeli Declaration of Independence did not mention the new state's borders (which, to this day, the Israeli state has never fully declared). By this time, Zionist forces had already pushed into parts of Palestine that the UN Partition Plan had designated for the 'Arab state'; after Ben-Gurion's Declaration, the newly formed Israeli army continued to do the same. All this provides strong evidence that the JA's acceptance of the Partition Plan was only ever intended as a stopgap on the way to a bigger land grab – executed in the first place mostly by the Haganah and then by its institutional successor in the form of the Israeli army. Violently ejecting more Palestinian communities, Israel extended its control further into Palestine's southern areas – including the Gaza sub-district, where it continued to carry out expulsions and seize territory into 1949.[53] Many of those targeted were peasants from the rural villages that characterised much of the Palestinian landscape.

Among this group was Zarifa Atwan, a young woman from the village of Isdud. Situated on the coast and located in the northern part of the Gaza sub-district, Isdud was home to fewer than 5,000 people in the early 1940s. Its residents were farmers who lived off the land and exchanged surplus produce with traders from further north in Palestine. Zarifa's family had their livelihood tied up in the land that they tended with their neighbours, as was typical for most Palestinian farmers at the time. This meant that when Israeli forces expelled them from Isdud, they had little of value to take with them into exile.[54]

Like the Khalafs, Zarifa and her family had been frightened by news of the Deir Yassin massacre. While some of their neighbours had left upon hearing of it, the Atwans initially chose to stay in their home, but when Israeli forces arrived in Isdud in October 1948 they were given no choice but to leave. Zarifa would recount later how Israeli soldiers forced them to evacuate at gunpoint, herding them onto trucks bound for Gaza. On arrival there, Zarifa, her husband and their four young children were forced to seek refuge in Deir al-Balah, one of the refugee camps being set up by the Egyptian military and the American Friends Service Committee (AFSC) to shelter the thousands of refugees streaming in from across Palestine.[55] The AFSC was a US-based Quaker organisation contracted by the UN to provide food, shelter and basic medical care to refugees in the Strip at this time.

By comparison, Salah Khalaf's family were relatively fortunate. As his father was originally from Gaza City, they could stay with his uncle and avoid the dire camp conditions. But they were far from comfortable. Khalaf, then aged fifteen, spent two years living in one small room with his parents and four siblings.[56] Like Zarifa, they were gradually coming to the realisation that they would not be able to return home any time soon.

The new Strip

At the same time as hundreds of thousands of Palestinians were being forced from their homes, the territory of the Gaza sub-district was being torn apart. Vowing to reclaim lost Palestinian land, the Egyptian army moved northwards through the area, joined by Palestinian volunteer fighters – among them a young

Yasser Arafat, who would go on to become the most prominent Palestinian leader of the twentieth century.[57]

Egypt also served as the primary sponsor of the All-Palestine Government (APG), which was established in Gaza in September 1948 and was made up of Palestinian nationalist leaders from the Mandate era. Intended to impede the new Israeli state by upholding Arab claims to the whole of Palestine, the APG set about mobilising the Mufti of Jerusalem's irregular forces from the early part of the war. It declared itself the government of independent Palestine and sought international recognition from its Gaza base.[58]

Yet both its diplomatic and its military efforts came to little. The APG had extremely limited resources, no real army and no real political power. What's more, it had powerful enemies: the British and the Jordanians were determined to quash any potential threats to their own power in Arab Palestine. In October, British officers forcibly disarmed the APG's fighters. By the end of that month, all members of the APG had left Gaza.[59] Israeli forces continued to sweep south, seizing more and more of what had been the Gaza sub-district. In February 1949, Egypt privately accepted defeat and signed an armistice agreement with Israel that formally placed Gaza under its administrative rule; it assured both the Palestinians and the rest of the Arab League that this military governance would end once Palestine was fully liberated.[60] By this time, Gaza had been reduced to a tiny sliver of land comprising less than 1.5 per cent of Palestine; the nearly 460 square miles of the Gaza sub-district shrank to a mere 214 square miles.[61]

In drawing an armistice line around the new territory, the 1949 agreement severed it from the towns and villages across Palestine with which Gazans had long traded and interacted. Legally, this demarcation line (also called the Green Line) wasn't a border, but both Israel and Egypt policed it as such.[62] The refugees who had sought safety in Gaza were now cut off from their homes and lands, which in many cases were only a few miles away and sometimes within sight. The Atwans, for example, were only around 30 miles from Isdud, but returning there was almost impossible. In a little-known addendum one year after the armistice, a war-weary Egypt agreed to Israeli requests for a 'buffer zone', ostensibly designed to prevent further fighting.[63] The resulting agreement reduced the area of Gaza by a further 20 per cent, to the 141 square miles that the Egyptian administration would subsequently dub the 'Strip'.[64]

By the end of 1949, the Gaza Strip had seen its population more than treble as it received at least 200,000 refugees from across Palestine. It was now home to more than one in four of all Palestinians who remained in the territory of Mandate Palestine.[65] Population density had risen from 500 people per square mile in 1944 to 2,300 in 1948.[66] Having received refugees from across the country, the Strip became something of a microcosm of Palestine writ large.

Geographically, the newly established 25-mile-long Strip was characterised by the eight refugee camps that now spanned its full length. The smallest, Deir al-Balah, was home to 9,000 Palestinian refugees in 1948; the biggest, Jabalia, accommodated 35,000.[67] Some were adapted from older structures; Bureij, Maghazi and Nuseirat were former British Army camps, with the latter having also housed Greek refugees fleeing the Second World War. By the end of the 1940s, Nuseirat was sheltering 16,000 Palestinian refugees on less than 1 square kilometre of land.[68] All the Gaza camps were characterised by poor conditions, overcrowding and insufficient supplies. In the winter of 1948, the International Committee of the Red Cross estimated that around ten children were dying every day from the appalling conditions in Khan Younis camp.[69]

In Deir al-Balah, Zarifa Atwan had to share a single tent with her husband, their four young children, her husband's parents, his three sisters and his two brothers. With no running water or sewerage system, there was a constant risk of disease spreading across the camp. In February 1950, less than eighteen months after being expelled from her home, Zarifa gave birth to her fifth child. The baby was delivered in the camp by the same midwife who had delivered her four older children back in Isdud; like the Atwans, the midwife had been forced into exile in 1948. Zarifa would go on to give birth to five more children in Deir al-Balah refugee camp.[70]

Palestinian refugees in Gaza initially received aid from the AFSC. In May 1950 – exactly two years after Ben-Gurion had declared the new state of Israel – a significant new actor arrived on the scene when the UN Relief and Works Agency for Palestine Refugees (UNRWA), created at the end of 1949, began operations across the Middle East. With the refugee crisis dragging on for longer than anyone had expected, the UN established UNRWA to provide a more comprehensive set of services to the thousands of displaced Palestinians across the Middle East. It was originally mandated to do so for eighteen months, but its mandate was continually renewed as Israel refused to implement Resolution 194, passed by the UN in December 1948 to formally recognise the Palestinian refugees' right of return.[71]

UNRWA became especially active in Gaza on account of the Strip's significant refugee population and high levels of impoverishment; in 1950, the agency's director, John Blandford Jr, described it as 'over-populated and lacking any considerable endowment in natural resources'.[72] Yet while UNRWA's services were doubtless needed, many refugees resented the presence of aid in their lives, especially if they had previously been self-sufficient farmers living off their own lands. Feelings of humiliation and shame are a common theme in refugee memoirs of the era.[73]

Long-term residents in Gaza were also suffering. Hekmat al-Taweel recalls widespread alarm among local Gazans as the catastrophe unfolded: 'it was a stressful time for everyone, including the local people of Gaza. Many of them panicked because they watched these tens of thousands of nearby villagers becoming refugees living in tents with nothing.'[74] As the crisis worsened, some of the poorest Gazans resorted to selling the doors and windows of their houses to survive.[75] Some residents had even been displaced by the fighting between Egypt and Israel, albeit within the Strip. With everyone struggling, some native Gazans felt aggrieved that the international relief efforts were ignoring their needs; as non-refugees, they were ineligible for many of the essential services being provided.[76]

Across Palestinian society, the Nakba created something of a levelling effect as the shared trauma of dispossession overshadowed internal divisions of class, region, religion and to some degree even political factionalism. In Gaza, more than 300,000 Palestinians were now surviving chronic physical hardship and suffering from both collective and individual traumas. All of them had lived through seismic upheaval. The vast majority had lost their homes. Many had experienced or witnessed horrific violence, been bereaved or separated from their loved ones. Some had survived rape or sexual assault.[77] On top of all of this, large numbers were now having to survive in makeshift shelters with no idea when they might be able to return home.

The new Israeli government, headed by Prime Minister Ben-Gurion, stated early on that the refugees' return was inconceivable, despite accepting Resolution 194 when joining the UN in May 1949. Instead, Ben-Gurion proposed an alternative deal. At the Lausanne Conference in 1949, he suggested that a limited and unspecified number of refugees be allowed to return – or as he put it 'resettle' – in exchange for Israel annexing Gaza. His proposal was overwhelmingly rejected by the Arab delegations, who understood it as a pitch for a further land grab while continuing to deny Palestinian national rights.[78] Meanwhile, the US and UK were quietly turning their attention to the possibility of permanently resettling the Palestinians elsewhere in the Arab world.[79] Yet standing firm on their right to return to their homes and land, the refugees decisively rejected such suggestions.

The refugees did not only yearn for return; they tried to make it happen. Soon after their arrival in Gaza, many – usually but not exclusively men – tried to travel back to the homes and villages they had been forced to flee. These were usually short trips – if caught, they could be killed by Israeli forces – but underpinning them was the hope of an eventual permanent return. It was with this in mind that many farmers visiting their former homes continued to cultivate their crops.[80]

Zarifa Atwan's husband Muhammad was among the returnees. He made two visits to the family home in Isdud, seeking to retrieve possessions they had been forced to leave behind in the terror of their expulsion. The first time he was successful, claiming lost belongings as well as the gun he kept for protection. The second time, he found that the family home had been demolished and the land claimed by Israelis.[81]

Muhammad may have had a lucky escape. As the years in exile rolled on, low-level Palestinian militants carrying out ambush operations made an increasing number of journeys across the armistice line. Israel didn't distinguish between refugees and militants, regarding any Palestinian crossing the line as an 'infiltrator' to be shot on sight. It is estimated that anywhere from 2,700 to 5,000 Palestinians were killed in this way in the years after the Nakba.[82] Egyptian forces, who were concerned about

Israeli reprisals and the perceived risk of Palestinians spying for Israel, also sometimes targeted Palestinians moving towards the armistice line.[83] Others died of heat, thirst and exhaustion during the arduous journey through the desert.[84]

Despite Muhammad making it safely back to Gaza after both his return visits, it is unlikely that the Atwan family felt particularly lucky. The sight of his home's destruction and the loss of his land dealt him a devastating blow. He later suffered a heart attack and never recovered his full health. He would eventually die young, leaving Zarifa a widowed mother of ten children at the age of thirty-eight. She was never able to return to Isdud.[85]

Gaza was utterly transformed by the Nakba. It went from being the largest city in a sub-district of just under 770 square miles to the namesake of a 141-square-mile enclave almost entirely closed in by an enemy state.[86] Refugees now composed more than 70 per cent of its population, as its landscape was transformed into a site of densely packed camps.[87] Its economy was crippled as residents could no longer trade with the rest of Palestine. And its people were traumatised, dispossessed and suffering.

In the end, the state of Israel had been established on 78 per cent of Palestine – significantly more than the 55 per cent allocated to the Jewish state in the Partition Plan. Zionist forces, which became the Israeli army, had expelled and displaced more than 750,000 Palestinians. Around 150,000 Palestinians remained in what was now Israel, the majority of them internally displaced.[88] The Israeli state gave them citizenship but of a decidedly second-class nature: they were placed under martial law for the next eighteen years. Among this group were some of the al-Naffar family, who had been displaced repeatedly after their initial expulsion from Jaffa and eventually settled in the central city of Lyd (renamed Lod by Israel).

The two remaining parts of Palestine, the West Bank and the Gaza Strip, didn't gain sovereign independence but instead came under the rule of neighbouring Arab regimes. Jordan's Abdullah I annexed the West Bank in 1950; as it happened, he had also wanted to annex the Gaza Strip but Israel had rejected this suggestion in the two parties' secret negotiations.[89] Instead, Gaza was now administered – but not annexed – by Egypt, meaning no state claimed sovereignty over the Strip. As such, it was the only part of historic Palestine not claimed by any state after 1948.

The Gaza Strip wasn't alone in receiving Palestinian refugees from the Nakba; large numbers also fled to the West Bank, Lebanon, Syria and Jordan, and some went even further afield. But, as we have seen, Gaza received more per head than any other region. Its centrality to the Palestinian refugee crisis lies at the heart of its ongoing importance to both Palestinian and Israeli politics. Its majority-refugee population served as a constant reminder of the expulsions and dispossession that had accompanied Israel's birth. From the periphery of Mandate Palestine, it now became a heartland of Palestinian nationalism.

To understand the history of a place, you have to go back to the start. For the Gaza Strip, that starting point is the Nakba. Nothing that happened subsequently – from the 1950s through to the 2020s – can be understood without it. Yet for the Palestinians of Gaza and beyond, 1948 was only the beginning of their dispossession and displacement, which continued to plague them for decades to come. The next round came only shortly after the seminal events of 1948.

2

THE EGYPTIAN ERA

Just eight years after the Nakba, the Palestinians of Gaza faced another Israeli assault when, in November 1956, Israel invaded and occupied the Gaza Strip for the first time. In the name of removing hostile militants, the Israeli army imposed a brutal regime on Gaza characterised by raids, war crimes and massacres. Ending after four months, this first Israeli occupation established many precedents for the military regime that would later occupy Gaza and the West Bank from 1967. Yet unlike the later occupation – which became the longest-running in modern history – Israel's encroachment on Gaza in 1956–7 ended in full withdrawal following international pressure. Rather than dominating the decade, this first occupation only interrupted the Egyptian rule that defined Gaza's immediate post-Nakba history.

For most of the two decades after 1948, Gaza functioned under Egyptian administration. During these years, the Palestinians of Gaza remained cut off from the rest of Palestine, meaning they were severed from both their homeland and many of their loved ones. But in contrast to what was to come, Gaza was fairly open to the rest of the world in this period, hosting visits from high-profile international figures including Simone de Beauvoir and Malcolm X. With Egypt a key actor in Global South politics for much of the 1950s and 1960s, people in Gaza could meet with activists from across the world.

Unsurprisingly, the Nakba and its aftershocks continued to dominate daily life for Palestinians everywhere. With Israel still refusing to allow the refugees to return – and often seizing even more land – the Palestinians lived through their dispossession every day. For this reason, many Palestinians spoke of 'ongoing Nakba' (al-nakba al-mustamirra), experiencing it as a long-term process, rather than a single event.[1]

LIFE IN GAZA AFTER THE NAKBA

The Nakba's comprehensive impact had economic as well as political elements. The Egyptian–Israeli armistice line had crippled Gaza's economy by severing it from domestic trade links and cutting off most of its cultivable land.[2] An estimated 80 per cent of the original inhabitants had lost their livelihoods after 1948 and now found themselves without work or job opportunities.[3] As late as 1959, unemployment stood at 87 per cent;[4] even in 1966, UNRWA was still contributing a fifth of the Strip's GDP.[5] Of the five geographical fields in which UNRWA operated – Syria, Lebanon, Jordan, Gaza and the West Bank – Gaza was the only one where refugees still relied on a general distribution of clothing and blankets in the mid-1960s.[6]

Of course, the poverty was at its most extreme in the Strip's eight refugee camps, where thousands of people were forced to survive with inadequate sanitation and insufficient food supplies.[7] By 1955, UNRWA had replaced all the tents in Gaza with pre-fabricated shelters and containers, but life remained extremely difficult.[8] Izzeldin Abuelaish, born in Jabalia camp that same year, describes life growing up in the 10-square-foot room where his family of eleven all lived:

There was no electricity, no running water; there were no toilets in the house. It was dirty. There was no privacy. We ate our meals from a single plate we shared. We had to wait in line to use the communal toilets and wait for water that was delivered by the United Nations. We were only allowed to fill our pots during certain hours of the day . . . We were usually barefoot, flea-bitten and hungry.[9]

What's more, the transition from tents to prefabs fuelled further alarm among the refugees that their displacement was becoming permanent. For many, this was their worst nightmare, and they were determined to prevent it. Despite the devastation of their circumstances, the Palestinian people were certainly not passive in accepting them, but instead responded to their dispossession with forms of activism that were variously political, cultural, creative or militant.

Salah Khalaf, whom we met in the previous chapter when his family were displaced from Jaffa, was among those in Gaza who embraced political activism at this time. In 1951, he enrolled at Dar al-Ulum teachers' college in Cairo. While there, he met a young engineering student named Yasser Arafat, and the two connected over their shared dedication to the cause of Palestine.[10] They successfully campaigned to lead the Palestine Students' Union (PSU, later the General Union of Palestinian Students or GUPS), beginning their lifelong political partnership while gaining critical experience of activism and organising.[11]

Despite, or perhaps because of, the Palestinian people's struggles, there was also a cultural flourishing in the period after the Nakba. Ismail Shammout was a Palestinian refugee surviving with his family in Khan Younis camp, after Israeli forces expelled them – along with as many as 70,000 others – from Lyd in 1948.[12] After a time making and selling sweets to supplement

REFUGEE CAMPS
IN GAZA c.1950

MEDITERRANEAN SEA

Shati

Jabalia

ISRAEL

Nuseirat

Bureij

Deir
al-Balah

Maghazi

N

Khan Younis

Rafah

EGYPT

0   5 Miles

0   10 Km

	Date established	Area Sq km (approx)	Original population
Shati	c.1948	0.52	23,000
Jabalia	1948	1.4	35,000
Nuseirat	c.1948	0.68	16,000
Bureij	1950s	0.5	13,000
Deir al-Balah	1948	0.17	9,000
Maghazi	c.1949	0.6	Data unavailable
Khan Younis	1948	1.27	35,000
Rafah	c.1949	1.23	41,000

his meagre income as a teacher in Gaza, Shammout began depicting the refugees' experiences in art. One of his most famous paintings, entitled *We Shall Return*, portrayed elderly and child refugees on the move. In 1953, the Employees Club in Gaza City hosted his first show, later described as the first contemporary art exhibition in Palestine's history.[13]

While Shammout captured the plight of the Palestinians with paint, the Gaza-born poets May Sayegh and Mu'in Bseiso turned to verse. Like Palestinian artists everywhere, Sayegh and Bseiso imbued their poetry with national themes. Sayegh fought for both Palestinian rights and women's rights; in common with anti-colonial feminists across the Global South, she saw these struggles as intertwined. At a young age, she became involved in the socialist Ba'th Party, heading up its women's section from 1954.[14] Meanwhile, Bseiso, a Gaza-based teacher, was one of the most prominent Palestinian communists of the era, at a time when the Communist Party had significant support among some refugees in Gaza.[15]

Alongside feminist, socialist, communist and anti-colonial movements, there were also Islamist expressions of Palestinian nationalism, most notably in the form of the Muslim Brotherhood. Founded in Egypt in 1928, it had become a significant actor in Palestine by the 1950s. Many of its members had fought in 1948, and in subsequent years its Gaza chapter would work to organise militant operations against Israel.[16]

Yet in the early aftermath of 1948, the most common form of activism among many Palestinians in Gaza was also the simplest: crossing the armistice line. As we saw in the previous chapter, many refugees did this to retrieve belongings, tend to their crops or find loved ones.[17] As time passed and destitute refugees increasingly found that their homes had been destroyed, some turned to stealing possessions from the Israeli communities who had taken their place.[18] In 1952, there were an estimated 5,000 journeys across the Gaza line alone (with a further 11,000 coming from Jordan and the West Bank).[19] As we'll learn, these crossings became increasingly organised and militant as the years in exile passed. Yet in seeking to return home, Palestinians came up against the Israeli state's brutal policy of shooting on sight anyone crossing the Green Line.

Though they treated Palestinian crossings as criminal, Israeli forces regularly crossed the line themselves on incursions into Gaza (the same was true in the West Bank). They typically framed these incursions as necessary clampdowns on Palestinian crossings, but the intrusions also took place in a context whereby many senior Israeli politicians saw the 1949 armistice lines as unsatis-factory. While Israeli expansionists were undoubtedly much more focused on the West Bank, in view of its religious, political and strategic significance, some Israeli leaders – most notably Ben-Gurion himself – also saw Gaza as part of *Eretz Israel* ('the Land of Israel') and were looking for ways to enclose it.[20] In 1955, Ben-Gurion (then serving as Defence Minister) even tried unsuccessfully to push through a cabinet proposal for Israel to occupy Gaza.[21] The following year, Foreign Minister Golda Meir said openly that the Gaza Strip was 'an integral part of Israel'.[22]

In other words, then, Israel's policy on the armistice line varied depending on who was trying to cross it. When Israeli forces approached the Gaza line, it was an open frontier to be crossed. When Palestinians sought to move in the other direction, it was a fixed and firm border. It was one of many cases whereby the Israeli state subjected Palestinians to a brutal double standard.

Gaza under Egypt

The Egyptian regime that ruled Gaza after 1948 was far removed from the independent self-government that Palestinians had fought for. Palestinians in Gaza were now under the authority of an Egyptian military governor who took his powers from the emergency regulations of the British Mandate.[23] The regime curtailed Palestinian political expression, banning political parties and publications.[24] It also systematically disarmed the population; only Palestinian auxiliaries serving under Egyptian military authority were allowed to bear arms.[25]

With Palestinian passports now defunct, the residents of Gaza received identity documents from the Egyptian military administration. And because Egypt maintained Gaza as a separate Palestinian entity, travel documents for Palestinians carried the name of the All-Palestine Government – a government in name only. The Egyptian regime also imposed controls to manage Palestinian movement from the Strip into Egypt.[26]

During the 1948 war, Egypt had been governed by King Farouk, a corrupt and ineffectual monarch largely reliant on support from Britain, the former colonising power. Egypt's humiliating defeat in 1948 – when it had failed to repel Israeli forces from all but a tiny sliver of southern Palestine – proved the final straw for his opponents. Four years later, a group of Egyptian soldiers known as the Free Officers overthrew the monarchy, exiled the royal family and established the Arab Republic of Egypt. Ostensibly led by Muhammad Neguib – who had served as Egyptian military governor of Gaza in 1951 – the new regime's *de facto* leader was Gamal Abdel Nasser, who became prime minister in 1954.

The Palestinian cause had helped shape Nasser's politics. He had served as a staff officer in Gaza in 1948 and was shocked by the mismanagement and corruption he witnessed there. He was particularly appalled to discover that the Egyptian regime was providing its soldiers with defective weapons.[27] Nasser's pan-Arab pride, outspoken criticisms of colonialism and promises of liberation all made him hugely popular with Palestinians across the Middle East.

After taking leadership of Egypt, Nasser reversed the previous regime's refusal to issue work permits for Palestinians from Gaza, and allowed Palestinian medical and legal professionals to practise in Egypt. Most importantly, he allowed Palestinians to study at Egyptian universities without tuition fees, opening up new prospects for many.[28] He created a free trade zone in Gaza for industrial and consumer goods that were unavailable in Egypt, which helped boost the Strip's economy.[29] Gaza became a magnet for small-scale Egyptian businessmen, and a tourist destination for Egyptians seeking cheaper goods. The policy generated economic opportunities for Palestinians in Gaza – although some benefitted far more than others.[30]

Yet Nasser was also an authoritarian leader who clamped down on all political movements besides his own – including those among Palestinians. Under his rule, Egypt was a one-party state, and the ban on political parties extended to Gaza. As such, he stopped short of supporting independent Palestinian political activism. In a move that caused considerable tension with the population in Gaza, he maintained the policy of disarmament and continued to suppress armistice line crossings, except when they were instructed by his regime directly.[31] As a result, many Palestinians in Gaza had a more wary view of Nasser than their compatriots elsewhere.[32] In fact, Nasser's motives had a lot in common with those of the previous Egyptian regime. Like them, he was concerned about provoking Israeli retaliation (Israel deliberately employed disproportionate retaliation as a warning to the Arab states). He was also suspicious that some Palestinians crossing into Israel might be working as spies.[33]

In contrast to his image in the West as a hard-line ideologue, Nasser negotiated directly with Israel in the early years of his leadership. Although Egypt and Israel formally remained in a state of enmity – and despite the Israeli government's displeasure at the Free Officers' revolutionary pan-Arabism – in the early 1950s there were tentative steps on both sides to reach an agreement. There were signs of progress during the Israeli premiership of Moshe Sharett (in office 1954–5), who favoured a more conciliatory approach than Ben-Gurion.[34] The talks gave Nasser another reason to suppress armistice line crossings.

All of this caused anger and outrage among many Palestinians in Gaza, who saw the Egyptian regime as claiming the mantle of their cause while suppressing the national movement on the ground. In accordance with the 1949 agreement, they understood the armistice line as a temporary measure designed to stop the fighting, rather than a fixed state border.[35] Frustrated by the Arab regimes' lack of action, Palestinians began organising themselves, acquiring arms where possible, and planning and implementing attacks on Israeli infrastructure, soldiers and civilians. In some cases, they returned to the sites of their own lost lands, confronting and attacking the Israeli communities now living there (some of whom, in turn, were Jewish refugees whom the Israeli state had forcibly placed close to the armistice line).[36] These Palestinian militants called themselves *fedayeen*, meaning 'the ones who sacrifice themselves'.

The fedayeen could be found across the region but they were especially prominent in Gaza. Although the Strip made up less than 1.5 per cent of historic Palestine, its high concentration of refugees and their close proximity to their former homes made it central to fedayeen activity.[37] Many of them would become key figures in Palestinian national politics. One of the most prominent was Khalil al-Wazir, who began organising fedayeen operations from Gaza in the early 1950s. Like the majority of the Strip's population, al-Wazir was a refugee; the Israeli army had expelled his family from Ramle in 1948, when he was a teenager. They sought refuge in Gaza's Bureij camp, where al-Wazir completed school and spent his later teenage years. In 1953, he formed his own commando organisation in Gaza and began orchestrating ambush operations against Israel.[38]

That same year, Salah Khalaf – another teenage refugee during the Nakba – returned to Gaza. His intensifying activism in the PSU had attracted the interest of the Egyptian secret police, who deported him back to Gaza two years into his studies.[39] When Arafat travelled to Gaza shortly afterwards to participate in commando raids on Israel, he reconnected with Khalaf and also met al-Wazir. Together the trio organised fedayeen operations across the Gazan armistice line, beginning what would become one of the most significant collaborations in Palestinian political history.[40]

The fedayeen had extremely limited resources and capabilities in the face of a fully armed state, so their operations had a minimal impact on the state itself – but not on the Israeli communities living in the country's south. Here, the fedayeen created panic and fear, which spiked after every attack. As well as sometimes directly attacking individuals, they mined roads and caused damage to other infrastructure. The resulting insecurity led many Israelis to avoid driving at night on main roads in the south.[41] In total, fedayeen from Gaza and Sinai killed 403 Israelis between 1951 and 1955; those entering from the West Bank, Jordan, Syria and Lebanon killed another 564 Israelis in the same period – both soldiers and civilians.[42]

As we have seen, Israel countered the crossings by enforcing a zero-tolerance policy. In the early 1950s, Israeli forces killed as many as 5,000 'infiltrators', the majority of whom were unarmed. Some Israeli kibbutzim in the south also planted mines to punish Palestinian crossers; in the first six months of 1950, eleven Palestinians were killed in this way in Erez kibbutz alone.[43] That year, Prime Minister Ben-Gurion recorded in his diary two cases of Israeli troops capturing and raping Palestinian women and girls who had crossed over, and more frequent cases of captured 'infiltrators' being tortured.[44] As Israel's shoot-on-sight policy started to deter people, especially those who were merely seeking to reclaim their possessions or harvest their crops, the number of crossings began to fall, from as many as 15,000 in the early 1950s to 5,000 by the middle of the decade.[45]

The measures didn't stop there. Israeli forces also carried out military incursions into Gaza to deter Palestinian crossings and pressure the Egyptian regime to clamp down on the fedayeen – moves that commander Moshe Bar-Kochba described as 'punish[ment]' for 'troublesome Gaza, home of saboteurs and attackers of Israel'.[46] Then, in 1953, the Israeli army created a special unit specifically designed to tackle the Gaza fedayeen. Unit 101 was led by Ariel Sharon, then a young Israeli soldier who had fought with the Haganah in 1948 and quickly became known as an effective and aggressive operator. In August 1953, he led Unit 101's first operation, an incursion into Bureij refugee camp that killed at least fifty Palestinians, including twenty civilians.[47] In response, Bureij residents organised demonstrations demanding the creation of a Palestinian national guard to protect the camps. The Egyptian regime ignored these calls.[48]

The following year, Israel codified its policy on armistice line crossings when it passed the Prevention of Infiltration Law. The legislation stated that 'a person who enters Israel without permission or who is in Israel unlawfully is . . . deemed to be an infiltrator so long as he has not proved [sic] the contrary.' The definition included 'a Palestinian citizen . . . who [since 29 November 1947, the date of the UN Partition Plan] left his ordinary place of residence in an area which has become part of Israel for a place outside Israel'. It imposed a punishment of minimum five years' imprisonment or a fine of 5,000 Israeli pounds.[49]

Mindful of such policies and determined not to become embroiled in another war, the Egyptian regime continued to curtail crossings throughout the early 1950s, meaning that those still seeking to cross the line risked being shot not only by Israeli forces but also by their Egyptian counterparts. They could otherwise be arrested; in one of the biggest clampdowns in 1954, Egyptian authorities arrested and detained around 200 Palestinians in Gaza, including Khalil al-Wazir.[50]

The watershed moment came in February 1955. A group of fedayeen from Gaza reached the Tel Aviv suburbs, where they killed an Israeli civilian. Unit 101 then attacked an Egyptian military base in Gaza, where they killed thirty-six Egyptian soldiers and two Palestinian civilians, including a young boy.[51] The Gaza Raid, as it became known, was the most violent attack since the Egyptian–Israeli armistice agreement, and the UN Security Council passed a resolution condemning it.[52]

Demonstrations erupted across the Strip in response. Palestinian protestors condemned the Egyptian regime's continual failure to defend their rights and protect them from Israeli attacks. A particular point of contention was Egypt's plan, devised in concert with UNRWA and the US, to resettle 12,000 Palestinian refugee families from Gaza to Sinai in violation of their right of return.[53] The organisers of these demonstrations were all key figures in the community-based groups and voluntary work that defined Gazan civil society: Mu'in Bseiso, the poet and teacher we met earlier in this chapter; physician and community leader Haidar Abd al-Shafi; and educator Yusra al-Barbari, Gaza's first female university graduate.

The demonstrators were a broad alliance of communists,

Islamists, independent activists and others. They demanded the training and arming of Palestinians in the camps, full civil freedoms in Gaza and the cancellation of the Sinai relocation scheme. As the protests grew, normal daily activity shut down across the Strip. In an unsuccessful bid to curtail the movement, the Egyptian authorities arrested and imprisoned hundreds of demonstrators, including Bseiso.[54]

Palestinians in Gaza called the 1955 demonstrations an *intifada*, which loosely translates as 'uprising'.[55] In later decades, more intensive intifadas would draw on this tradition of grassroots organisation. The movement spread across the border into Egypt itself, where the PSU – at the time the only democratically elected Palestinian organisation[56] – organised strikes, sit-ins and demonstrations that eventually won union leaders an audience with Nasser himself.[57]

The demonstrations were ultimately successful. The Gaza Raid proved a turning point in Nasser's policy towards Israel. Humiliated and undermined, he abandoned his conciliatory approach and the possibility of a peace agreement.[58] Swearing that from now on no Israeli attack would go unanswered, the Egyptian government shifted to a policy of support for the fedayeen, recruiting and training its members.[59] In turn, the Israeli government increasingly came to see Nasser's government as an enemy that had to be removed.

THE FIRST ISRAELI OCCUPATION

From 1955 onwards, violence between Israel and Egypt escalated exponentially. After another Israeli raid in August, Egypt deployed ten groups of fedayeen into Israel, where they killed as many as seventy people, among them unarmed workers and a family of four.[60] In response, Israeli forces attacked Khan Younis police station, killing seventy-two Egyptians and Palestinians.[61] By the end of the year, 216 Arabs and 47 Israelis had been killed in the Gaza frontier area.[62] The following year saw another spike of violence and more fatalities, culminating in the Israeli shelling of Gaza City in April, which killed fifty-eight civilians including ten children.[63] Fedayeen from Gaza then launched their own raid, killing ten Israelis, the majority of them civilians.[64]

Matters came to a head in July 1956, when Nasser announced that he was nationalising the Suez Canal Company. The move was a strike against the European former colonisers, who had used their control of the company to continue extracting wealth from Egypt after decolonisation in 1922. As Britain and France considered an offensive against Nasser in response, Ben-Gurion saw an opportunity. In October, the three countries' leaders met in secret and agreed to launch a co-ordinated offensive against Egypt.[65] The resulting conflict is known variously as the Second Arab–Israeli War, the Suez Crisis (in Britain), the Sinai War (in Israel) or the Tripartite Aggression (in the Arab world). Like the war of 1948, its name is contested in the battle of narratives.

This war was much briefer than that of 1948, lasting less than a fortnight, but its consequences were hugely significant for Britain, France, Israel – and Gaza. As Israeli forces attacked Egypt and moved towards the Suez Canal, they quickly took control of Gaza. On 1 November 1956, Israel began its first military occupation of the Gaza Strip.[66] In Ben-Gurion's eyes, this was a chance to remake Gaza, which had been so central to the fedayeen's emergence and growing strength. So, while Britain and France succumbed to international pressure and withdrew from Egypt the following month, the Israeli occupation of Gaza lasted until March 1957.

Military occupations are never benign and this one was especially brutal. On its first full day, Israeli radio announced that the civilian population of Gaza would be held collectively responsible for any attacks on Israeli civilians and property.[67] This policy set the tone for what was to come. Israel imposed a strict curfew on residents and ordered them to surrender all arms, as the military went door to door conducting extensive house searches. Some fedayeen escaped on small boats to Egypt, while others went to the West Bank; those caught in Gaza were summarily executed, as was anyone else suspected of having borne arms.[68]

Determined to root out all fedayeen, the Israeli army carried out 'screening' operations. Ostensibly, these were designed to identify and locate militants; in practice, they entailed widespread violence and war crimes. Over three weeks in November 1956, Israeli forces massacred at least 275 people in Khan Younis camp, 111 in Rafah and 66 across camps elsewhere. Some sources place the number of fatalities upwards of 500.[69] Testimonies highlight the ruthlessness of the operations; in Khan Younis, the army lined men and boys up against the wall to shoot them, some as young as fourteen.[70] Some men were forcibly disappeared, their bodies discovered later in mass graves. The majority were undeniably civilians; UNRWA Director Henry Labouisse reported that in one case, Israeli forces had simply opened fire on a crowd in Rafah.[71]

As they enforced the occupation across the Strip, Israeli forces arrested all males aged fifteen to sixty, publicly searching them and incarcerating many. Despite its claims to be fighting militants, as the months passed, Israel also targeted Palestinians involved in non-violent civil disobedience campaigns.[72] Occupation forces transferred some Palestinian detainees to Atlit prison camp inside Israel, in contravention of the Fourth Geneva Convention, which prohibits the forcible transfer of people from occupied territory into the territory of the occupying power.[73] Word quickly spread of the massacres and other atrocities committed by Israeli forces, including their use of Palestinian children as human shields when moving through booby-trapped spaces.[74] Hearing such accounts, many Palestinians hid in terror, while others escaped to Egypt on foot, camel or donkey.[75]

For Palestinians across Gaza, the echoes of 1948 were unmistakable. During the Nakba, the Israeli army had expelled the Atwan family at gunpoint from their home in Isdud. Eight years later, they found themselves living through another war. Abdel Bari Atwan recalls what happened when Israeli tanks entered their camp of Deir al-Balah on 14 November:

> The refugees in Deir al-Balah had heard about the massacres in Khan Younis and Rafah, and were paralysed with fear . . . the door burst open and five heavily armed Israeli soldiers marched in [to our home] . . . They hit [my father] with their gun butts until he nearly fell, then they told him to get out of the house, pushing him with their rifles. We were all screaming and crying and we followed them . . . my father, together with the rest of the men from the camp, [was] being kicked and shoved towards the empty bit of wasteland.[76]

It was, perhaps surprisingly, US opposition that put an end to the first Israeli occupation of Gaza. With the Cold War at its height, President Eisenhower was furious that the Suez–Sinai invasion had distracted international attention from Soviet aggression in Europe and handed the USSR a PR victory by enabling it to speak about Western neo-colonialism in the Middle East. Concerned about the Arab world falling into the Soviet sphere, Eisenhower demanded an unconditional withdrawal, which Israel executed on 7 March 1957. Although Israel handed over authority to the UN Emergency Force (UNEF), this new arrangement didn't last long. Nasser was now so popular that the Palestinians of Gaza demanded his government replace UNEF's international observers. Egyptian authorities returned to the Strip on 14 March 1957.

Israel's first occupation of Gaza had lasted four months. Compared to the decades-long occupation that began in 1967 and continues more than half a century later, this four-month period may seem momentary. But it was far from insignificant, politically, militarily and in its human cost. In total, Israeli forces killed as many as 1,500 Palestinians during the occupation, out of a total population of around 300,000. Including those injured, detained or tortured, this means that at least 1 per cent of the Strip's population suffered first-hand from Israeli violence during the first occupation.[77] And while Israel claimed its purpose in Gaza was to eliminate the fedayeen, the majority of those killed were civilians.[78]

In the end, and as we shall see, these four months would also serve as a laboratory for the longer occupation that was to come. In 1956–7, Israeli officials investigated the possibility of exploiting the Strip's agricultural resources and even zoned off part of the territory for future settlement-building.[79] Israel also destroyed infrastructure that connected Gaza to Egypt, most notably the railway line.[80] And in another sign that it had been planning to stay for the long haul, it changed the Strip's legal tender from the Egyptian pound to the Israeli pound, imposing a harsh exchange rate that compounded the economic crisis for Palestinians in Gaza.[81] As we'll see, the events of 1956–7 would be formative in what came next.

Between the occupations

With the end of the Israeli occupation, Gaza erupted in joy. Sahbaa al-Barbari, a Gazan native in her mid-twenties at the time, described the scenes:

> There were celebrations everywhere in the Gaza Strip, and tens of thousands of people danced in the streets, crying from happiness and celebrating the withdrawal of the Israelis and the end of the occupation. They danced and sang on Omar Al Mukhtar Street [a main street in Gaza City] until two in the morning to welcome the return of the Egyptian administrative governor.[82]

Al-Barbari was an activist herself. The niece of prominent Gazan educator Yusra al-Barbari, Sahbaa had become involved in politics when she joined the PSU during her time at Cairo University in the 1950s. In 1956, she had joined fellow PSU members Yasser Arafat and Salah Khalaf on a delegation to a conference in Warsaw. Engaging with various political circles in Cairo, Sahbaa became committed to communism and has described herself as 'one of the first women who knew about and studied Marxist ideology in Gaza'.[83] After graduating in 1958, she worked as a teacher at her aunt Yusra's school, all the while continuing her political activism. The following year, she was part of a group of students who visited Palestinian political prisoners in Egypt, meeting fellow communist and educator Mu'in Bseiso on one such visit.

As al-Barbari recalls, the Palestinians of Gaza were delighted by the return of the Egyptian authorities in 1957. Nasser's success in standing up to Britain and France had made him an unqualified hero across the Arab world and much of the Global

South in general. As a young schoolboy in Gaza at the time, Abdel Bari Atwan wrote a fan letter to Nasser, and briefly became a local celebrity when the Egyptian president replied to him directly.[84] Nasser's nationalisation of the Suez Canal Company served as an inspiration to anti-colonial movements everywhere and the Palestinians in particular. As Khalaf put it, 'Everything [now] seemed possible, even the liberation of Palestine.'[85]

Khalaf himself returned again to Gaza after Israeli forces withdrew in 1957. He had spent the occupation in Egypt, working with Arafat to organise a Palestinian fighting unit.[86] The two of them had also smuggled funds, arms and political tracts into the Strip. On his return, Khalaf began teaching in Bureij refugee camp, while secretly setting up his own fedayeen group to carry out attacks in southern Israel.[87]

Yet Khalaf and his comrades in Gaza continued to come up against Nasser's authoritarian rule. Now the undisputed champion of anti-colonial Arab nationalism, Nasser still allowed little political independence to the Palestinians of Gaza. Partly for this reason, many fedayeen increasingly based themselves outside Gaza – and all of historic Palestine – at this time. In 1959, Arafat asked Khalaf to leave Gaza again and join him in the Gulf. That year the two of them, along with Khalil al-Wazir and others, regrouped in Kuwait to form the Palestinian Liberation Movement (*harakat al-tahrir al-filistiniyya*), more commonly known by its reverse Arabic acronym, Fatah ('victory'). As a fedayeen group, Fatah had two primary aims: to establish a sovereign Palestinian state and to regain its homeland by armed struggle.[88]

Khalaf later reflected that it was no coincidence Fatah was founded in Kuwait, away from the immediate region of Palestine-Israel where regimes were more hostile to Palestinian activism.[89] The move gave them more freedom to operate.[90] At the same time, Fatah – which would become the most prominent Palestinian party of the twentieth century – could trace its genesis to Gaza.[91] The Strip was where Arafat (also known as Abu Ammar), Khalaf (Abu Iyad) and al-Wazir (Abu Jihad) had first connected as a trio.[92] Arafat and Khalaf came from Gazan families on their fathers' sides; Khalaf and al-Wazir belonged to families that had fled to Gaza during the Nakba. In other words, Gaza was core to their personal and political journeys.

Fatah's Kuwaiti base didn't mean that activism in Palestine ceased at this time. Gaza remained a hub of Palestinian nationalism, and Fatah officials themselves maintained close contacts with sympathisers and activists across the Strip, the West Bank and Israel.[93] Mu'in Bseiso, Haidar Abd al-Shafi and Yusra al-Barbari – the organisers of the 1955 uprising – all continued their political work after the Israeli withdrawal. Abd al-Shafi was elected to Gaza's legislative council in 1962 and participated in the first Palestine National Council in Jerusalem in 1964. That same year, al-Barbari played a key role in establishing the Women's Union of Gaza; she went on to lead the Gaza women's delegation to the founding conference of the General Union of Palestinian Women. Both al-Barbari and Abd al-Shafi sat on the first Palestinian delegation to the UN in 1963.

As a communist, Bseiso had a harder time. Communists remained opposed to Nasser after 1956, and Nasser in turn saw them as a threat to his regime. During a crackdown in 1959, the Egyptian authorities arrested both Bseiso and Sahbaa al-Barbari, now his fiancée; the two had become engaged after getting to know each other during her prison visits.[94] Al-Barbari became the first woman held in Egypt's military prison.[95] After sixteen months' incarceration she was released and returned to Gaza, where the authorities banned her from teaching or travelling.[96] Meanwhile, Bseiso remained imprisoned in Egypt until 1963.[97] Upon his release, the pair finally married after four years of engagement.

Meanwhile, Nasser continued to both support and seek to control the Palestinian cause. In 1962, his regime granted Palestinians in Gaza some internal autonomy by establishing a partially elected legislative council to run municipal affairs, although Nasser retained all major powers. Two years later, the Arab League created the Palestine Liberation Organisation (PLO) at Nasser's behest. Its fifteen-member Executive Council included five from Gaza, among them Abd al-Shafi.[98] Ostensibly, the PLO was an umbrella body to unify Palestinian nationalists, but it also served as a mechanism for Nasser to contain the movement; his regime had full control over the attached Palestine Liberation Army (PLA).[99] While the PLA was militarily insignificant, Fatah – which remained outside the PLO's structures at this time – was wary of Egypt's potential takeover of Palestinian politics and began organising directly in Gaza in response. This in turn led to another Egyptian clampdown.[100]

At the same time, Nasser's status as a hero and inspiration to oppressed people everywhere was drawing visitors from around the world. Maya Angelou, the African-American civil rights activist and writer, had first visited Egypt in 1955, when she remarked that Nasser was 'brown-skinned . . . without a doubt, he was one of us'.[101] She returned to Cairo in 1961 to work as a journalist there.[102] While Angelou didn't cross the border into Gaza, many others did. Among the highest-profile were Argentinian revolutionary Che Guevara, Indian Prime Minister Jawaharlal Nehru, African-American radical activist Malcolm X, and French philosophers Jean-Paul Sartre and

Simone de Beauvoir. All of them visited refugee camps there, signalling the camps' ongoing centrality to Palestinian life and politics.[103]

These international visits to Gaza demonstrate the long-running global solidarity with the Palestinian cause, particularly among colonised, minoritised and other oppressed groups.[104] More recently, demonstrations of Palestinian solidarity have included the international Boycott, Divestment and Sanctions (BDS) movement, formally founded in 2005, and the large-scale protests around the world following October 2023.[105] But in stark contrast to the twenty-first century, mid-twentieth-century Gaza was also open to visits that served as physical acts of solidarity, and were warmly welcomed by many Palestinians. Although Gaza was cut off from the rest of Palestine, its connection to Egypt served as a gateway to the rest of the world – meaning that Gaza could become a hub for Palestinian politics not only locally, but also internationally.

In some ways, the Egyptian era was an aberration in the Gaza Strip's modern history. Unlike the rest of the twentieth century, this period saw the Strip separated from the rest of Palestine by a different regime. At the same time, it bore many features that would characterise Palestinian history in subsequent decades: cultural enmeshment with politics; grassroots civil disobedience efforts; political organisation and militancy; the Israeli strategy of disproportionate retaliation; and the complicated stance of neighbouring Arab states on the Palestinian cause. Israel's 1956 invasion and subsequent four-month occupation was an interruption of the Egyptian era in Gaza. Although Israel withdrew in 1957, the next decade would only prove an interval before

Israel occupied the Strip again. The second occupation would bring the entirety of historic Palestine under Israeli control and last much longer than the first, with serious ramifications for Gaza — as we'll see next.

3

ISRAELI OCCUPATION

In 1967, simmering tensions between Israel and its Arab neighbours erupted into another war. Months of escalating conflict saw Israel and Syria do battle in the air; in a show of Arab solidarity, Nasser closed the Straits of Tiran to Israeli shipping shortly afterwards, blocking them from a crucial strategic sea passage. Then, on 5 June, Israel launched an airstrike against Egypt that marked the beginning of the third regional war in twenty years. Unlike in 1956, this war was a resounding victory for Israel. Over six days, it defeated the Arab alliance of Egypt, Syria and Jordan, and seized land from all three to more than treble its territory. Crucially, it occupied the two remaining parts of Palestine: the West Bank and Gaza Strip (now the occupied Palestinian territories or oPt). The oPt's 1.4 million Palestinians – many of whom were Nakba refugees – now found themselves living under an Israeli military regime, headed by a governor with absolute power.[1] As a stateless people without citizenship, they were subject to martial law and had little recourse to demand their rights.

Upon conquering the oPt, Israel immediately faced a quandary. It wanted the land but not the people – in the words of Prime Minister Levi Eshkol, 'the dowry is followed by a bride whom we don't want'.[2] In many ways, this was a return to Zionism's original problem: how to create a Jewish state in a place with a non-Jewish majority. Annexing the oPt would undermine Israel's Jewish majority, but repeating the mass expulsions of 1948 would risk international condemnation.[3] Israel therefore limited itself to annexing East Jerusalem – an act that was illegal under international law[4] – and opted for an incremental approach in the rest of the oPt, which it occupied without annexation.

The Israeli occupation brought the West Bank and Gaza back together under the same regime – albeit one of military oppression – and therefore created new potential for solidarity movements and shared political organisation. At the same time, it cut off Palestinians in the oPt from their compatriots elsewhere in the Middle East.

Nasser referred to the devastating Arab defeat of 1967 as the *naksa*, or setback: a deliberate attempt to downplay the extent of the loss and reframe it as part of a long-term struggle. While some Palestinians use that term, others refer to the events simply as *harb 1967*, or the 1967 War; in Israel and the West, it's referred to as the Six-Day War. With the Arab states having failed so badly, many Palestinians lost their faith in Nasserist pan-Arabism. They concluded that they needed to lead their own struggle for liberation, through a movement that focused exclusively on the cause of Palestine. With the Arab armies largely discredited, the fedayeen became increasingly prominent, particularly Yasser Arafat's Fatah. In 1968, fedayeen groups took control of the PLO and wrested it from Nasser's grip; Fatah was now its biggest member organisation, followed by the Popular Front for the Liberation of Palestine (PFLP), a Marxist revolutionary organisation created in the early aftermath of the 1967 war.

After Arafat was elected PLO chair in 1969 – a position he retained until his death in 2004 – the organisation adopted a noticeably more radical and militant agenda. It called for the

liberation of Palestine through armed struggle and the establishment of a secular democratic state replacing Israel.[5] The fedayeen
now leading the PLO based themselves in the Palestinian refugee
camps of Jordan and Lebanon, where exile created a different
set of problems from the Israeli military occupation that perme-
ated every aspect of Palestinian lives in Gaza and the West Bank.
This divergence reinforced the oPt's post-'67 isolation from the
rest of the Arab world.

Depopulation

Of the two Palestinian territories it seized in 1967, the Israeli
government saw Gaza as the bigger 'threat', on account of its
dense population and high proportion of refugees.[6] At a meeting
shortly after the war, the director of Israel's Central Bureau of
Statistics told Eshkol, 'If the [occupied Palestinian] area remains
in our hands, then you'll have less trouble from those in the
West Bank than in the Gaza Strip. Because in Gaza they're
presented as refugees for all the world to see.'[7]

Eshkol himself had long viewed Gaza's large refugee population as a major concern, saying 'Gaza is the problem . . . I was
there in 1956 and saw venomous snakes walking in the street'.[8]
Defence Minister Moshe Dayan went further, calling it 'a swarm
of bees'.[9] The prime minister was keen to annex the Strip, but
only after permanently resettling the refugees elsewhere.[10]

The war had given such plans a head start. Around one in
ten of Gaza's population – 45,000 Palestinians – had already
fled the Strip during the six days of war and its immediate
aftermath, many fearing a repeat of the 1956 massacres.[11] Of
this number, around 38,000 ended up in Jordan and the
remainder went to Egypt.[12] With Gaza's population already
depleted, Israel compounded the effect by precluding anyone

who had been outside the Strip during the war from returning. After conducting a census of Palestinians across the oPt, Israel issued identity cards to those who were present at the time. Those who were absent – be it for work, study or tourism – subsequently struggled to get such a card, without which they were denied the right to live in Palestine.[13] The people left stranded outside Gaza as a result included communists Mu'in Bseiso and Sahbaa al-Barbari, who had been in Syria at the time of the war and now had no choice but to spend decades in exile from their homeland.[14]

All the while, Israel was considering more heavy-handed moves. Barely a week after the end of the war, the Israeli cabinet discussed the possibility of 'transferring' Gaza's Palestinian population to Jordan en masse.[15] To aid this goal, it opened the Allenby Bridge border crossing between the West Bank and Jordan and arranged special coaches to transport Palestinians there from Gaza.[16] With clear echoes of 1948, those who tried to slip back into the Gaza Strip without permission were deported, and sometimes shot dead. Between June and September of 1967, Israeli forces killed 146 Palestinians who were trying to cross the River Jordan into the West Bank, and arrested and deported more than 1,000. In total, the population of Gaza fell from 400,000 in June 1967 to 325,900 by the end of that year, and would not return to pre-1967 levels until the mid-1970s.[17]

With such significant numbers at play, Israeli depopulation efforts unsurprisingly came up against regional resistance. In December 1967, the Jordanian government denied entry to several hundred Palestinians at the Allenby Bridge on the grounds that they were being transferred against their will.[18] At the end of 1968, Jordan banned Palestinians from Gaza from entering the country altogether.[19] Yet the Israeli government was undeterred, merely looking to alternatives. Eshkol had initially favoured expelling Gaza's population to Iraq.[20] He also considered forcibly relocating some of them to the West Bank housing vacated by those displaced during the war, which would have the added 'benefit' of blocking the latter's return. The scheme was never carried out because the government, fearing the potential loss of US support, concluded that it would be impossible to implement large-scale forced transfer in the open.[21]

The Israeli government then opted for a different approach. In 1968, it set up so-called 'emigration offices' in Gaza's refugee camps, deliberately targeting the camp populations whom Eshkol saw as so problematic.[22] With the tacit approval of US President Lyndon Johnson, the offices offered money and foreign passports to Palestinian refugees who agreed to permanently relocate abroad, primarily to Canada, Australia and Brazil.[23] On departure, they had to forfeit the ID cards that proved their Gaza residency and Palestinian identity. Eshkol himself had long supported such a policy; as Israeli finance minister during the 1956–7 Gaza occupation, he had allocated half a million dollars to fund the emigration of 200 Palestinian refugee families from the Strip. But the post-'67 initiative had limited success. Few Palestinians accepted the 'offer'.[24]

Despite this failure, Israel's depopulation policies in the wake of the 1967 occupation had a significant demographic impact on Gaza. In the first six months of 1968, 20,000 Palestinians had departed the Strip under varying degrees of coercion. Around 80 per cent of them were already refugees from 1948.[25] They included one branch of the al-Naffar family, whom we met in Chapter One when they were expelled from Jaffa during the Nakba. Having found shelter in Shati refugee camp on the Gaza coast, they were now displaced again by the onset of Israeli occupation. Forced to flee to Jordan and later moving to Syria, they found themselves further and further removed from their hometown of Jaffa. Saleem al-Naffar, born a refugee in Gaza in 1963, had never seen his ancestral home and was just four years old when his family had to leave Palestine altogether. His displacement typified the Palestinian experience as a whole.

THE FOUR YEARS' WAR

Those Palestinians who remained in the Gaza Strip felt the full force of Israel's military occupation. Among them were Yusra al-Barbari and Haidar Abd al-Shafi, who had continued their civil society activism after the 1955 uprising. In 1964, al-Barbari had co-founded the Women's Union of Gaza and the following year she was involved in setting up the General Union of Palestinian Women (GUPW).[26] Women's activism became increasingly important during the Israeli occupation, when large numbers of Palestinian men were deported and detained (the male proportion of the Strip's adult population under forty-nine fell to 41 per cent as a result).[27] In subsequent years, the GUPW intensified its organising work, becoming particularly active in labour relations.[28] Al-Barbari also worked through the Women's Union to provide aid to the families of political detainees and fedayeen.[29]

Having served as a founding member of the PLO, Abd al-Shafi drew on his expertise as a doctor to establish the Gaza branch of the Palestine Red Crescent Society (PRCS) in 1969, with al-Barbari serving as executive secretary. After finally gaining the Israeli governor's authorisation three years later, the PRCS operated a free dispensary, medical services and a public library. Abd al-Shafi used his role to bring together different Palestinian factions, including both armed groups and non-violent civil society organisations.[30] In 1973, he liaised with leading figures across the oPt to issue a direct appeal to the UN for Palestinian autonomy.[31]

But with the PRCS so important in the Palestinian national struggle, it also became a target of Israeli repression.[32] The Israeli authorities variously denied its members their freedom of movement or forced them to move, depending on whichever measure was deemed more effectively punitive at the time. After frequent periods of house arrest, Abd al-Shafi was exiled to Sinai in 1969, where Israel detained him for three months alongside Ibrahim Abu Sitta, the former mayor of Khan Younis who had refused to serve under the occupying regime.[33] In 1970, Israel deported Abd al-Shafi again, this time to Lebanon for two months.[34] Meanwhile in 1974, the regime barred al-Barbari from leaving the Strip for several years.[35] They later imposed the same measure on Abu Sitta, forcing him to remain in the Strip to prevent him from meeting with PLO activists elsewhere.[36]

The activism of Abd al-Shafi and al-Barbari reflected the wider reality of Gaza's centrality to the Palestinian struggle. The Israeli view of the Strip as more 'radical' than the West Bank wasn't entirely inaccurate. After 1967, Israel faced much fiercer resistance in the Strip than elsewhere in Palestine. Civil disobedience in late-1960s Gaza included student demonstrations, consumer boycotts of Israeli goods and widespread refusal to serve in administrative roles under the occupying regime, as well as acts of spontaneous violence such as throwing stones at Israeli vehicles.[37]

Resistance to the Israeli occupation in Gaza also took an organised militant form. In what has been called the 'four years' war', from 1967 to 1971 fedayeen groups used bombs, grenades and sabotage operations to attack Israeli soldiers, civilians and infrastructure from the very first day of the occupation. While the fedayeen were active in Palestinian communities across the region at this time, Gaza proved especially fertile ground for their operations – they were so active in the Strip that, according to a popular saying, 'Israel controlled Gaza during the day but the fedayeen ran it at night.'[38] In the first half of 1970, fedayeen groups in Gaza claimed responsibility for a total of 352 armed operations.[39] Their operations were indiscriminate, and they killed unarmed Israeli civilians as well as soldiers.

Gaza's refugee camps were particularly important to the fedayeen's campaign. In addition to producing a large number of fedayeen, the camps also served as their bases – something particularly significant in the Strip given its lack of available hinterlands. Jabalia, where the fedayeen were especially active, was nicknamed Liberation Camp or Vietnam Camp.[40] The Palestinian campaign gained added impetus from 1969, when Palestinian refugees in Lebanon ousted state security forces from their camps and took control of the spaces themselves, in a movement called the *thawra* ('revolution').[41] News of the refugees' takeover in Lebanon sparked unrest at camps in Gaza, as well as student demonstrations that continued for several weeks.[42]

Nearly all nationalist organisations in Gaza joined the fedayeen campaign against Israel – with one notable exception. Although it had carried out violent attacks against Israel in the 1950s, the Palestinian Muslim Brotherhood now took a different path as Sheikh Ahmed Yassin directed it away from armed struggle. His Mujamma organisation favoured an 'Islamisation' agenda that focused on building social institutions and mosques, based on the rationale that only a truly Islamic society could overthrow the occupation. In stark contrast to its rhetoric today, the Israeli state actually backed the Islamist movement. Seeing it as a valuable counterweight to the PLO's secular nationalism, Israel provided the Muslim Brotherhood with both administrative approval and financial support.[43] The Israeli military governor even attended the opening of Yassin's new mosque in 1973.[44]

Yet elsewhere, Israel's management of Gaza was merciless. It responded to the fedayeen campaign with a ruthless clampdown in the shape of mass arrests, deportations, public beatings, torture and summary executions.[45] The military authorities imposed twenty-four-hour curfews on the refugee camps and severe restrictions on Palestinian movement in policies that amounted to collective punishment.[46] The resulting figures were stark. In 1970, 110 Palestinians (including 71 fedayeen) and 17 Israelis (including 8 soldiers) were killed, while 667 Palestinians and 109 Israelis were wounded. By this time, 1 per cent of the Strip's population was incarcerated.[47] Abu Hassan, a teacher in Gaza, would later reflect, 'I don't think any of us escaped the suffering.'[48]

Israeli repression intensified in the early 1970s, when Ariel Sharon, in his capacity as head of the Israeli army's southern command, was given carte blanche to crush the fedayeen. Applying the same ruthlessness he had shown during the Gaza Raid, he immediately sealed off the entire Strip using a ring of fences with few entry points.[49] He then directed Israeli forces to carry out a brutal campaign against the whole population that involved forcible expulsions, house demolitions and indiscriminate violence. In violation of international law, Israeli forces summarily executed suspects rather than arresting and prosecuting them; they also breached the Geneva Convention by transferring wounded fedayeen by ambulance for interrogation in Israel.[50] Sharon's tactics were so brutal that even the Israeli military governor of the Strip raised concerns – although he took no action to stop it.[51]

Like many Israeli leaders, Sharon saw the refugee camps as the root of the problem. The occupation regime had already tried to annex some of the camps to neighbouring towns, aiming to reduce the population density that it saw as a 'radicalising' force.[52] Sharon went further, seeking to dismantle the camps altogether.[53] From July 1971, his forces demolished more than 2,500 houses in Jabalia, Rafah and Shati camps, and cleared 200 miles of road to enable military access;[54] fittingly, Sharon would later be nicknamed 'the Bulldozer'.[55] The demolitions almost completely destroyed Shati camp,[56] and displaced nearly 16,000 refugees that summer alone.[57]

Izzeldin Abuelaish, who was a teenager at the time, was among the victims of Sharon's campaign. He recalls:

It was midnight. Families rushed to doorways to see long guns pointing at us from the turrets of the tanks . . . The soldiers ordered the people on my street to leave our houses and stand together and wait. About eight hours went by. At dawn they said we had a couple of hours to empty our houses . . . They wanted us to move to al-Arish, a town in the northern part of the Sinai Desert, where there were empty houses because the Egyptians who had lived there had run away when the Israelis arrived and occupied the region. But how were we to do that? We were Palestinians. We grew up in the Jabalia refugee camp . . . We decided to stay. But because we refused to relocate, Sharon denied us compensation for our home . . . The bulldozers started their calamitous work on our street at eight a.m. . . . in one hour we witnessed the demolition of our house.[58]

For the Abuelaish family, Ariel Sharon's demolition of their refugee home had a further twist; it was he who had taken over their land in Huj, the village they had fled during the Nakba.[59]

The demolitions and displacements continued into the following year, with Sharon's troops killing hundreds of Palestinians and detaining thousands more.[60] In another act of collective punishment, Israel forcibly transferred as many as 12,000 relatives of suspected militants to detention camps in Sinai.[61] And on a single night in January 1972, Sharon ordered the expulsion of thousands from an area around Rafah – an act that Israeli general Shlomo Gazit would later describe as 'ethnic cleansing and a war crime'.[62] In total, Sharon's campaign uprooted 38,000 Nakba refugees for the second time.[63]

The Israeli government justified these actions as necessary security measures. But in private conversations with the US embassy, sources at the Israeli Ministry of Foreign Affairs acknowledged that the demolitions formed 'the first phase of a larger plan to thin out the population of the Gaza Strip'.[64] To this end, Israel transferred some of the displaced Palestinian refugees to Sinai and the West Bank, and forcibly dispersed others across towns and cities in Gaza. The occupation regime encouraged them to move into newly built city flats, but often came up against resistance.[65] Seeing the policies as part of a plan to dissolve the refugees' political identity and undermine their right of return, many Palestinians refused to accept the new housing.[66]

By the end of 1972, the Israeli government judged that Sharon's campaign had broken the back of the fedayeen in Gaza. Attacks on Israel – both its military and civilians – were down. His mission supposedly accomplished, Sharon retired from the army the following year and entered politics, helping establish the right-wing Likud party. When Egypt and Syria attacked Israel in 1973 and there were no resulting major insurrections in Gaza, Israel concluded that it had succeeded in pacifying the Palestinians.[67] On this basis, it stepped up efforts to install client authorities in the Strip – but with limited success. Israel twice appointed Rashad Shawwa as Gaza mayor in a bid to counterbalance the power of Yasser Arafat's PLO. Shawwa hailed from a prominent local family – his father had served as Gaza City's first ever mayor in the late Ottoman era[68] – but he faced an immediate backlash and Israel reimposed direct rule shortly afterwards.[69]

At the same time, Israel's brutality between 1967 and 1972 had created new grievances. It had not addressed the underlying causes of Palestinian resistance, in Gaza or anywhere else; the occupation continued across the oPt, the refugees remained displaced and the Palestinian people were still dispossessed. And the fedayeen, though weakened, had not disappeared. In fact, the shared experience of Israeli oppression fostered an even greater sense of unity among Palestinians from a range of backgrounds, helping blur the differences between town and camp communities.[70] As the occupation wore on, many Palestinians felt that remaining on the land and preserving their communities was itself a form of resistance, referring to it as *sumud* – an Arabic word that loosely translates as 'steadfastness'.[71]

Under the occupation regime, every type of resistance – from militancy to music – faced Israeli repression. The regime stifled Palestinian politics by suppressing freedom of expression and freedom of assembly.[72] It punished anyone campaigning, even peacefully, for national self-determination and the right of return. Civilians could be arrested for simple non-violent acts like flying the Palestinian flag or listening to Fatah Radio.[73] Palestinians were forbidden from publishing political material without specific military approval, and Israel censored teaching and reading materials. With the military able to shut down educational and cultural institutions at any time, Palestinian academics also had to struggle against restrictions on research and a lack of funding, as the Israeli authorities often barred organisations from accepting external donations. Festivals, exhibits and public lectures were prohibited.[74]

All the while, the threat of detention hung over Palestinians across the oPt. As non-citizens subject to military law, they could be held in administrative detention for months or even years without charge or trial – all completely legally under the terms of the occupying regime. From 1967 to 1982, this happened to more than 300,000 Palestinians in the territories.[75] Their offences could be vanishingly minor: in 1984, Israel detained an artist from Jabalia camp for seven months on the grounds that his paintings' colours – red, white, green and black, the colours of the Palestinian flag – constituted incitement.[76] It also violated the Geneva Convention again by holding some Palestinian detainees at prisons inside Israel.[77] When detainees were eventually released, many bore the scars of being tortured.[78]

Across the oPt, Israel also made heavy use of local collaborators to enforce the occupation, mostly by gathering intelligence. The presence of collaborators, whom Israel often recruited by blackmail or coercion, sowed mistrust and suspicion across Palestinian society.[79] If found out, collaborators could be killed by the fedayeen. From 1967 to 1971, the PFLP claimed responsibility for twenty-nine such executions.[80]

In the late 1970s, Israel tried again to depopulate the camps by offering residents subsidised 'build your own' housing opportunities in exchange for the demolition of their camp homes. While 10,000 refugees took up the offer, the programme was fiercely opposed and condemned by both the PLO and the UN.[81] Ultimately, the camps remained in place, and Israel continued to target them in its periodic crackdowns, imposing curfews and carrying out raids and demolitions at will.[82] As Israel had calculated, some Palestinians responded to these impossible living conditions by leaving the country.[83]

THE SETTLEMENTS

Israel sought not only to empty Gaza of Palestinians but to fill it with Jewish Israelis. In the aftermath of the 1967 war, Israeli politicians and citizens called for Jewish settlements to be built across the oPt. With religious Zionism boosted by

Israel's overwhelming military victory, the settler movement initially focused on the West Bank, which had a wealth of Jewish holy sites.[84] In 1968, the Israeli government formally established Kiryat Arba settlement on the outskirts of Hebron, after lobbying by a group of religious Zionists who had moved into a hotel in the city.[85] Many more followed, the majority engineered by the Israeli state, which provided settler communities with political, economic, fiscal, military and judicial support.[86]

When the Israeli government discussed settling Gaza the language was less messianic. Sharon was the driving figure here, seeing settlement as the next step after his mass demolitions. Describing Gaza as 'our southern security belt',[87] he envisioned 'fingers' of Jewish settlements that would shatter Gaza's territorial contiguity by cutting it into five zones.[88] Deputy Prime Minister Yigal Allon agreed, saying, 'These settlements are of supreme importance to the political future of the Gaza Strip, because they split up the Strip south of Gaza City. There is great security importance in a Jewish presence in the heart of Gaza.'[89]

At the same time that the first Israeli settlement was underway in Hebron, Allon was proposing two military outposts in Gaza.[90] In 1970, Israel established Kfar Darom near the centre of the Strip, on the site where the JA had built a settlement in the 1940s.[91] Two years later, it built Netzarim settlement between Gaza City and Bureij and Nuseirat refugee camps, cutting through the Strip's most densely populated stretch and further hemming in the Palestinians.[92]

Each one of these settlements is illegal under international law.[93] The Fourth Geneva Convention forbids occupying powers from transferring their population into occupied areas.[94] Despite this, the Israeli courts have consistently endorsed settlement-building across the territories seized in 1967.[95] In 1972, a group of Bedouin (nomadic pastoralist Arabs) went to the High Court of Justice to contest their eviction by Israeli forces seeking to make space for Jewish settlements. The Israeli justices ruled against the Bedouin, enabling the military to forcibly evacuate more than 6,000 people.[96] Subsequent Palestinian attempts to challenge the settlements in the courts have been similarly unsuccessful. On the world stage, consistent US support for Israel has impaired Palestinian efforts to challenge Israel in the international courts – not only when it comes to settlements, but regarding any Israeli crimes.[97]

The settlement project in Gaza intensified from 1977, when Israeli elections returned a majority for Likud for the first time. New prime minister Menachem Begin was notorious among Palestinians for his 1940s leadership of the Irgun Zvai Leumi militia, which had killed as many as 250 unarmed Palestinian civilians in the Deir Yassin massacre of 1948. Three decades later, Begin remained unrepentant and committed to establishing a 'Greater Israel' across all of historic Palestine. Deeply against any notion of political rights for the Palestinians, his party had close ties to the settler movement Gush Emunim.[98] As leader of the opposition, he had promised never to return any territory gained in 1967 or allow a Palestinian state.[99] In his first speech as premier, Begin pledged to build more settlements, rhetoric he quickly acted on by removing all limits on the Jewish colonisation of Arab lands.[100]

The minister for agriculture in Begin's cabinet was none other than Ariel Sharon, who used the office to realise his plan for 'fingers' of settlements in Gaza.[101] By this time, many settlements across the oPt were fully fledged residential neighbourhoods, with shops, schools, synagogues and cafes, as well as their own armed security details alongside the Israeli army.[102] Specially built roads connected them to Israel, enabling the settlers to pretend they lived in Israel proper.[103] For Jewish Israelis, the 1949 armistice line (or Green Line) was increasingly invisible.

ISRAELI SETTLEMENTS
IN GAZA c.1985

To encourage migration to the settlements, the government launched an advertising campaign feting Gaza as the 'Hawaii of Israel'.[104] Some Israelis were enticed by the tax concessions and subsidies on offer. These so-called 'economic settlers' joined the ideologues in Gaza's growing settler population.[105]

For the Palestinians, of course, the individual settlers' motivations made little difference. Either way, the settlements took more land from them – often the most fertile and desirable land – and caused even more displacement. By the mid-1980s, Palestinians had lost a third of the Strip's land to Israeli expropriation. Adjusting for population, this meant that a settler had 400 times as much land at their disposal as a Palestinian refugee living in the same territory.[106] It was the ongoing Nakba in action again.

The settlers and the Palestinians lived under different political, economic and judicial regimes. As Jewish Israeli citizens, the former enjoyed rights and privileges denied to the latter – including the right to elect the Israeli government that ruled over them all. What's more, the settlers were subject to Israeli criminal law as civilians, while Palestinians living in the occupied territories were tried in military courts where army officers served as judges.[107] The resulting inequalities were manifold; for example, a settler could be arrested and detained for no more than twenty-four hours without charge, while for a Palestinian the equivalent period was eight days – with the potential for endless renewals adding up to months or even years in detention. A Palestinian convicted of manslaughter could expect life imprisonment, while the equivalent punishment for a settler was twenty years at most. And while an imprisoned settler could be eligible for early release after serving two thirds of their sentence, there was no such break for an imprisoned Palestinian.[108]

Access to water was a particular flashpoint in this two-tier society. Forbidden from developing any new water resources,

Palestinians faced strict water quotas and harsh fines for overuse.[109] With no such restrictions placed on Israeli settlers, there was a stark difference in consumption rates. In 1985, settlers in Gaza used 2,326 cubic metres of water per capita, while Palestinians used just 123.[110] Settlers' swimming pools and lush green lawns signalled the inequality as Palestinian farmers struggled to water their crops.[111] The visible injustice became an underlying everyday grievance for Palestinians.

THE CAMP DAVID ACCORDS

When it came to settlement-building, Israel didn't only target the occupied Palestinian territories. In 1967, it had also captured Sinai from Egypt and the Golan Heights from Syria.[112] It soon began building settlements in both territories. In fact, in the 1970s the Israeli settlement project was more expansive in Sinai than in Gaza; by 1977 there were thirteen settlements in the former compared to six in the latter. Concentrated in the north of Sinai, these settlements cut off the Palestinians not only from the Egyptian support that had previously been so significant, but also from their entry point to the wider world.[113] Palestinians could still travel to Egypt, but only in very particular circumstances – usually with student visas – and under tightly controlled conditions. Izzeldin Abuelaish, who left Jabalia in 1975 to study at the University of Cairo, recalls travelling through Sinai in an Israeli bus with blacked-out windows, before being transferred by the Red Cross when reaching Egyptian-controlled territory.[114]

Egypt, however, was adamant that this would not become the new status quo. Having lost more than 10,000 soldiers in the 1967 war, it was determined to mend its national reputation and regain Sinai.[115] In 1973, Anwar Sadat – who had become Egyptian president following Nasser's death three years earlier – allied with Syrian President Hafez al-Assad to launch a surprise attack on Israel and restore Arab honour. Deliberately timed to coincide with the Jewish holiday of Yom Kippur, when much of Israel was shut down, the attack led to what became known as the Yom Kippur War in Israel, the Ramadan War in the Arab world, and otherwise simply the October War or the 1973 War.

Somewhat complacent after its overwhelming victory in 1967, Israel was caught off guard by the attack, which until 2023 was the worst in its history. It found itself on the back foot as the Egyptian and Syrian armies advanced from either end of the country. As international pressure mounted, the three governments agreed to a ceasefire after three weeks of war. What happened next took much of the world by surprise.

When planning the surprise attack, Sadat had assured Assad that their goal was to fully recapture the Arab territories lost in 1967. This was in keeping with the Khartoum Resolution agreed by the Arab League shortly after that defeat: no peace with Israel, no recognition of Israel, no negotiations with Israel.[116] Yet unbeknownst to Assad, Sadat had a secret plan: he wanted to regain Sinai via peace talks with Israel, as a prelude for closer Egyptian ties to the US, and he saw the war as a way to make this happen. After gaining leverage with the surprise attack of 1973, Sadat used his advantage to push for a comprehensive Egyptian peace agreement with Israel. As a stunned Arab world looked on, he even travelled to Jerusalem in 1977 to directly address the Knesset (Israeli parliament).

The following year, US President Jimmy Carter hosted Sadat and Begin at Camp David, where they agreed on a framework for peace known as the Camp David Accords.[117] Its terms became the basis of the 1979 Egyptian–Israeli peace agreement: full diplomatic relations between the two states, the return of Sinai to Egypt and guaranteed Israeli shipping rights through Suez.[118]

By the end of 1982, Israel had withdrawn all 8,000 settlers from the peninsula and Egyptian sovereignty was re-established.[119]

The Camp David Accords also included a framework for the oPt, envisaging limited Palestinian autonomy without full Israeli withdrawal, with Gaza to act as an initial testing ground for the plan.[120] With the PLO excluded from Camp David, despite now being recognised by both the UN and the Arab League as the Palestinian people's 'sole legitimate representative', this strand of the Accords went nowhere. It was a far cry from the fully fledged independence that Palestinians wanted, and was met with fierce protests on the ground. In October 1978, Palestinians from across the political spectrum attended a rally in Gaza denouncing the Accords and demanding the PLO's inclusion in any negotiations.[121] A few months later, Gaza's political figures and local representatives issued a strongly worded condemnation of the Accords, and Haidar Abd al-Shafi joined with West Bank mayors to form a National Orientation Committee in opposition to Camp David.[122] Once the Egyptian–Israeli agreement was finalised in 1979, Sadat became *persona non grata* in Palestine.[123] Gaza refugee Ramzy Baroud recalls how his father Mohammed would throw his shoes at the television whenever Sadat appeared on the news.[124]

While Palestinians everywhere opposed the Egyptian–Israeli agreement, those in Gaza felt its impact most keenly. The withdrawal from Sinai freed up Israeli resources and intensified Jewish settlement-building in the Strip, partly to absorb some of the Sinai settlers who now relocated there.[125] What's more, Sadat responded to the PLO's condemnation by banning Palestinians from studying in Egyptian universities. The fall-out was particularly bad in Gaza, where Palestinians had relied on Egyptian higher education – and specifically the free-tuition policy introduced by Nasser[126] – as an important lifeline of opportunity.[127]

Perhaps worst of all, the establishment of the Israeli–Egyptian border divided Gaza's southernmost city of Rafah into Palestinian and Egyptian parts, separated by barbed wire and fences. To achieve this, Israel destroyed more than 300 houses in Rafah camp and forcibly transferred their residents northwards.[128] At the same time, it uprooted and displaced some of the same refugees whom it had ejected from Gaza to Sinai in 1971; they were now placed in the Tel al-Sultan gathering* north of Rafah. With families divided in the process, some were reduced to communicating with their relatives by shouting across barbed wire.[129] It was a devastating symbol of the Palestinian people's continuing displacement, dispersal and dispossession.

CROSSING THE LINE

Meanwhile, the armistice line that had been so central to Gaza's politics in the 1950s and 1960s took on a different status under the occupation. After treating it as an impenetrable border and shooting Palestinian crossers on sight in the decades after the Nakba, from 1967 Israel switched to an 'open door' policy under the direction of Defence Minister Moshe Dayan. Dayan believed that partial integration into the Israeli economy would hinder Palestinian resistance and pacify the oPt population. On this basis, Israel began allowing armistice line crossings in the early years of the occupation. In 1972, after Sharon's campaign had kneecapped the fedayeen, Israel issued a general exit order that allowed Palestinians to move freely between Gaza, Israel and the West Bank during the daytime.[130]

The exit order meant that Palestinians in Gaza could visit their brethren in the West Bank, and vice versa, for the first time

---

* Tel al-Sultan is a refugee camp in Rafah that UNRWA does not formally recognise and therefore refers to as a 'gathering'.

in two decades.[131] They could also reunite with the Palestinian community inside Israel (also known as '48 Palestinians), who had lived under military rule until just six months before the 1967 war and continue to face prejudice and discrimination to this day.[132] These reunions may have been the only positive that Palestinians could take from the naksa, as many refugees took the opportunity to visit their lost homes for the first time since the Nakba.[133] In her memoir, Gazan-born Hekmat al-Taweel recalls visiting Jaffa with her husband, where they found that his parents' home had been converted into an Israeli kindergarten.[134]

Of course, family reunions were not the intended purpose of Dayan's 'open door' policy. By enabling Palestinians to enter Israel, he sought to use the occupied populations as a cheap labour pool, a set-up that drew comparisons to South Africa's Bantustans.[135] Dayan would prove sorely mistaken in his belief that this limited integration would quieten the Palestinians and undercut their resistance movements. But with so few opportunities inside Gaza, many Palestinians did begin to cross into Israel for work. A new form of 'integration' began – one that was inherently unequal in every way.

Categorised as temporary guest workers, and without the protection of their own state, Palestinian labourers inside Israel were highly vulnerable to exploitation. Barred from joining unions, they had no means of advocating for better conditions and had to work without health insurance, sick leave, paid breaks, pensions or any other basic labour rights. Indeed, their appeal as employees was premised precisely on this status, which allowed employers to pay them lower wages while demanding more labour from them.[136] On average, Palestinian workers from Gaza earned less than half the wages of their Israeli counterparts.[137] Unsurprisingly, this generated serious grievances, although Israeli policymakers continued to dismiss them in their calculations.[138]

Around a third of Gaza's workers in Israel were employed illegally, hired from informal open air 'markets' where they would gather in front of prospective Israeli employers.[139] The experience could be humiliating, with workers sometimes forced to run alongside employers' moving cars as a way of proving their stamina.[140] As Palestinians were not allowed to stay in Israel or East Jerusalem overnight, their options were to either sleep there illicitly – and risk imprisonment if caught – or get up as early as 4 a.m. to make it to the 'markets' on time. In the mid-1970s, Izzeldin Abuelaish spent months doing casual labour in Israel to earn money for his studies in Egypt. He once missed out on an agreed job because he didn't arrive sufficiently early at the 'market', and another Palestinian labourer took it in his absence. On occasion, Palestinian workers had happier experiences; Abuelaish also recalls a summer he spent working on a family farm in southern Israel, where he developed a warm relationship with his Israeli employers.[141]

Typically, casual labourers from Gaza had to start their days no later than 5 a.m. and didn't get home until 6 p.m. at the earliest. Their absences had knock-on effects. As those working in Israel were predominantly men, it often fell to their wives to take on additional domestic and financial burdens while they were away. Many children grew up with their fathers rarely present.[142]

Palestinians who worked in Israel also faced hostility from the fedayeen, who saw them as collaborators and sometimes threw grenades at Israeli buses transporting the workers.[143] From 1970 to 1971, the fedayeen's violent intimidation caused the number of Gaza-based Palestinians working in Israel to almost halve, from 10,000 to less than 6,000. But with opportunities in the Strip remaining so limited, many had little choice but to continue labouring for Israeli employers. By 1973, the figure was back up to 25,000 and by 1977 it was 53,000.[144] By 1986, an estimated two fifths of the oPt workforce were employed in Israel, but this didn't include casual labourers – those who did irregular and insecure work, usually menial tasks for under-the-table payment – meaning the true figure was likely much higher.[145] The situation was especially pronounced in Gaza, where more than half of the salaried population were employed in Israel at this time.[146]

As well as a cheap labour pool, Israel used the oPt as a captive market for its exports: it removed all restrictions on the flow of Israeli goods into the oPt, while tightly regulating Palestinian commodities. As Israel also restricted imports from neighbouring countries like Jordan, Gaza became flooded with cheap Israeli goods.[147] By 1979, more than 90 per cent of Gaza's imports originated in Israel. In the 1980s, the oPt was second only to the US as the biggest importer of goods from Israel and, as a result, the Palestinian economy became increasingly shaped by the interests and priorities of the Israeli economy.[148]

To make matters worse, Israel limited competition by curbing Palestinian economic activity. Military orders and curfews seriously damaged Gaza's once-thriving fishing industry; in the first two decades of the occupation, Israel reduced the area available to Gaza's fishermen by 75 per cent, and their annual haulage of fish dropped by 59 per cent.[149] Meanwhile, Gazan agriculture, once key to its economy, was undercut by Israeli restrictions on water and fertiliser usage and planting; military orders made it illegal for Palestinians to plant fruit trees on a commercial scale without a permit. By the 1970s, Gaza's famous citrus fruits were no longer profitable.[150] And while government grants enabled Israeli investors to easily set up businesses inside the oPt,[151] Palestinian businesses had little access to investment and working capital – made worse by the heavy taxes that Israel imposed on Palestinians across the oPt.[152]

On top of all this, Israeli export restrictions meant that Palestinians were mostly limited to selling their goods in Israel, where they faced tough quotas and prohibitions. While Israeli producers had unlimited access to Gazan markets, Gaza's farmers were prohibited from marketing most fruit and vegetables inside Israel. Worse still, Arab boycott laws prevented most Arab countries from importing any goods that may have used raw materials or facilities originating in Israel – which included many products from the oPt. Palestinian producers were therefore left with the highest production costs and the fewest markets, pushing many to seek work in Israel instead.[153] The overall effect was to buttress Israeli control and boost its industry while weakening the Palestinian economic base – with the long-term goal of preventing any chance of a Palestinian state.[154] Palestinians were left reliant on Israel for their basic food and agriculture, in stark contrast to the self-sufficiency of their farming culture before 1948.

Israel claimed that Palestinians benefited economically from the occupation, pointing to the higher wages they could earn in Israel. But this was offset by the increased cost of living, inflation and the lack of investment or savings infrastructure.[155] Israel also invested very little in Gaza's public services and didn't build any housing.[156] In fact, government expenditure inside the Gaza Strip more than halved relative to GNP between 1967 and 1983.[157] The exception, of course, was the Jewish settlements, where the government invested heavily in all kinds of infrastructure, including roads, water, electricity and social institutions.[158] Meanwhile, Palestinians were left with inadequate public services, increasingly overstretched provisions from UNRWA (which didn't cover all of Gaza's population), and a very limited private sector that few could afford.[159]

As we've seen, it wasn't the Palestinians but Israel that benefited from the occupation, on multiple fronts. As well as providing a cheap solution to manpower shortages, in the mid-1980s workers from Gaza who were employed in the formal economy contributed $2–3 million per month to the Israeli government in taxes and social security. Strikingly, this produced an annual total that exceeded Israel's $17.5 million yearly contribution to Gaza's budget – meaning that the occupation cost the Israeli taxpayer nothing.[160] At the same time, Palestinian labour was boosting the Israeli economy, with the Palestinians themselves feeling next to none of the benefits.[161]

What's more, the occupation opened up new territory for Israeli citizens, who now moved freely back and forth over the Green Line – not only as settlers but also as tourists. An estimated 35,000 Israelis descended on Gaza's shops on the first Saturday that the Strip was open to them, with the crowds so large that many parked their cars on the beach. In the 1970s and 1980s, Israelis continued to visit the Strip to go to the beach, eat its famous seafood, and take advantage of its cheaper goods and services.[162] Gaza was known for its car mechanics and many Israelis took their cars to garages there.[163] Some young Palestinians, among them Izzeldin Abuelaish, made money by carrying Israeli visitors' shopping bags and running errands for them.[164]

While for many Jewish Israelis visits to Gaza were about tourism and shopping, movement across the Green Line was ultimately rooted in the unequal dependency model the Israeli regime imposed on the Strip. Palestinian labourers working inside Israel were a stateless population subject to the military rule of occupation; Israelis in Gaza, whether settlers or visitors, had all the benefits of full citizenship and civil rights.

In the years after 1967, a small minority of Jewish Israelis began to agitate against this injustice. Oded Lifshitz was an Israeli leftist from Nir Oz kibbutz, a few miles from Gaza. In 1972, he joined with other Israeli activists to campaign against the forced eviction of the Bedouin from the Rafah Salient in northern Sinai. When they failed to stop it, Lifshitz and fellow activist Latif Dori started a new initiative called 'Rafiah Tours', in which they took groups of Israelis around Sinai and Gaza to show them what their army was doing there.[165] Unfortunately, such anti-occupation activism remained very much the exception among Israelis visiting Gaza – and the West Bank – at this time.

The Arab defeat of 1967 had ushered in a devastating new reality for the Palestinian people. With Israel now controlling the whole of historic Palestine, they were further away than ever from their dream of independent statehood. Instead, they faced what many described as the next phase of the Nakba, as Israeli settlement-building and land seizure caused further displacement and dispossession, and the settlers' lifestyles highlighted the systemic injustice that deprived the Palestinians of their rights while protecting Israeli violations. It was the same injustice that allowed any individual with Jewish ancestry to move to an illegal Israeli settlement in Gaza (or the West Bank), while denying their Palestinian neighbours the right to return to their lost homes only a few miles away. And it was exactly this injustice that would ultimately provoke a mass Palestinian uprising, twenty years into the occupation.

4

THE FIRST INTIFADA

By the mid-1980s, a whole generation of Palestinians had grown up under Israeli occupation. They had never lived in Palestine before the Nakba and had little or no memory of Egypt's period of governance in Gaza. Instead, their lives had been dominated entirely by Israel's occupation and its total control over Palestinian lives. As they reached adulthood, young Palestinians across the oPt faced limited opportunities alongside continuing oppression, violence and discrimination. And this group was in the majority; by 1987, 59 per cent of Gaza's population was aged under nineteen.[1] At the end of that year, their grievances would erupt into the biggest Palestinian uprising since the 1930s: the first intifada.

Intifada is an Arabic word literally meaning 'shaking off', though it is usually translated as 'uprising'. The term is not religious and has been used in various settings to describe collective movements; as we saw in Chapter Two, some Palestinians described the 1955 Gaza protests as an intifada. In the context of 1980s Palestine, the *intifada* referred to the Palestinians' collective desire to *shake off* the occupation and take power into their own hands. Through collective action, they demanded an end to the occupation, no more disunity in the PLO, and a renewed focus on Palestine in the Arab and international agendas, with the ultimate goal of an independent Palestinian state.

The first intifada, as it became known, was a spontaneous grassroots uprising – a popular outburst after twenty years of occupation and four decades of dispossession. It was also mostly non-violent, especially in its early years. Instead of militancy, activists relied on a strategy they called national disobedience; across the oPt, Palestinians resigned from the public sector, withdrew their labour from Israeli employers, stopped buying Israeli products and refused to pay taxes to the occupying authority. In this way, they used the limited leverage they had against Israel: as labourers, taxpayers and consumers. Public demonstrations and widespread raising of the Palestinian flag became common.

Why did the intifada erupt in 1987, two decades into the occupation? The younger Palestinian generations, many of whom played a leading role in the uprising, were crucial here. After enduring humiliation and oppression throughout their lives, they came of age during a fresh series of crises for the Palestinian people in the 1980s.

In 1982, Israel had launched its second invasion of Lebanon, under the direction of Ariel Sharon, now minister of defence. By this time the PLO had been based in Lebanon for over a decade and controlled significant parts of the country, using it as a base for attacks on Israeli infrastructure, military personnel and civilians.[2] Some of these attacks proved fatal: in 1974, Fatah militants entered the Israeli coastal city of Nahariya, where they killed three civilians and one soldier. Most seriously, in 1978, Abu Jihad planned the hijacking of a bus in central Israel, in which Palestinian militants killed thirty-eight Israeli civilians on board, including thirteen children, in what became known as the Coastal Road Massacre. Many more PLO attacks didn't cause any fatalities, but nevertheless spread fear and panic among Israelis and destabilised communities living near the Lebanese border in the north. By invading Lebanon, Israel sought both to destroy the PLO and to install its own anti-Palestinian Lebanese allies in government.[3] Sharon believed that doing so would also curtail Palestinian nationalism in the oPt and therefore make it easier for Israel to annex the remainder of historic Palestine.[4]

The Israeli offensive, culminating in a seven-week siege of Beirut, devastated the country's capital and, according to Lebanese statistics, killed more than 19,000 Palestinians and Lebanese, mostly civilians, as well as 364 Israeli soldiers.[5] Under intense pressure from Israel and the US, and with no meaningful support from any Arab government, the PLO eventually agreed to leave Lebanon in exchange for American pledges to protect the thousands of unarmed Palestinian civilians left behind.[6] At the end of August, around 10,000 PLO fedayeen departed by sea, including Yasser Arafat, Salah Khalaf (Abu Iyad) and Khalil al-Wazir (Abu Jihad).[7] Four Palestinian civilians joined one of the boats, including the Gazan communists Mu'in Bseiso and Sahbaa al-Barbari, whom we met in Chapter Two. Their activism made it unsafe for them to remain in Lebanon, so they travelled with the PLO to its new base in Tunisia.[8]

But the US didn't follow through on its promises of protection.[9] On 16 September, the Israeli military surrounded the Palestinian refugee camps of Sabra and Shatila, left vulnerable after the fedayeen's departure. Israeli soldiers sent up flares to illuminate the camps while their Lebanese allies, the Kata'ib militia, killed no fewer than 1,400 unarmed Palestinians inside, mostly women, children and elderly people.[10] Sabra's main hospital – incidentally called Gaza Hospital – became a centre of horror, struggling to treat hundreds of victims as the Kata'ib committed mass murder and Israeli forces prevented escape from the camps.[11] The massacre was meant as revenge for the killing of Lebanese President-Elect Bachir Gemayel two days previously (whose assassin, it later turned out, wasn't Palestinian but Lebanese).[12]

When news spread of the massacre, Palestinians everywhere were horrified and outraged.[13] Transnational Palestinian solidarity ran deep; some families in Gaza had relatives in Lebanon, and during the Israeli siege many had donated blood for the Red Cross to transport to war victims there.[14] The Sabra-Shatila massacre carried strong echoes of the original Nakba: the targeting of innocents, the sense of Israeli impunity, and the international disregard for Palestinian lives as none of the foreign armies present in Lebanon moved to protect the refugees. Israel faced a rising international backlash after the event, alongside the biggest protests in its history, as the organisation Peace Now brought 400,000 Israelis – 10 per cent of the population – to the streets of Tel Aviv to protest against the massacre and demand an inquiry.[15] After the government acquiesced to this demand, the resulting Kahan Commission found that both Menachem Begin and Ariel Sharon bore responsibility for the massacre and recommended Sharon's resignation – a strikingly mild penalty given the crime.[16] In the end, his punishment was even milder: he stood down as defence minister but remained in the cabinet.[17]

Among Palestinians, the Sabra-Shatila massacre added to a rising sense of disillusionment with the PLO, which had failed in its promise of liberation and was now increasingly beset by internal fractures.[18] Over the course of the 1970s, the PLO had become more prominent on the global stage, and in 1974 it gained international credibility when first the Arab League and then the UN officially recognised it as the 'sole legitimate representative' of the Palestinian people (as discussed in Chapter Three).[19] That same year, the UN admitted the PLO as a non-member observer entity, giving it a similar status to the Vatican.[20] But by the time it was routed from Lebanon in 1982, the PLO seemed less and less relevant to many Palestinians. Those in the oPt felt both literally and figuratively distant from the ageing PLO leadership, thousands of miles away in Tunis. To make matters worse, the Palestinian issue had slipped down the agenda for many Arab governments. There were even rumours that some Arab states were considering following in Egypt's footsteps and forging their own separate agreements with Israel.[21]

Meanwhile, Gaza and the West Bank were nearing twenty years of Israeli occupation and losing ever more land. In 1985, Minister of Defence Yitzhak Rabin – a Labor politician in a coalition government – had pledged on a visit to settlements in Gaza that the Strip would remain 'an inseparable part' of Israel. The following year, Minister of Housing David Levy visited Gaza to announce the establishment of more settlements there.[22] By 1987, 2,500 Israeli settlers controlled 28 per cent of the Strip, with the support of both main parties.[23]

The settlers' land seizure intensified Gaza's population density, which was already among the highest in the world, by driving Palestinians into smaller and smaller areas.[24] The Strip's population had more than doubled in the four decades since the Nakba, but the occupation had prevented the economy from growing accordingly.[25] Escalating tensions over water and other resources fuelled Palestinian grievances about the manifest inequality between their rights and those of the settlers. The result was rising agitation in Gaza.

Increasingly, attacks on Israel were carried out by Islamists. Political Islam was surging across the Middle East, emboldened by the success of the Islamic Revolution in Iran and the mujahideen's struggle against the Soviet occupation of Afghanistan. In this context, the Muslim Brotherhood's failure to confront the Israeli occupation was increasingly compromising its standing in Palestinian society.[26] In 1981, a renegade from the Brotherhood had set up a militia called Palestinian Islamic Jihad (PIJ), which called for immediate jihad against Israel.[27] PIJ carried out significant attacks on Israeli soldiers and civilians, both within the oPt and in Israel itself.[28]

On the ground in Palestine, civil society also mobilised at this time. In 1982, Palestinians formed voluntary work committees (VWCs) to clean public spaces, rebuild houses, arrange medical trips and organise extra classes for students.[29] Women's work committees (WWCs) ran literacy and health education classes in refugee camps and villages, provided skills training for women, and set up nurseries to enable them to work outside the home.[30] Some Palestinians also organised strikes withdrawing their labour from Israel.[31]

In response to both the militancy and the non-violent resistance, Defence Minister Rabin intensified collective punishment practices in Gaza. From 1985, the Israeli military carried out mass arrests and house demolitions that typically targeted the refugee camps, while resuming deportations to Jordan and Lebanon. At the beginning of 1986, Israel imposed a curfew on the entire Strip after Fatah announced celebrations for the twenty-first anniversary of its first fedayeen campaign. Shortly afterwards, Fatah killed two settlers in Gaza. The following year, Israel arrested so many Palestinians in Gaza that a new detention camp had to be created to hold them.[32]

The final spark came on 8 December 1987. An Israeli vehicle crashed into four Palestinians walking home from work, killing all of them. The crash took place near Jabalia, a camp with a longstanding reputation as a hub of Palestinian resistance and home to three of the four men killed.[33] While Israel insisted the crash was an accident, many Palestinians suspected it was a revenge attack for the killing of an Israeli settler in a Gaza market two days earlier. Ramzy Baroud, a relative of some of the deceased, who were from the same extended family, said that their deaths 'represented the grievances of a whole generation'.[34] Their

funerals brought thousands onto the streets of Jabalia to demonstrate, with some in the crowd throwing stones at Israeli soldiers,
who opened fire in response. After soldiers shot and killed
fifteen-year-old Hatem Sisi, demonstrations spread across the
entire Strip.[35]

The fatal crash was the trigger but not the cause of Palestine's
first intifada. In the words of Izzeldin Abuelaish, himself from
Jabalia:

> the unrest came mostly from the fact that nothing was
> being done to alleviate the situation for Palestinians. There
> was no sign of establishing a Palestinian state . . . The
> leadership needed from the Arab states in order to resolve
> this issue was faltering. Palestinians had been waiting for
> change, for relief from intimidation and harassment, for
> twenty years since the Israelis took over in Gaza.[36]

The demonstrations quickly spread to the West Bank, East Jerusalem
and Palestinian communities inside Israel – who constituted nearly
20 percent of Israeli citizenry.[37] The intifada, as they were now
calling it, would ultimately last six years. It was no coincidence
that it began in Gaza; as activist Ihab al-Ashqar reflected, 'if something doesn't start in Gaza, it just won't get off the ground. Whoever
suffers the most is always the one to force change.'[38]

RESISTANCE: THE PALESTINIAN UPRISING

In January 1988, leading Palestinian activists formed the Unified
National Command of the Uprising (UNC) to co-ordinate the
intifada. It brought together members of the biggest Palestinian
factions, including Fatah, the PFLP, communists and Islamists.
The UNC sought to focus on political rather than military

strategy in order to compel Israeli withdrawal, and in the early period it was effective in holding even militants to non-violence, calling on the Palestinian people to boycott the occupation authorities by withholding their labour and their taxes.[39] With a decentralised leadership, the UNC circulated its instructions via popular committees – community-based grassroots organisations that provided social services and, from 1988, used graffiti and leaflets to spread the word of intifada activities.[40]

Activists both within and beyond the UNC also worked to establish Palestinian autonomy and move away from dependence on Israel – a first step towards independent statehood.[41] Women were particularly significant in establishing the intifada's new institutions: they ran underground classes to replace the schools shut down by Israel, set up mobile health clinics to reach Palestinians with no access to hospitals and grew local produce to counter Israeli economic domination. The WWCs extended their nurseries' hours so that more women could get involved. They also worked with the UNC and its popular committees to organise relief and emergency services and support bereaved families, as well as distributing leaflets, recruiting new activists and contacting lawyers for detainees.[42]

Through these acts, Palestinian women asserted themselves as equal partners in the national struggle.[43] Their agitation often struck at two fronts: the occupation and society's sexism. Sometimes they met both goals at once; for example, by setting up co-operatives they could simultaneously support the boycott of Israeli produce and promote women's economic independence.[44] Alongside slogans calling for an independent Palestinian state and an end to the occupation, some activists promoted slogans calling for women's liberation.[45]

Among the women activists was Naila Ayesh. Born in the West Bank, she had been six years old when the occupation began and eight years old when Israel demolished her family home. As a young adult she joined the Democratic Front for the Liberation of Palestine (DFLP), a splinter group from the PFLP, and in the mid-1980s she began working as women's and children's officer for Save the Children in Gaza. Ayesh's activism brought her to the attention of the Israeli military authorities, and in early 1987 she was arrested. She was pregnant at the time. Detained in Jerusalem for forty-five days without charge or trial, Ayesh suffered a miscarriage after being beaten, dragged along the ground and denied medical care. When her husband informed a human rights group in Israel of Ayesh's miscarriage in detention, her story reached the news and Israel released her to avoid negative international press.[46]

When the intifada erupted shortly afterwards, Ayesh immediately became involved in the national disobedience campaign. To spread the word, she hid pamphlets in loaves of bread and delivered them through the camps. Along with other Palestinian women, she also forged ties of solidarity with Israeli women activists who campaigned against the occupation; the Israeli peace movement had been steadily growing over the 1980s.[47]

Many of the most active participants in the intifada were Palestinian children. In fact, in a mostly unarmed uprising, Palestinian violence usually took the form of young boys throwing stones at Israeli tanks, in an image that became an icon of the conflict's asymmetry – especially as the Israeli military often punished stone throwers with disproportionate force. Some of the stone throwers were older teenagers, but others were young children; in total, around 60 per cent were aged between six and fourteen.[48] And stone-throwing was just one among many acts of protest. Ramzy Baroud, who was a high school student in Gaza when the intifada began, remembers how some youths in Gaza would put blankets down on the roads to entangle the chains of Israeli tanks and render them immobile.[49]

Baroud's own involvement in the intifada began on its very first day. As he describes it:

> Following our morning exercise, the school principal ordered us into class, but we, for once, refused to comply. Flyers distributed by student political groups urged all students to march in protest of the killing of the four laborers and the violence that followed in Jabaliya . . . All it took was one daring student to stand up in the centre of the schoolyard and start waving a Palestinian flag. The students began chanting, praising the martyrs of Jabaliya . . . Within a few minutes, the entire school was marching, followed by students from nearby schools, and within an hour, thousands of refugees throughout the Nuseirat refugee camp were moving in one large, unprecedented mass. Many such protests had taken place in the past in our refugee camp, but the speed at which thousands gathered, the intensity of the chants, the tears of the many women who marched alongside [us] were such that once the protest reached the camp's central market, all vowed that today would not be like any other.[50]

While the Palestinian grass roots were mobilising so effectively, the PLO leadership was looking increasingly detached. Struggling to keep up, the PLO tried with limited success to exert control over the uprising.[51] In a radio interview in January 1988, Khalil al-Wazir (Abu Jihad) told an outright lie, claiming that he had given the order to start the intifada.[52] In reality, power was shifting from the exiled PLO leadership to Palestinian civil society inside the oPt, including Haidar Abd al-Shafi, the longstanding community leader in Gaza.

There was another force emerging too. We have already seen how the rise of political Islam across the wider region had led to growing disillusionment with the Muslim Brotherhood's apolitical stance in Palestine. The intifada provided the final impetus. On 9 December 1987, Mujamma leader Sheikh Ahmed Yassin hosted a group of men at a meeting in Shati camp, where he had lived ever since being displaced from al-Jura village during the Nakba.[53] They decided the time had come to form an offshoot organisation that would take up arms against Israel. The next month, they formally launched the Islamic Resistance Movement (*al-haraka al-Islamiya al-muqawwama*), which went by its Arabic acronym: Hamas.[54]

Hamas' activities were expansive; it set up political, military and administrative wings to go alongside the Mujamma's substantial welfare network, which it would eventually subsume. As a result, many Palestinians came to know the organisation not only as militants but also for its social, cultural and educational projects – particularly in Gaza, where it ran the strongest and best organised social service network, including medical care, food aid and youth clubs.[55] But it had ultimately been set up to directly confront the occupation with militancy, and this was its main focus.

On creation, Hamas had immediately pledged its commitment to the intifada. Yet in August 1988, its ideological and strategic divergence from the UNC became clear when it announced its Charter.[56] In contrast to the UNC's discourse, the Hamas Charter framed the Palestinian struggle in Islamic terms and cited jihad as the only route to liberation, meaning not just armed struggle – although that was key – but also political, economic, social and cultural Islamisation. Crucially, the Charter defined historic Palestine (meaning the Mandate territory) as a *waqf*, meaning an inalienable Islamic endowment. On these grounds, Hamas contended that the territory's man-made partition – and accordingly the state of Israel – were illegitimate.[57]

Notoriously, Hamas' Charter was full of antisemitic tropes and caricatures. Conflating Judaism with Zionism and Jewish people worldwide with the state of Israel, it stated that Israel's success was down to Jewish control of world affairs. Citing the infamous *Protocols of the Elders of Zion* – a fabricated tract from early twentieth-century Europe that popularised racist notions of an international Jewish conspiracy – the Charter claimed that a global Jewish plot had been behind every war in history, including both world wars, as well as the creation of the League of Nations and the UN. It also talked about Jewish financial power and influence over the media, and described Israeli policies as 'Nazism of the Jews'.[58]

After issuing its Charter, Hamas increasingly diverged from the UNC in both messaging and tactics.[59] It issued its own communiqués and had a separate schedule of activities, which gave the impression that it was competing with the intifada activists.[60] And while the UNC held to a message of national unity and civil resistance, some of Hamas' graffiti attacked Jews, Christians and secular nationalists.[61]

From 1988, Hamas also demanded that all Palestinian women wear the hijab, graffitiing slogans like 'Daughter of Islam, abide by *shar'ia* dress!' across Gaza. Those who resisted risked street harassment or even assault. The UNC condemned attacks on 'uncovered' women as it emerged that some of the attackers had been planted by the Israeli military to sow divisions among Palestinian society; others were ideologically committed to the hijab campaign; and others still were young boys seeking an outlet to show their 'activism'. All this came after decades of Israeli forces using sexual harassment, and sometimes outright assault, alongside gendered ideas of 'modesty' to force false confessions from Palestinian women detainees.[62] The hijab campaign piled even more pressure on Palestinian women by seeking to turn their clothing into signs of nationalist commitment.[63]

As the intifada went on, Hamas increasingly disregarded the UNC's call for unarmed resistance. As a result, its relationship with Israel became openly confrontational. This marked a shift; in Hamas' early months, it had had several pragmatic exchanges with Israel. While this may seem surprising from today's stand-point, it was consistent with Israel's longstanding support for Palestinian Islamists as a counterweight to Yasser Arafat's secular PLO. Hamas also showed flexibility in its approach; in March 1988, its co-founder Mahmoud Zahar met with Foreign Minister Shimon Peres to propose direct Palestinian–Israeli negotiations on the basis of Israeli withdrawal from Gaza and the West Bank.[64] Reports of similar exchanges with Defence Minister Yitzhak Rabin have never been confirmed, but Israel maintained direct communications with Islamist officials for over a year after Hamas was established.[65]

Yet the dynamics between the two parties shifted soon after-wards. In early 1989, Hamas captured and killed two Israeli soldiers. Israel responded with a full-scale crackdown: it designated Hamas a terrorist organisation, criminalised any dealings with it and arrested hundreds of its members. Among the latter was Sheikh Yassin himself, whom Israel later sentenced to life imprisonment plus fifteen years. Seeking to escape the Israeli crackdown and remain functional, Hamas now shifted much of its decision-making to an external leadership structure it set up in the Palestinian diaspora across the Middle East.[66]

In 1991, Hamas established its armed wing, the Qassam Brigades – named after Izzeldin al-Qassam, the anti-colonial preacher and nationalist we met in Chapter One – and launched a campaign of stabbings known as the 'war of the knives'.[67] Stepping up its use of violence, the group also developed its military capabilities and detonated car bombs to target army posts and settler communities across the oPt.[68] At this time, Hamas stated that it was seeking to minimise civilian casualties and would only attack the Israeli military and settlers, who it argued were legitimate targets. But in reality, even in the early 1990s some Hamas members targeted Israeli civilians. In December 1990, for example, two of them had stabbed three Israeli workers in Jaffa to death, and the number of such attacks on Israeli civilians only continued to rise in the early years of the decade.[69] In April 1993, Hamas carried out its first suicide bombing, targeting a settlement in the West Bank. Other than the bomber himself, there was one fatality: a Palestinian civilian who worked in the settlement. As we shall see, suicide bombings against civilians inside Israel would become central to Hamas' campaign later in the decade.

REPRESSION: THE ISRAELI CRACKDOWN

Israel was caught off guard by the first intifada. Despite the rising tensions in 1980s Gaza, the authorities believed – wrongly – that they had largely pacified the Palestinian population. So when the uprising began, Israel assumed that its long-term *bête noire*, the PLO, must be responsible. When Abu Jihad falsely claimed to have started the intifada, the Israeli government readily believed him – not least because removing a single man was far easier than addressing the Palestinian people's real grievances – and Defence Minister Rabin gave the order to assassinate him. In April 1988, a group of operatives from Mossad (Israel's external intelligence and espionage agency) travelled undercover to Tunisia, entered his house, killed his Tunisian gardener, and shot Abu Jihad himself fifty-two times in front of his wife Intissar and their children.[70]

Abu Jihad was a leading PLO operative who had commanded many attacks against Israel over the years, killing civilians as well as military targets. Most notably, he had orchestrated the Coastal Road Massacre, with its deliberate targeting of civilians. Israel had first placed him on a kill list twenty-three years earlier, and his assassination was a victory for Mossad. But he wasn't behind the first intifada and killing him did nothing to stop the unrest in Palestine. On the contrary, news of his death provoked an upsurge in agitation, as 'the sacrifice of martyr Abu Jihad' became a recurring theme in nationalist propaganda.[71] In fact, many of the Israeli officers involved in the assassination later expressed regret over the operation, reflecting that by weakening the Fatah leadership they ended up enabling the rise of Hamas.[72]

Israel's response to the intifada on the ground showed the same tunnel-visioned approach. Despite the uprising's largely non-violent character, especially in its early period, Israeli forces used punitive violence against demonstrators. Its coalition government, headed by Prime Minister Yitzhak Shamir (Likud) and Defence Minister Yitzhak Rabin (Labor), agreed on an 'iron fist' policy that included shoot-to-kill orders.[73] Rabin told the *Jerusalem Post*, 'The first priority of the security forces is to prevent violent demonstrations with force, power and blows . . . We will make it clear who is running the [occupied Palestinian] territories.'[74]

On this basis, Israeli forces frequently fired live ammunition into crowds of protestors. The violence was consistently disproportionate, with soldiers using M16 assault rifles against young boys throwing stones.[75] In the first week of the intifada alone, Israeli forces killed six Palestinians across the oPt, and the number rose dramatically in subsequent months, reaching 289 over the course of 1988.[76] As was so often the case, the violence was worst in Gaza: twenty-six of the forty-one Palestinians killed in the intifada's first month died in the Strip.[77]

In January 1988, Rabin ordered Israeli soldiers to 'break the bones' of demonstrators.[78] Ramzy Baroud recalls what this meant: 'The event was customary. Soldiers often stormed into people's homes and broke the arms and legs of men and boys so as to send a stern message to the rest of the neighbourhood that they would receive the same fate if they continued with their Intifada.'[79] Baroud goes on to say that a soldier would often ask 'Which hand do you write with?' before breaking it with a club, followed by the other arm and the legs.[80]

As Baroud's account shows, children were not spared the brutality of Israel's response. In fact, in 1990, the Swedish branch of Save the Children issued a damning report on the experiences of Palestinian children during the intifada. It found that Israeli shootings, beatings and teargas had injured 7 per cent of all Palestinians under eighteen in the intifada's first two years.[81] A third were aged under ten.[82] In the same period, more than 23,600 Palestinian children (aged under sixteen) had needed medical treatment after being beaten by soldiers; and Israeli violence had killed 159 children, with an average age of ten. And while it was unusual, children as young as five could be held in detention centres where their basic human rights were violated. Again, the suffering was particularly intensive in Gaza, where children were 40 per cent more likely to die a violent death than children in the West Bank.[83] Over the full course of the first intifada, 85 per cent of Gaza's children had their homes raided by the Israeli army, 55 per cent witnessed their fathers being beaten and 42 per cent were beaten themselves.[84]

Israeli forces also inflicted brutality on women.[85] We saw above that Naila Ayesh had suffered a miscarriage in Israeli detention before the intifada. In 1988, Israeli forces arrested and detained her for a second time on account of her political activism. Like all Palestinians, she had limited rights under the occupation regime and could be detained for long stretches without charge. By this time, her husband had been deported on account of his own activism, and their baby son Majd joined her in jail, where he cut his first tooth and took his first steps. After six months' imprisonment, Ayesh was exiled to Egypt, where she reunited with her husband. Like so many others, they were denied the right to return to Palestine.[86]

We see from Ayesh's story that the Israeli authorities were merciless in their treatment of activists, both militants and non-violent campaigners. The most-wanted Palestinian targets could face summary execution or deportation.[87] In one notable case at the end of 1992, Israel retaliated for Hamas' killing of four Israeli soldiers and a frontier guard by deporting 415 Islamist militants, including 164 from Gaza, to southern Lebanon – in breach of international law.[88] Militants' families were also targeted, as Israeli forces regularly raided their homes and sometimes beat their relatives.[89] Asmaa al-Ghoul, who was five when the first intifada began, remembers Israeli soldiers regularly 'bursting in on us in the middle of the night, terrorising me' because her uncles belonged to Hamas.[90] In some cases, Israel demolished houses without giving any prior warning.[91]

Yet not even those without ties to the intifada were safe, because Israeli forces regularly used collective punishment to suppress the resistance, as they had done for much of the occupation.[92] They conducted mass arrests and searches and sometimes cut off essential services to civilians. At other times, Israel re-directed water away from Palestinian towns and villages, sometimes to supply Jewish settlements that would subsequently sell it back to the Palestinians at a higher price.[93] Israeli forces also imposed more extensive curfews than ever, confining Palestinians across Gaza to their homes from 8 p.m. to 6 a.m. every night.[94] Anyone found breaking curfew could be shot by the Israeli military.

The curfews were often more intensive in the refugee camps. In the first 500 days of the intifada, Shati was under curfew for 190 days, Jabalia for 164 days, Deir al-Balah for 116 days and Khan Younis for 105 days.[95] During this period, camp residents were confined indoors and often ran out of essential supplies. Ramzy Baroud, who lived through these curfews as a teenager, recalls that the fedayeen would throw desperately needed bags of tomatoes, potatoes, bread and sugar through open windows to the people inside.[96]

The occupation regime also drew on its vast powers to repress the intifada in more underhand ways. Observing that the UNC committees distributed information via leaflets, it banned Palestinians from owning fax machines and closed all the printing shops in Gaza. When the UNC resorted to spreading messages via graffiti instead, Israel carried out reprisals against anyone whose house was marked with such graffiti. And with Palestinians refusing to pay taxes, in 1989 it introduced new magnetic-strip ID cards that Palestinians needed to enter Israel and that were only issued upon evidence of tax payment.[97]

In 1991, Israel cancelled the general exit permit that it had issued for Gaza nineteen years earlier; personal exit permits were now required.[98] Palestinians who could still work in Israel found themselves even more vulnerable than before, facing the constant threat of their permits being cancelled if they engaged in even very minor forms of activism. The separation, isolation and closure that have come to characterise Gaza in the twenty-first century – characteristics that are usually attributed to Hamas taking power – thus had their roots in the Israeli response to the first intifada.

Israel's immobilising measures added to the Palestinian suffering already caused by years of collective punishment and repression. Curfews and immobilising closures seriously damaged the Palestinian economy and standards of living dropped across the oPt.[99] As usual, the impact was particularly severe in Gaza, due to its isolation, lack of agricultural land and absence of major industry.[100] Over the first three years of the intifada, the Strip's GNP dropped by a third. As the Strip fell into poverty, hunger became a rising problem for the first time.[101]

The most serious suffering, though, resulted from the intifada's human cost. Its first year alone saw 142 Palestinian fatalities in Gaza, killed either by gunfire, beatings, teargas, vehicle collisions or torture during detention. Over the entire six years of the intifada, Israeli forces killed 523 Palestinians in Gaza, demolished 462 houses there and inflicted injuries resulting in 78,338 hospitalisations.[102] Overall, the Strip accounted for around half of the Palestinian death toll even though less than 40 per cent of the oPt population lived there.[103]

Increasing intra-Palestinian violence towards the end of the intifada also caused serious damage to the Palestinian social fabric. The early 1990s saw a rise in the number of suspected collaborators being killed, with militants from Fatah, Hamas and the PFLP all carrying out such attacks at a time when Israel had stepped up its recruitment of collaborators in a bid to counter the uprising.[104] Out of every ten Palestinians killed during the intifada, an estimated two lost their lives at the hands of other Palestinians.[105] The UNC explicitly condemned this campaign, and in Gaza, civil society veteran Haidar Abd al-Shafi called for an end to intra-Palestinian violence, which also involved factional score-settling and almost certainly targeted some individuals who were not collaborators at all.[106] The internal violence and factional conflict, which was especially bad in Gaza from 1992 to 1993, lowered Palestinian morale and fuelled divisions – which served the interests of the occupation.[107]

Throughout the intifada, Israel's long-term goal of depopulation was never far away. Describing the attacks on Palestinian infrastructure and the punitive measures imposed on people's daily lives, Shlomo Gazit, now the head of Israeli military intelligence, said in 1988 that Israel wanted the Palestinians to 'face unemployment and a shortage of land and water and thus we can create the necessary conditions for the departure of the Palestinians from the West Bank and Gaza'.[108] In this way, we can see a connecting line between Israel's approach to the intifada, its occupation policies since 1967 and the original Nakba of 1948.

RESULTS: POLITICAL BREAKTHROUGH

Despite the intra-Palestinian violence of its later years, the first intifada still did a great deal to boost Palestinian morale, restore a sense of national dignity and fuel social cohesion. It affirmed Palestinian solidarity, as communities defied Israeli separation policies to organise across the oPt and within Israel. The diaspora also drew strength from the intifada. Watching it from Tunis, Sahbaa al-Barbari found that 'it brought us back to life . . . The Intifada returned our dignity and pride, and our belief in ourselves.'[109]

The intifada also gave Palestinians a new level of political capital on the world stage. Images of young Palestinian boys throwing stones at huge Israeli tanks had reversed the conventional Western view of who was David and who was Goliath, after decades in which the West had seen Palestinians (and Arabs in general) as the aggressors.[110] Now, even the US broke with its usually unquestioning support for Israel.[111] As American news programmes broadcast footage of Israeli soldiers beating Palestinians,[112] the State Department criticised Israel's 'excessive use of force' and its avoidable killings of Palestinian civilians.[113] It withheld its usual veto at the UN Security Council, enabling the passage of several resolutions criticising Israel's human rights violations against Palestinians. In one, the Security Council 'strongly deplore[d] those policies and practices of Israel, the occupying Power, which violate the human rights of the Palestinian people in the occupied territories, and in particular the opening of fire by the Israeli army, resulting in the killing and wounding of defenceless Palestinian civilians'.[114] In 1992, the US actually voted in favour of a resolution condemning Israel's deportation of hundreds of Islamist militants to southern Lebanon, in breach of international law.[115]

The first intifada also returned Palestine to the top of the Arab agenda. Widespread support for the uprising on the Arab streets forced governments to confront the issue's importance and dampened any furtive plans for separate agreements with Israel. In July 1988, the intifada scored a clear victory when Jordan's King Hussein renounced his claim to the West Bank in the name of Palestinian self-determination.[116] His declaration that 'Jordan is not Palestine' put an end to the 'Jordanian option' that for decades had been floated for both Palestinian territories by Israel, the US and even the Jordanian regime itself, suggesting that the Palestinians could either be permanently resettled in Jordan, or placed under full Jordanian sovereignty in limited parts of the West Bank. Not long before Hussein's statement, Israeli Foreign Minister Shimon Peres had proposed that the Jordanian police force take over security in Gaza.[117]

Later that year, the PLO acted on the intifada's momentum when its legislative body, the Palestine National Council (PNC), convened in Algiers for a three-day 'intifada meeting'. Following deliberations, the PNC approved a new strategy that recognised the state of Israel for the first time. Yasser Arafat then issued the Palestinian Declaration of Independence, which laid the ground-work for what would become known as the 'two-state solution' by calling for independent Palestinian statehood in the oPt.[118] By pursuing this new vision for a future Palestine, the PLO responded directly to one of the key demands of intifada activists: that it recentre the oPt in its strategy, after decades of focusing on politics in the diaspora.[119]

Hamas immediately opposed the Declaration. Despite describing the PLO as a 'brother' in its Charter, it condemned the organisation's recognition of Israel and positioned itself as the PLO's more authentically Palestinian rival. Rising tensions would eventually lead to open clashes between Hamas and Fatah in Gaza, injuring dozens.[120] But in its condemnation of the PLO's move, Hamas was out of step with Palestinian opinion. Far from opposing it, Palestinians in Gaza defied curfew and risked their lives to dance on the streets when they heard about the Declaration, hopeful that the concessions would finally bring them a state after decades of dispossession. 'I will never forget my home in Palestine; it will always be in my heart. But now, all I want is a factory and a flag,' one Gaza-based refugee told an American researcher at the time.[121]

The PLO's strategic shift towards diplomacy rather than armed struggle was a momentous step for an organisation that had previously refused to recognise Israel. It had been several years in the making, with the intifada providing the final impetus. The following month, Arafat addressed the UN General Assembly in Geneva – having been denied a visa to travel to New York – and confirmed explicitly the PLO's recognition of Israel and its renunciation of violence. The US deemed the Geneva statement satisfactory in meeting its declared pre-conditions for working with the PLO.[122]

And yet the Israeli government ignored the milestone statement, maintaining that the PLO was a terrorist organisation. On the ground, it continued to suppress the intifada while expanding

Jewish settlements – overruling a call from Shimon Peres for a freeze on settlement activity in Gaza.[123] In 1990, the Jewish settler population across the oPt increased by a quarter; the following year saw 13,000 new residential units under construction for settlers.[124] At the same time, the settler movement doubled down on the most extremist elements of its ideology, calling for mass expulsions and violence. Settlers across the oPt carried out vigilante attacks on Palestinians, either as reprisals for specific assaults or simply outbursts of anti-Palestinian violence.[125]

But while far-right extremism was on the rise among settlers, the ongoing intifada was subtly changing the discourse elsewhere in Israel. The years of unrest put an end to any suggestion that the occupation was benign, and restored Israeli awareness of the Green Line; as Yitzhak Rabin put it, 'Jews simply don't visit the [occupied Palestinian] territories as they used to. No one's wandering around the garages of Gaza any more these days.'[126]

What's more, as the intifada went on the Israeli death toll was slowly creeping up. In total, Palestinians killed 160 Israelis during the first intifada, of whom 100 were civilians, including four children. The majority of Israeli fatalities occurred in the later part of the intifada, and the accelerating death toll increased public pressure on the government to put a stop to it.[127] After force failed to quell the uprising, Defence Minister Rabin started to believe that the answer lay in a political, not a military solution.[128] The polls showed rising Israeli support for withdrawal from Gaza.[129]

The Israeli government was also under pressure from the US. Determined to see progress on the diplomatic front, in 1991 the Bush administration insisted that Israel participate in a peace conference it was organising in Madrid, also including Syria, Jordan, Lebanon and the Palestinians. When Prime Minister Shamir demurred, President Bush threatened to cancel $10 billion in loan guarantees to the Israeli government.[130] The threat worked, but Shamir held to a condition that no one associated with the PLO could participate. Instead, a Palestinian delegation was allowed to join the Jordanians, and only Israeli-vetted delegates could participate in face-to-face talks with the Israeli team.[131] Despite these highly restrictive terms, many Palestinians welcomed the talks; ignoring Hamas' calls to strike in protest, thousands filled the streets of Gaza City and Khan Younis to show their support for the negotiations, hopeful that they would bring about real change.[132]

The Palestinian delegation consisted of leading figures from civil society in the oPt, headed by Gaza's Haidar Abd al-Shafi. It was a sign of the shifting dynamics brought on by the first intifada, with the momentum increasingly held by Palestinians inside the oPt (the 'insiders') rather than the Tunis-based PLO leadership. In his opening speech to the conference, Abd al-Shafi called for equality and justice:

> Our intifada is a testimony to our perseverance and resilience waged in a just struggle to regain our rights . . . In the name of the Palestinian people, we wish to directly address the Israeli people with whom we have had a prolonged exchange of pain: Let us share hope, instead. We are willing to live side by side on the land and the promise of the future. Sharing, however, requires two partners, willing to share as equals. Mutuality and reciprocity must replace domination and hostility for genuine reconciliation and coexistence under international legality.[133]

Elsewhere in the speech, Abd al-Shafi cited the PLO's Declaration of Independence from three years earlier, reminding listeners of the organisation's centrality to the Palestinian struggle despite its exclusion from the conference.

This exclusion came at a time of diminishing stature for the PLO. In 1990, Arafat had made what turned out to be a catastrophic decision: when Saddam Hussein invaded Kuwait, he broke ranks with other Arab leaders and sided with the Iraqi dictator against US intervention. In response, Gulf Arab governments cut off their payments to the PLO. Some redirected the money to Hamas, which had condemned the Iraqi invasion.[134] Making matters worse still, the Kuwaiti government went on to expel its significant Palestinian population of 400,000.[135] An estimated 20,000–30,000 returned to Gaza, placing further strain on its already faltering economy.[136]

Then, in January 1991, Arafat's deputy Salah Khalaf (Abu Iyad) was assassinated by the Abu Nidal group, a Fatah splinter organisation probably acting on behalf of the Iraqi regime. Abu Iyad had been an outspoken critic of Saddam Hussein and one of the few senior PLO voices to strongly oppose Arafat's stance on the war.[137] The death of Khalaf, whom we first met in Chapter One as a teenager fleeing Jaffa, came three years after Abu Jihad's assassination and left Arafat the sole survivor of the original group of Gaza fedayeen. Increasingly isolated and friendless, the PLO had less leverage than at any other point in at least two decades.

It remained excluded when Abd al-Shafi led the Palestinian delegation again at talks in Washington in 1993. There, the delegation proposed the creation of a Palestinian Interim Self-Governing Authority (PISGA) as a stepping stone towards full statehood. While not having sovereignty, the PISGA would have jurisdiction over the oPt and the Palestinian population therein, while Israel would be obliged to freeze settlement activity and withdraw its troops. The Israeli delegation now represented a new administration, after 1992 elections had returned a Labor government and made Rabin prime minister. While he was more open to negotiations than Shamir, the Israeli delegation never-theless rejected the proposal and the talks reached a stalemate.[138]

Then, over the summer of 1993, word began to spread of separate negotiations happening between Israel and the PLO, initiated by a group of Norwegian academics in Oslo. Recognising the historic weakness of the PLO, the Israeli government had sensed an opportunity to secure better terms than it could get in Washington; at the same time, forging an agreement with the PLO would have the added advantage of winning Israel international approval for its peacemaking efforts. From the PLO's perspective, it was an opportunity to reassert its dominance and counter its marginalisation in the Palestinian struggle. In August, news emerged from Oslo of a landmark agreement between Israel and the PLO. It was regarded as the formal end of the intifada.

But when the Palestinian delegation in Washington saw the terms of the Oslo agreement, they were horrified.[139] The PLO's negotiators had accepted a proposal far more limited than the PISGA, whereby Israel would retain control of land, water, borders and much else, without any freeze on settlement expansion. Palestinian scholar Rashid Khalidi, who served as an advisor to the Washington delegation, later said, 'Every pitfall, every trap, every Israeli scheme we had avoided, they walked blindly into. They made every single mistake. They made every single one.'[140] When he learnt that the US had deliberately kept his delegation in the dark about the parallel negotiations, Abd al-Shafi walked out of Washington and refused to attend the signing ceremony for Oslo.

The Oslo Accords were greeted with international fanfare despite the obvious shortcomings. On 13 September 1993, Rabin and Arafat shook hands on the White House lawn and signed the Declaration of Principles. The PLO recognised the state of

Israel's right to exist in peace and security, and Israel recognised the PLO as the Palestinian people's representative. In so doing, Israel formally acknowledged the Palestinian people for the first time, although not their right to statehood. The two parties pledged to work together to achieve a 'just, lasting and comprehensive peace' and agreed on a plan whereby Israel would withdraw its troops first from Gaza and then, in phases, from limited parts of the West Bank. A self-governing Palestinian Authority would govern for an interim five-year period, pending a final permanent settlement.[141]

Many Palestinians in Gaza cheered when they heard of the agreement. A poll found that 76 per cent supported it.[142] After forty-five years of dispossession, twenty-five years of occupation and six years of a taxing uprising, many dared to hope they were about to find freedom. Unfortunately, the serious problems with Oslo would quickly become evident.

5

THE OSLO YEARS

In July 1994, Yasser Arafat returned to Gaza. After decades in exile from Palestine, he was returning triumphantly as president of the council of the new Palestinian Authority (PA, known in Arabic as the *sulta*). Hopeful that they finally had their own government ahead of independent statehood, hundreds of thousands of Palestinians turned out to greet him. Arafat set up his new headquarters in Gaza City and moved into Mansion House, the former residence of the British governor in Mandate times.[1] Later that year, he received the Nobel Peace Prize jointly with Yitzhak Rabin and Shimon Peres.[2] Yet even at this early stage, doubts about the Oslo process were setting in on the streets of Palestine.[3] By the time Arafat was elected Palestinian president in 1996, Oslo's flaws were manifest.

Arafat had a long history with Gaza; it was his father's birthplace and the site where he had first connected with the fedayeen forty years earlier. But his return to Gaza, rather than anywhere else in Palestine, was like so much else determined by Israeli designs. The Oslo framework followed the 'Gaza first' formula that Begin had first proposed at Camp David, with the Strip providing an initial testing ground for limited Palestinian self-rule.[4] This approach was based on the longstanding Israeli view that Gaza was less desirable than the West Bank, on account of its refugee demographics, tiny size, absence of religious sites and limited geo-strategic value. Accordingly, the first stages of the Oslo process established limited Palestinian autonomy in the Strip – along with the West Bank city of Jericho, which was added to the terms after Arafat baulked at Israeli efforts to contain Palestinian self-governance to Gaza only.[5]

The limitations placed on this autonomy cannot be overstated. The Oslo Accords – which some of Arafat's senior associates claim he never fully read[6] – heavily restricted Palestinian self-rule while maintaining ultimate Israeli control over the entire oPt. Palestinian 'territorial jurisdiction' excluded Israeli settlements and military zones, which made up nearly a quarter of the Strip.[7] Israel continued to control all water resources and entry and exit points, with Rabin declaring, 'We will not give you control of *our* borders.'[8] It had power of veto over every function of the PA, which was allowed a police force but not an army.[9] The issues of central importance to the Palestinian struggle – particularly refugee rights and the status of Jerusalem – were to be discussed as part of 'permanent status negotiations' five years into the future, with no guarantee of Israeli withdrawal and no mechanism for resolving conflict or crisis. And with Israel still refusing to define its borders, Oslo also placed no limits on its settlement expansion, allowing the occupier to continue seizing more land in the meantime.

Crucially, the Oslo set-up created the illusion of an even-handed conflict between two opposing sides, obscuring the reality of continuing occupation of a dispossessed people and the ongoing colonisation of their land by a military power. The establishment of the PA suggested a territorial distinction between two powers, whereas in fact a single power dominated the entire territory, with unequal rights given to the people living there depending on their religious and ethnic identity.

These limitations led many Palestinian activists to oppose Oslo. Haidar Abd al-Shafi, who had led the Palestinian delegations at Madrid and Washington, was particularly critical of the agreement's silence on the settlements.[10] Intifada activist Naila Ayesh condemned it as a 'coup', pointing out that, unlike the Madrid delegation, the Palestinian team at Oslo didn't include a single woman.[11] Edward Said, perhaps the most prominent Palestinian intellectual of the twentieth century, famously called Oslo 'an instrument of surrender, a Palestinian Versailles'.[12] And Palestinian refugee communities across the Middle East were outraged that after their camps had driven the PLO's struggle for decades, its leadership had now relegated their rights and future to unspecified 'final status' talks.[13] By excluding both the diaspora and the Palestinian minority inside Israel, Oslo shrank the Palestinian nation demographically to less than half its total.[14]

Despite the agreement's clear tilt in favour of Israeli power, many Israelis still opposed it as a bridge too far. Some disagreed with legitimising the PLO, which until Oslo had been designated a terrorist organisation in Israel; others opposed any idea of Palestinian self-rule. Polls showed that around half of the Jewish Israeli public supported Oslo when it was signed, compared to more than 75 per cent of Palestinians in the oPt.[15] Opponents included powerful figures in the Knesset; Benjamin Netanyahu, who had succeeded Shamir as Likud leader in 1993, disagreed with any notion of Palestinian national rights, however limited. He described the agreement as 'a crime against Zionism' and vowed to destroy it.[16] In Jerusalem, he joined demonstrations calling for Rabin to be executed for treason.[17]

Settler communities were especially forceful in their opposition to Oslo. Longstanding settler violence against Palestinians intensified in response to the agreement, culminating in some horrific crimes. Most notably, in February 1994, during the month of Ramadan, American-born Jewish settler Baruch Goldstein forced his way into the Ibrahimi mosque in Hebron.[18] Wearing an Israeli army uniform, Goldstein used an automatic rifle to open fire on the unarmed Muslims in prayer. As Israeli soldiers failed to intervene, some of the worshippers managed to overpower Goldstein and kill him in self-defence.[19] By that time, he had murdered 29 Palestinians and injured around 150. Rabin condemned the massacre but ignored calls to evacuate Jewish settlers from Hebron's Old City. Goldstein became a hero to many Zionist extremists, and hundreds of people attended his funeral in Jerusalem.[20]

Among the mourners was a 23-year-old law student named Yigal Amir. During the intifada Amir had served in the Israeli army in Gaza, where he became known for his brutality in catching Palestinian children on the streets of Jabalia during curfew.[21] A religious nationalist bitterly opposed to Oslo, Amir was involved with the pro-settlement movement in Hebron and took inspiration from Goldstein's crime. Fifteen months after the Hebron massacre, he shot and killed Rabin at a peace rally in Tel Aviv. Hearing of Rabin's death at his office in Gaza, Arafat broke down in tears, despairing of what it would mean for negotiations and telling aides, 'It's over, it's over.'[22] Amir later told police of the direct connection between Goldstein's crime and his own: 'It began after Goldstein . . . It's then that it dawned on me that someone must put down [Rabin].'[23] Israeli violence, which had tormented Palestinians for decades, had turned on itself.

The Hebron massacre also precipitated a new campaign of Palestinian violence.[24] Once the Muslim mourning period for Goldstein's victims had passed, Hamas sent a bomber to a bus stop in northern Israel. There, he detonated a suicide vest that killed seven Israelis and wounded fifty-two. A week later, another bomber struck at a different bus stop, this time killing five Israelis and wounding thirty.[25] It was the beginning of a new wave of horrendous attacks in which both Hamas and PIJ deliberately struck at civilian targets inside Israel. Despite widespread opposition from the Palestinian public, the two organisations went on to kill 171 Israelis in twenty-seven suicide bombings over the next six years.[26]

As Israelis faced the threat of bombings while going about their daily lives, public opinion moved to the right. Support for Likud swelled as Netanyahu attacked Labor for failing to protect Israel's security interests.[27] His tactics paid off; in May 1996, Israeli voters narrowly elected Netanyahu as prime minister on a margin of less than 1 per cent.[28] He was the youngest prime minister in Israeli history, and the first to be born after the state's establishment. In keeping with his long-held opposition to any negotiations or agreements with the Palestinians, Netanyahu immediately set about obstructing further talks, seizing more Palestinian land and fomenting violence.

That year had also seen Palestinian elections for both the PA president and the parliamentary body, the Palestinian Legislative Council (PLC). While Hamas, the PFLP and the DFLP all boycotted the elections as part of their opposition to Oslo, many Palestinians took a different view and chose to vote.[29] Turnout was especially high in Gaza, reaching 87 per cent in the Strip against 74 per cent in the West Bank.[30] The results were a clear victory for Fatah. Arafat was elected president on a landslide, with 87 per cent of the vote.[31] Fatah became the biggest single party in the PLC – although the single most successful parliamentary candidate was Gaza's Haidar Abd al-Shafi, who ran as an independent and received more votes than anyone else.[32] Other successful candidates in Gaza included Rawya Shawwa, whose father and grandfather had both served as Gaza mayors; and Intissar al-Wazir, Abu Jihad's widow and a lifelong activist who had been the first female member of Fatah and had co-founded the GUPW in 1965. As minister of social affairs, she became one of seven cabinet ministers from Gaza, out of a total of twenty-three.[33]

The PLC's inaugural meeting took place in Gaza City in March 1996. Israeli travel restrictions meant that it took West Bank members more than twelve hours to travel the 30 miles to the Strip.[34] Their immobility portended a bigger reality, in which the PA would find that its ability to effect change was seriously curtailed from the beginning.

CHANGE? THE PA IN GAZA

In May 1994, the Israeli army had vacated its bases in Gaza City. Coming five months later than originally planned, the military redeployment nevertheless caused Palestinians to rejoice at the move towards freedom.[35] Thousands came out onto the streets to celebrate as the public mood lifted. Israeli soldiers were replaced by a new Palestinian police force, the majority of whom came from the diaspora.[36]

The terms of Oslo allowed for a brief window in which an approved list of Palestinian exiles – mostly those associated with the PLO leadership – could return to Palestine. Among them was Saleem al-Naffar, whom we met in Chapter Three when his family were forced to leave Gaza at the onset of the Israeli occupation. Born in Shati camp in 1963, he had spent most of his life in exile, moving from Jordan to Syria. Now a poet and writer, he returned to his birthplace full of hope, later telling a friend, 'I was forced to leave my land. In exile, we felt suffering . . . [In 1994] the only important thing was that I came back to my land. Without a doubt, I knew tomorrow would be better. But these things flew away.'[37]

Al-Naffar was not the only Gaza-born activist to return to the Strip at this time. Intissar al-Wazir, born in Gaza City seven years before the Nakba, went back in 1995, as did Sahbaa al-Barbari, the Palestinian communist we first met in Chapter Two. Like al-Wazir, al-Barbari was now a widow; her husband Mu'in Bseiso had died of a heart attack in London in 1984.

Yet al-Naffar, al-Wazir and al-Barbari were atypical in being Gaza-born. The majority of the 10,000 returnees at this time were Tunisian-based PLO figures with no particular ties to the Strip. Mahmoud Abbas (Abu Mazen) was a refugee from Safed who had fled to Syria during the Nakba. Ahmed Qurei (Abu Alaa) was from Abu Dis and had served in the PLO in Lebanon. The returnees became known among the local population as 'the Tunisians' – a term that was rarely complimentary.[38]

For the returnees, Oslo provided some of the trappings of statehood to salve their decades of exile. In the words of al-Barbari:

In 1996, I obtained a Palestinian passport issued by the Palestinian National Authority (PNA). I am proud of it and have used it in my travels, and I feel like it has returned part of my identity to me . . . when I was given a Palestinian passport, then I felt that I had an identity, my real identity, the identity that I had lost but dreamt of for many years. With this passport I felt that I regained myself. I can now travel as a Palestinian.[39]

Al-Barbari used her Palestinian passport to fly with Palestinian Airlines, which was created in 1995 and operated from Egypt until Yasser Arafat International Airport opened in Gaza in 1998.

The opening of a Palestinian airport provided a brief moment of hope for Palestinian statehood and the chance of direct independent connections between Palestine and the wider world. For Nabil Shurafa, whose family had run a travel agency in Gaza since 1952, there was a short-lived boom in business after decades of decline.[40] 'It may look like a little airport to you, but to us it's bigger than John F. Kennedy,' Shurafa told the *New York Times*.[41]

Yet al-Barbari also describes the restrictions of her return to Palestine, noting that 'even after the peace agreement we still needed permission from the occupier authorities to get back to our homes'.[42] The terms of Oslo allowed Israel to veto all Palestinian returnees to Gaza, and in 1996 it halted the entry of PLO personnel altogether. It also denied several governments' requests to open embassies or consulates in Gaza; in November 1994, it prevented Pakistani Prime Minister Benazir Bhutto from visiting Arafat at his headquarters there.[43] Such moves were an early indication that Oslo would not bring the freedom Palestinians had hoped for.

At the same time, PA governance in Gaza fell far short of the open democracy that Palestinians had struggled for during the first intifada. Instead, they observed cronyism and nepotism in the sulta, as the route to power and status appeared to lie through loyalty to Arafat.[44] The local activists who had organised the intifada found themselves largely excluded from the new regime, despite – or perhaps because of – their significant standing among the people.[45] Dominated by PLO figures from the Tunisia era, the PA cabinet didn't include anyone from the camps, disregarding their enduring centrality to the Palestinian struggle.[46]

A divide quickly emerged between the longstanding Gaza population and the Tunisians, many of whom were now enjoying elite lifestyles as Oslo gave them the trappings of power.[47] New resorts and villas sprang up across the Strip to house the returning leaders.[48] Some outraged locals marked Abu Mazen's villa, worth more than $2 million, with graffiti declaring 'This is your reward for selling Palestine'.[49] The PA elites were also exempt from the worst suffering caused by the ongoing occupation, as their Israeli-issued VIP passes gave them the freedom of movement denied to the rest of the Palestinian population.[50] As the decade went on they spent most of their time in the West Bank, with Arafat largely basing himself at his *muqata* (headquarters) in Ramallah.[51] Gaza, which had started the intifada that ultimately led to the PA's creation, was being relegated.

Worst of all was the PA's intensive focus on protecting Israel's security interests. This had been a key part of Oslo from the start. In September 1993, just as the agreement was being finalised, Rabin had told an Israeli newspaper:

> I would prefer to see the Palestinians take upon themselves the problem of keeping order in Gaza. They will be more effective than we have been, since they will not allow appeals to the Supreme Court. They will prevent the Association for Civil Rights in Israel from entering the territory to criticise them . . . more important, they will take over responsibility for the task from the Israeli military.[52]

In other words, Rabin's intention for Oslo was less about achieving a just and lasting peace and more about using the Palestinian leadership to control their own people on Israel's behalf. The effects of this quickly became apparent on the ground; almost half of all PA employees performed a security function.[53] Arafat put Fatah fighter Mohammed Dahlan in charge of the sulta's security forces in Gaza and gave him carte blanche to recruit as he wished.[54] By the end of 1994, PA security forces numbered more than 30,000, exceeding the number of teachers in the oPt.[55] By 1996, the figure had reached 40,000.[56]

The Palestinian security forces co-ordinated closely with Israel, which required them to suppress any activity deemed a threat to Israeli security interests. In practice, this included protecting Israeli settlers and military infrastructure. Activism that resisted the occupation was classed as a security threat to be put down, in a process that served Israeli interests while transferring costs and liabilities to the Palestinian leadership.[57] The effect was to nullify dissent and plurality in Palestinian politics.

Unsurprisingly, this situation led many Palestinians to see the PA as simply an outsourcing of the occupation. Concerns arose early on about Palestinian forces' brutality. In November 1994, PA police opened fire on a Palestinian demonstration, killing fourteen people and injuring hundreds in what became known as the 'November massacre'.[58] The PA subsequently placed Gaza under curfew and began rounding up anti-Oslo activists, in moves that echoed the typical actions of the occupation authorities.[59] Protests against the PA's collaboration with the Israeli military, and particularly its complicity in suppressing Palestinian dissent and demonstrations, intensified over the course of the decade.[60]

To make matters worse, Arafat's leadership took on a clear authoritarian character. Whenever possible, he brought the sulta's infrastructure under his direct control – a process enabled by his appointment of cronies to senior positions. The PLC, which was meant to represent Palestinians as their elected parliament, found its efficacy restricted by the president as he increasingly concentrated power in his own hands.[61] In August 1997, Haidar Abd al-Shafi resigned from the PLC in protest at Arafat's power grab.[62] Civil society suffered as the sulta pressured international donors to channel their funding via PA institutions, meaning that independent NGOs and grassroots organisations lost out.[63]

The PA's human rights violations included arbitrary arrests, detention without trial, censorship, suppression of dissent, restrictions on freedom of assembly and repression of organised activism.[64] From early on, it censored and repressed Palestinian media that was insufficiently supportive of Arafat or Oslo. Journalists who had struggled for years against the Israeli occupation now found themselves silenced, arrested and even detained by the Palestinian leadership. The regime's clampdown targeted not only militants and rival politicians but trade union leaders, civil society figures and public intellectuals. Over the course of the 1990s, Arafat's forces arrested and detained renowned human rights activists including Raji Sourani and Bassim Eid.[65] In July 1997, university lecturer Fathi Subuh was arrested and detained for five months after setting his students an exam paper that included questions on PA corruption and mismanagement.[66] Arafat even sought to ban Edward Said's books, in retaliation for the writer's outspoken criticism of his leadership.[67]

Worst of all, PA security forces tortured some of their detainees, using the very same techniques that they had endured themselves during earlier Israeli interrogation. Torture was a particularly common feature in the PA's treatment of Hamas suspects, creating a new level of enmity that would have lasting consequences.[68] Yet Hamas fighters were far from the only victims. Human rights activists like Bassim Eid were also abused and tortured in PA detention.[69] In June 1997, violent demonstrations broke out in Gaza when a man died in detention after being tortured by Arafat's presidential guards – a fatality that followed twelve other deaths in PA detention facilities.[70] In the disgusted words of Mohammed Baroud, a Nakba refugee who had fought with the fedayeen, 'those who resisted [the occupation] and lost everything are fought at every corner, thrown in jail and tortured; not by Israel, but by the Palestinians themselves.'[71]

In time, Arafat's critics would come to call him a dictator. There was a certain irony to the accusation. If Arafat was a dictator, he was perhaps the least powerful one in the world. The Israeli authorities still held ultimate control over Palestine.

CONTINUITY: ISRAELI OCCUPATION

For all the hope that Oslo would begin a new era, most Palestinians quickly found it changed little that mattered. As Edward Said had pointed out in 1993, the agreement didn't end the occupation but rather enabled its continuation.[72] This meant that Palestinians still had to endure Israeli military raids, land seizures, house demolitions, school and business closures, curfews and unchecked violence.[73] Even in the optimistic early days of Oslo, the number of Palestinians killed and wounded by Israeli forces didn't decrease.[74] In fact, just two weeks after Rabin and Arafat shook hands in Washington, Israeli forces responded to disturbances in Gaza by demolishing seventeen houses, arresting sixteen people and carrying out the summary executions of two Hamas members. While the army's chief of staff, Ehud Barak, defended the operations as targeting militants, some Israeli violence clearly targeted civilians.[75] In February 1994, Israeli soldiers shot dead ten-year-old Ayman al-Suri as he went to return a book to Jabalia library.[76]

What's more, Israel's much-touted military 'withdrawal' from Gaza City in May 1994 wasn't in fact a withdrawal at all. After evacuating their headquarters, Israeli forces merely moved a few miles north and repositioned themselves at a new headquarters near the illegal settlement of Nisanit. Other military bases relocated to the vicinity of the Gush Katif settlement.[77] In total,

ISRAELI PRESENCE IN
GAZA IN LATE 1990s

MEDITERRANEAN SEA

Ele Sinai
crossing

Beit Hanoun/
Erez
crossing

Shati
Camp

Jabalia
Camp

Jabalia

Gaza City

Al Shujaiah/
Nahal Oz crossing

Al Muntar/
Qarni crossing

Nuseirat
Camp

Bureij
Camp

Deir al-Balah
Camp

Maghazi
Camp

ISRAEL

Al Karara/Kissufim crossing

Khan Younis
Camp

Khan
Younis

Oslo-defined Israeli military
installation area

Oslo-defined Israeli
settlement area

Rafah
Camp

Rafah

Israel security perimeter

N

Rafah
border
crossing

Al Awdah/Sufa crossing

Gaza International Airport

Karem Abu Salem/Kerem Shalom crossing

EGYPT

0   5 Miles

0   10 Km

more than 5,000 Israeli soldiers were still deployed inside the Strip – and Palestinians still had to pass through Israeli check-points within the territory.[78]

Most significantly, Israel maintained and intensified the closure of Gaza that it had first imposed during the intifada. Both Gaza and the West Bank were increasingly sealed off from Israel, from external markets and from each other.[79] In 1994 – the year that Arafat returned to Palestine, during a period of supposed hope and peace – Israel began building a wall around the Gaza Strip, deepening its control over the movement of both people and goods.[80] This, combined with new checkpoints and an ever more complex permit system, meant that Gaza Palestinians were increasingly confined to the Strip.[81] To visit loved ones in the West Bank, they had to fill out endless paperwork, acquire various permits and sometimes wait months to be allowed to go.[82] They were losing not only their land but also their time, as it became impossible to either plan ahead or act spontaneously.[83]

As the years went on, most Gaza-based Palestinians found that they simply could not get the required permits; between March 1996 and June 1997, for example, only 500 people were permitted to move between Gaza and the West Bank.[84] The majority were trapped in the 141 square miles of the Gaza Strip, as Palestinian territory became more and more fragmented.[85] Nor could those living outside Gaza straightforwardly access it, as the permit regime cut off the territory from the rest of the world.[86] To this day, Israel argues that the closure of Gaza is a necessary security measure against Hamas' violence, but it had already made the Strip into an open-air prison long before Hamas came to power. And as we saw in the previous chapter, it had removed Gaza Palestinians' right to access Israel as early as 1991, two years before Hamas began its campaign of suicide bombings.

Israel's intensifying closure policy caused serious damage to the Palestinian economy, already harmed by decades of military occupation and land seizure. Closure prevented most Palestinians from working inside Israel or exporting goods, both of which were crucial to the Strip's economy.[87] The impact offset any economic benefits from Oslo: from 1994, the loss of revenue due to closure exceeded the inflow of international aid to Gaza.[88] In 1996, the closure policy caused losses amounting to nearly 40 per cent of Gaza's GNP. By that time, unemployment in Gaza already stood at 28 per cent.[89] The terms of the Oslo process also locked in Palestinian economic dependence on Israel, requiring the PA to adhere to Israeli regulations on import duties, taxation, trade and investment.[90]

There was worse to come. After Israel completely banned any entry from Gaza in 1996, two thirds of the Strip's workforce found themselves either unemployed or severely underemployed.[91] By 2000, nearly a third of the population were living below the poverty line. Child labour increased and school enrolment rates dropped. Beggars and pedlars, some of them children, started to appear on the streets.[92] There was little debate that closure was responsible: in a report by the State Department, even the US government attributed Gaza's economic woes to Israeli policies.[93]

There was, of course, one crucial exception to the closure of Gaza: the settlers. They remained exempt from Israel's restrictions on movement, continuing to cross the Green Line as they desired. More than 20 per cent of the Gaza Strip was designated for the settlers, who composed 0.5 per cent of the population, as well as the Israeli military apparatus that protected them.[94] Throughout the Oslo years, Israel continued to expand its illegal settlements on the very land supposedly earmarked for a Palestinian state – just as Haidar Abd al-Shafi had predicted.[95]

While defenders of the Oslo process have often attributed its failure to Rabin's demise, the truth is that Israel's settler population rose by 20,000 in the period that he was supposedly pursuing peace with the Palestinians.[96] In the months immediately after Arafat and Rabin shook hands in Washington, 850 new settlers moved to Gaza.[97] During Rabin's premiership, Israel began building more than 6,400 new housing units in settlements, demolished at least 328 Palestinian homes and structures, and committed $600 million to constructing new Jewish-only roads in the oPt.[98]

After Netanyahu came to power in 1996, government support for the settlements intensified. Shortly after becoming prime minister, Netanyahu formally eased restrictions on settlement expansion.[99] In November 1998 alone, he approved a thousand new housing units, the fortification of thirty settlements and the construction of thirteen new Jewish-only bypass roads.[100] At the same time, Ariel Sharon, who held various portfolios in Netanyahu's cabinet, maintained his reputation as the settlers' staunchest supporter in government. In 1998, he went on Israel Radio and urged settlers to 'grab more hills, expand the territory. Everything we don't grab will be in their hands.'[101] Overall, from 1993 to 2000, the number of Israeli settlers living in Gaza more than doubled to 6,700.[102]

Settler violence also continued. It included violent rampages in Palestinian towns and villages, as well as shootings, stonings and harassment. Refugees in Khan Younis camp had to endure violence, abuse, threats and vandalism from settlers from the nearby Gush Katif settlement, which had continued to expand throughout the 1990s.[103] The Israeli authorities did little to curtail it or to bring the culprits to justice, while condemning Arafat for failing to clamp down on Palestinian militancy.[104]

All of this meant that rather than establishing a Palestinian state, the PA helped entrench the occupation – which continued to impose repression, humiliation and violence on the Palestinian people. Theoretical Palestinian autonomy came without the basic required access to land, water and space. Across Gaza and the West Bank, the Palestinians continued to endure restrictions on their movement, arbitrary human rights violations and frequent collective punishment.[105] Oslo had simply become another instrument of their oppression.

COLLAPSE: THE SECOND INTIFADA

The Oslo framework had named 1999 as the year for proposed 'final status negotiations' between Israel and the Palestinians. Supposedly, these talks would resolve the conflict's thorniest issues and bring an end to decades of violence. Yet by this time Palestinians were widely disillusioned with Oslo. Those international figures still committed to it were encouraged by Israeli election results that year, which put an end to Netanyahu's first premiership and brought Labor's Ehud Barak to power. Pinning its hopes of a final peace agreement on Barak, the Clinton administration hosted him and Arafat at Camp David in July 2000. When these talks failed, both President Clinton and Barak blamed Arafat – but later document leaks showed that Israel had refused to compromise in the negotiations.[106] Like Rabin before him, Barak was unwilling to countenance a fully sovereign Palestinian state.[107] In fact, immediately after winning the 1999 election, he had named four 'red lines' in his approach to peace talks: full Israeli sovereignty over all of Jerusalem; no Palestinian national army; the retention of most West Bank settlements under Israeli sovereignty; and no return to the 1967 borders.[108]

As Barak declared that Israel had 'no partner' in peace after the Camp David summit, the Israeli right surged again.[109] Ariel Sharon had succeeded Netanyahu as Likud leader, to the horror of many Palestinians. Never having repented for the Sabra-Shatila massacre or the crimes he had committed as a military commander in Gaza, he remained hardline in his opposition to Palestinian rights.[110] In September 2000, Sharon visited the Haram al-Sharif (the Noble Sanctuary), known to Jews as Har ha Bayit (Temple Mount), in Jerusalem's Old City. It was a deliberately provocative move: the military commander who had committed war crimes against Palestinians visiting the third holiest site in Islam, in the city that Israel denied to Palestinians as their capital.[111] Hammering home his point, Sharon declared, 'The Temple Mount is in our hands and will remain in our hands.'[112] His visit triggered Palestinian protests across Jerusalem, with disruption quickly spreading throughout Palestine. It was the beginning of the second intifada.

The initial protests against Sharon's visit involved the same stone-throwing and civil unrest that were seen in the first intifada.[113] But the Israeli army responded with characteristic disproportionate retaliation, firing 1.3 million bullets in the oPt in just the first few days.[114] On only the second day of the intifada, cameraman Talal Abu Rahma filmed twelve-year-old Muhammad al-Durrah crouching terrified behind his unarmed civilian father in Gaza, before slumping to the ground upon being hit by Israeli gunfire. The footage was beamed across the world, with al-Durrah's death becoming a symbol of Palestinian suffering.[115]

Israeli military brutality had predictable consequences. During the intifada's first fortnight, the fatality rate was marked by a 20:1 ratio of Palestinians to Israelis. Before long, Israel was using heavy weaponry, including tanks, helicopters, air force jets and artillery.[116] At the same time, the Palestinian unrest quickly became militarised as armed groups mobilised. At the end of October, PIJ carried out the intifada's first suicide bombing, which caused no Israeli fatalities but instigated a new campaign of Palestinian violence.[117] In contrast to the first intifada, the second would see sustained, deliberate Palestinian attacks on Israeli civilians.

Once again, Israeli society moved to the right in response. In February 2001, the electorate voted by a landslide for Sharon to become the new prime minister – a result which many Palestinians took as evidence that Israelis were not serious about peace. Less than a month later, Hamas launched its first suicide bombing of the second intifada, killing three Israelis and wounding sixty-six at a shopping centre in Netanya. Shortly afterwards, it fired its first rocket from Gaza into Israel.[118] From the end of 2001, Fatah joined in too, creating a deadly inter-factional competition as various Palestinian forces targeted Israeli civilians on buses, in cafes and at nightclubs.[119] In total, Palestinian attackers – mostly suicide bombers – killed more than a thousand Israelis over the five years of the second intifada, two thirds of whom were civilians.[120] In the month of March 2002 alone, seventeen Palestinian suicide bombers killed ninety-nine Israelis inside the Green Line.[121] It marked a devastating escalation in violence, with innocent civilians paying the price.

Hamas and other proponents of suicide bombings claimed that the tactic could fragment Israeli society and deter Israeli violence.[122] In reality, the opposite was true. The suicide attacks were strategically counterproductive as well as morally heinous. Far from extracting any Israeli concessions, the bombings increased Sharon's ruthlessness against Palestinians and provided him with cover on the world stage. Declaring that Hamas must be destroyed, Sharon ignored its leadership's sporadic ceasefire proposals and pursued a strategy of total military suppression.[123]

Sharon also refused to engage with the Arab League when it put forward the groundbreaking Arab Peace Initiative (API) in 2002. Endorsed by Arafat's PA, the API proposed full recognition and diplomatic relations between all Arab states and Israel, in exchange for Israeli withdrawal from the oPt and the establishment of an independent Palestinian state there.[124] It should have been a game changer for Arab–Israeli relations; instead, it became little more than a footnote. Deliberately trying to scupper the plan, Hamas sent a suicide bomber to kill sixteen people at a Passover dinner in an Israeli hotel, and Israel responded with a full-scale invasion of the oPt.[125]

The second intifada saw some of the worst violence that Palestinians and Israelis had ever endured. Yet it was also marked by continuities. As had been typical since 1948, the death toll was far higher among Palestinians than Israelis, with just under 4,000 Palestinians and just over 1,000 Israelis killed from 2000 to 2005.[126] Just as typically, the Palestinians in Gaza bore the brunt of it. From 2000 to 2008, the Israeli military killed 4,792 Palestinians; more than 3,000 of them were in Gaza.[127] In fact, Israel openly acknowledged that Gaza was the worst place to be, by announcing that it would deport West Bank suicide bombers' families there as punishment.[128]

Israel also used the second intifada to step up the closure of Gaza. In 2001, it declared that any Palestinian found within a kilometre of the Gaza armistice line was now considered a 'legitimate target', further shrinking the already tiny area in which Palestinians could move around.[129] The Strip's residents became more and more isolated as Israel closed down Yasser Arafat International Airport in October 2001 and destroyed it with airstrikes the following year. Sahbaa al-Barbari, who had joyfully returned to Gaza in 1995, now found herself isolated from her relatives in Egypt, who could no longer visit.[130]

Even within Gaza, Israeli measures divided many families. During the second intifada Israel divided the Strip into four disconnected sections, physically separated by concrete blocks.[131]

This policy left Palestinians unable to see loved ones just a few miles away: Mohammed Baroud was cut off from his adult daughter, who lived a mere 25-minute drive from his home.[132]

As ever, those in the refugee camps often suffered the most. Camp residents endured the same curfews, demolitions and raids as during the first intifada, but at a higher level of intensity.[133] In 2004, Israel targeted Jabalia camp during a particularly brutal operation in northern Gaza that killed 105 Palestinians, including thirty-three children.[134] The decades-long threat of expulsion was never far away: after the Israeli military bulldozed homes in Khan Younis, Defence Minister Binyamin Ben-Eliezer said on the radio, 'These are points we don't want the Palestinians to return to.'[135]

Gaza returned to international headlines at the end of 2003, when Sharon made a shock announcement: Israel would evacuate all its settlers from Gaza and a very small number from the West Bank, as part of a new strategy of 'unilateral disengagement'.[136] It was a striking move from the man who had done more than any other Israeli minister to champion the settlement project across the oPt. His supporters in Israel and the US cited it as evidence of Sharon's evolution from hawk to dove.[137] This narrative was fuelled by internal Israeli politics: large-scale opposition to the plan from Sharon's own Likud party led him to break away and form his own new party – Qadima – while former prime minister Benjamin Netanyahu returned as Likud leader and held firm in his opposition to settler evacuation. As Qadima brought together dissenting Likud and Labor politicians in support of the Gaza disengagement, it was easy for outsiders to cast Sharon in the role of peacemaker. Yet Palestinians, living under the reality of his regime, were far more sceptical.

In fact, Sharon's decision was based on the calculations of realpolitik.[138] We have seen throughout this book how Israeli politicians deliberated for decades over Gaza's 'demographic problem' and its 'threat' to the state's Jewish majority. With large-scale expulsion deemed unfeasible, since the first intifada Israel had turned instead to an alternative approach: cutting Gaza off. Yet the presence of thousands of Jewish settlers always curbed the degree of separation Israel could impose. By evacuating the settlers, the state would be able to definitively sever the Strip and 'solve' the 'demographic problem'. At the same time, the move would serve as a sacrifice to Israel's Western allies, chiefly the US, who continued to see the settlements as an obstacle to peace. By unilaterally disengaging from Gaza, Israel could present itself as a willing peacemaker – all the while using its acquired political capital to expand its illegal settlements in the West Bank, making use of the security and material resources freed up in Gaza.

Sharon made his true motives clear in numerous statements. He openly discussed the 'demographic problem', speaking of Israel's need to 'free ourselves from control over three and a half million Palestinians whose numbers are rising all the time'.[139] Shimon Peres, who became Sharon's deputy in 2004, said that 'we are disengaging from Gaza because of demography.'[140] It is also clear that Sharon had no intention of enabling an independent Palestinian state – quite the opposite. In the very same speech where he announced the disengagement, he vowed that 'Israel will strengthen its control over those same areas in the Land of Israel which will constitute an inseparable part of the State of Israel in any future agreement' – meaning, the West Bank.[141] With disengagement, he sought to create new facts on the ground that would supersede the US-backed plan for a two-state solution. Indeed, he told Israeli journalists that 'the disengagement plan releases Israel from adopting a diplomatic plan that is dangerous.'[142]

Dov Weisglass, Sharon's close advisor, spoke in even starker terms. In a wide-ranging interview in 2004, he said that the disengagement 'supplies the amount of formaldehyde that's necessary so there will not be a political process with the Palestinians.'[143] Weisglass also spoke openly about Sharon's plans for the West Bank, which he referred to by the Biblical name of Judea and Samaria: 'The withdrawal from Samaria [the northern part of the West Bank] is a token one. We agreed to [it] only so it wouldn't be said that we concluded our obligation in Gaza. Arik [Sharon] doesn't see Gaza today as an area of national interest. He does see Judea and Samaria as an area of national interest.'[144] Elsewhere in the same interview, Weisglass acknowledged that the disengagement plan was designed to guarantee lasting US support for Israel by positioning it as a peaceful and concilia-tory actor. It was, in the words of the interviewer, 'the manoeuvre of the century'.[145]

While recognising the ominous signs about Sharon's true motives, Hamas nevertheless argued that the disengagement plan was a victory for its militant strategy. In May 2000, Israel had withdrawn from southern Lebanon, ending its eighteen-year occupation of the territory without a peace agreement and following a years-long militant campaign by Hizbollah.[146] Ever since, Hamas had cited this when claiming that its militancy, rather than the PA's approach of negotiation, would liberate Palestinian land.[147] Now, it claimed Sharon's announcement as vindication.

Unsurprisingly, Israel was determined to dampen this narra-tive. In March 2004, it assassinated Hamas leader Ahmed Yassin, who had been released from prison as part of an Israeli–Jordanian deal in 1997. Dropping bombs as he returned home from dawn prayers, Israel killed Yassin, his two bodyguards and nine bystanders. The following month, Israel assassinated Yassin's successor, Abdelaziz Rantisi, with missiles that also killed his son and two bodyguards.[148] Hamas' decentralised structure limited the impact of the deaths on the organisation, but the assassinations were nevertheless a powerful show of Israeli strength.[149]

As with the earlier assassination of Abu Jihad, some Israeli security figures would later doubt the wisdom of killing Yassin. Like Abu Jihad, Yassin had masterminded attacks that targeted Israeli civilians, including children, and on these grounds most Israelis saw their assassinations as justified. But their deaths had unintended consequences that were often undesirable from the Israeli perspective. In particular, Yassin had been strongly opposed to Hamas allying with Iran. His assassination opened the door for the Tehran regime to significantly extend its power in Palestine in general and Gaza in particular.[150] Zvi Sela, the former chief intelligence officer of the Israeli Prisons Service who interrogated Yassin every week for three years in prison, later shared his reflections in an interview with the Israeli newspaper *Haaretz*. Revealing that Yassin had recognised the state of Israel in their exchanges, Sela added, 'I tend to think that if we had tried for an agreement with him, we would have succeeded.'[151]

A few months after Yassin and Rantisi, there was another major Palestinian death. In October, Yasser Arafat collapsed at his compound in Ramallah and was airlifted to Paris, where he died shortly afterwards.[152] It was a grim ending for the man who had led the Palestinian struggle for decades. By this time of his death, Arafat had been under Israeli siege in Ramallah for more than two years, unable to leave the muqata to travel even short distances. Barred by Israel from returning to his Gaza office, he had started to lose his grip over the territory as Hamas increased its power base there. Touting both its militancy and its extensive social service network – the most effective one in Gaza – Hamas sought to present itself as a functional alternative to the failing PA.[153] Meanwhile Arafat's final years – surviving under siege and then dying in exile – seemed to encapsulate the worst elements of the Palestinian experience. To underline his dispossession, Israel denied his wish to be laid to rest in Jerusalem.[154]

Sharon openly welcomed Arafat's death, having expressed his regret at not killing him in Beirut twenty years earlier.[155] In Arafat's final years, Sharon had worked closely with the George W. Bush administration to isolate him politically while also besieging him militarily. In 2003, the US had demanded a full restructuring of the PA, culminating in the creation of a Palestinian prime minister with responsibility for appointing the cabinet and overseeing the day-to-day working of governments. In reality, the post was designed to curtail Arafat's power by enabling Israel and the US to circumvent him in negotiations.

Mahmoud Abbas, Arafat's deputy and the favoured candidate of Israel and the US, was named prime minister in March 2003 and given responsibility for peace talks. He resigned just four months later, citing Israeli intransigence, American partisanship towards Israel, and a power struggle with Arafat that made his job impossible.[156] Ahmed Qurei, another Tunisian returnee and longtime Fatah activist, succeeded Abbas as the second Palestinian prime minister.

Yet Abbas remained a prominent figure in Palestinian politics. As secretary general of the PLO's Executive Committee, he was still technically the number two in charge. This meant that when Arafat died in November 2004, Abbas immediately succeeded him as PLO chair as well as Fatah leader. The US and Israel welcomed his leadership, but to many Palestinians he was unimpressive; Abbas lacked Arafat's credibility as a fedayeen fighter and was sometimes nicknamed *al-muwazzaf* ('the administrator').[157] In the words of Rashid Khalidi, a Palestinian scholar and former advisor in negotiations, 'Abbas was neither charismatic nor eloquent; he was not renowned for personal bravery or considered a man of the people. Overall, he was one of the least impressive of the early generation of prominent Fatah leaders.'[158]

Regardless, in January 2005 Abbas was elected as PA president with 62 per cent of the vote.[159] Once again, Hamas boycotted the election. The following month, Abbas travelled to Sharm El Sheikh to meet with Sharon, and the two agreed to a truce that formally ended the second intifada – while doing nothing to address its underlying causes.[160]

Later that year, Sharon carried out his disengagement plan in Gaza. In August and September, Israel unilaterally evacuated 8,500 settlers, dismantled all twenty-one illegal settlements and demolished 2,530 houses in the Strip.[161] It marked only the second time that Israel had dismantled settlements, and the first time it had done so anywhere in Palestine. On 12 September 2005, Israel moved its military units out of the Strip in a disengagement far more sweeping than the limited 'redeployment' of 1994. Now, for the first time in thirty-eight years, Palestinians could move around Gaza without encountering Israeli soldiers. As Gaza-born journalist Asmaa al-Ghoul put it, 'there was no longer the Israeli checkpoint between north and south where you could sometimes get stuck for hours on end – a real liberation!'[162]

Yet the Gaza disengagement was not tied to any wider peace efforts – on the contrary. In the run-up to it, Israel destroyed 1,500 Palestinian homes in Gaza's Philadelphi corridor (the area between Rafah and the Egyptian border) and constructed a 7-metre-high wall there.[163] Its military operations in the area at that time killed forty-three Palestinians, wounded hundreds and displaced thousands once again.[164] Around the same time, it installed two new fences – one with razor wire and one with electronic sensors and surveillance cameras – that surrounded the Strip entirely.[165] It was a further intensification of the closure policy that Israel had originally imposed on Gaza during the first intifada. Meanwhile, over the following year, 12,000 new Jewish settlers arrived in the West Bank, upending any suggestion that the Israeli government had embraced a two-state solution.[166]

Most importantly, the dismantling of the settlements – while undoubtedly significant – didn't mean the end of Israel's occupation of Gaza. Although it evacuated its settler and military presence, Israel retained full control over the Gaza Strip's 'borders', including all of its commercial crossing and entry points, and its airspace and territorial waters.[167] It continued to control the Strip's water supply, communications, fuel, electricity, sewerage networks, currency, trade and population register.[168] As a result, many international lawyers argued that Gaza remained under Israeli occupation. They pointed to Israel's ongoing control of Gaza; the fact that its vast technological superiority enabled it to quickly launch a ground invasion; and, crucially, that it remained fully in charge of all movement in and out of the Strip even after the disengagement.[169] In other words, the Palestinians of Gaza were now living under a new, 21st-century form of military occupation.

While the first intifada had strengthened Palestinian morale and won their cause new international standing, the second did the opposite. Palestinians across the oPt endured deaths and destruction as well as worsening poverty and escalating inter-factional rivalry on the streets. Over the six years of the first intifada, 18,000 Palestinians were injured; in just the first five months of the second, the equivalent figure was more than 11,000. In that same period, Israel bombed the homes of more than a million Palestinians.[170] Meanwhile, Palestinian activism turned significantly more violent, with suicide attacks killing more than 600 Israeli civilians, wounding many more and spreading fear and panic among the entire population.[171]

In the decade between Arafat's return to Palestine and his death, the moment of hope around the peace talks had turned to bitter disillusionment. Palestinians were now more oppressed than ever, by the new forces of the PA as well as the continuing Israeli occupation. Those in Gaza found themselves largely confined to the Strip, where they suffered from rising poverty and worsening living conditions, alongside intensifying violence and everyday terror. And with the conclusion of the disengage-ment plan, the scene was set for whole new levels of violence.

6

THE RISE OF HAMAS

At the beginning of 2006, Palestinians went to the polls again. In the decade since their last legislative election, they had lived through the collapse of the Oslo process, the second intifada and the death of their first president. Now they had to decide who would run the Palestinian legislature, the PLC, alongside the executive of Mahmoud Abbas' presidency. This time, there was a crucial difference from the 1996 elections: Hamas had chosen to participate. Israel, the US and the PA leadership all publicly reacted to this news with dismay, issuing statements of concern and thinly veiled threats about the end of the peace process.[1] When the results were announced, it seemed their fears had been realised: Hamas had won the elections with 44 per cent of the vote, making it the largest party and giving it the right to form the next government.[2]

Few events in 21st-century Palestine would prove more consequential than Hamas' electoral victory of 2006. The result set in motion a chain of events that fundamentally changed life in Palestine, precipitating the fracturing of the oPt, Israel's full-scale shutdown of the Gaza Strip and the region's descent into the worst violence in its history. To understand the origins of all this, we need to look back to 2006.

Hamas' decision to stand for the PLC aligned with the group's increasing political engagement. In 2004, a Hamas delegation had participated in talks in Cairo, joining with Fatah and eleven other Palestinian organisations in vowing to support the democratic process, resist the occupation and establish a fully sovereign Palestinian state with Jerusalem as its capital.[3] Hamas had long participated in municipal, student and union elections, with its moderate and pragmatic factions calling for involvement in the PLC too. After it won a third of seats in the oPt in the 2004–5 municipal elections, these factions were able to prevail in internal deliberations.[4]

In a bid to maintain coherence, Hamas' leadership insisted that its participation in the PLC elections was simply another element of its resistance strategy, alongside armed struggle.[5] It would later emerge that the George W. Bush administration had actually asked the Qatari regime to persuade Hamas to stand for election, with the aim of taming the movement and bringing it under control – but with the expectation that it wouldn't win.[6]

When Hamas' electoral victory was announced, critics cited it as evidence of majority Palestinian support for violent extremism.[7] The reality is more complex. Hamas never won a majority of the Palestinian vote; its 44 per cent showing put it ahead of all other parties but still meant that most voters didn't support it. And although Hamas undeniably had a base in Gaza, it only achieved a majority in one of the Strip's five electoral districts.[8] These figures should give pause to anyone claiming that Palestinians overwhelmingly supported Hamas in 2006. As late as March 2005, a poll had found that 33.9 per cent of Palestinians in Gaza supported Islamist parties like Hamas, while 35.3 per cent supported Fatah.[9] Nevertheless, Hamas was victorious in 2006 and could justly speak of electoral credibility. What, then, were the sources of its support?

Hamas ran its 2006 electoral campaign on a platform of 'Change and Reform', which it had also used in the municipal elections. This emphasised its commitment to cleaning up corruption, reforming Palestinian political institutions and developing civil society. It had little to say about either religion or militancy, although it remained an Islamist organisation committed to combat and opposed to Zionism and the state of Israel.[10]

During the campaign, Hamas' leaders also softened some of their rhetoric. Engaging directly with the Israeli media for the first time, co-founder Mahmoud Zahar granted interviews to Israeli state radio and the left-leaning *Haaretz* newspaper.[11] He told the latter that Hamas' notorious antisemitic Charter was 'a matter for interpretation' and could be changed; he also acknowledged the widespread Palestinian consensus in favour of a two-state solution along the 1967 lines (which, of course, ran counter to Hamas' ideology).[12]

There is strong evidence that Palestinian voters were influenced primarily by Hamas' electoral platform when casting their ballots. Opinion polls repeatedly showed that most Palestinians favoured a negotiated peace settlement with Israel, and voted for Hamas on grounds of its anti-corruption stance, rather than hardline anti-Israel or Islamist positions.[13] In fact, an exit poll found that three-quarters of Palestinian voters wanted Hamas to change its stance on Israel.[14] Accordingly, most observers concluded that Palestinians' vote for Hamas in 2006 was driven by despondency over their situation and widespread disillusionment with the PA, Fatah and the Oslo process.[15] Even Bush took this view, describing the election result as 'a wake-up call to the [Palestinian] leadership. Obviously people were not happy with the status quo.'[16]

As we saw in Chapter Five, in the decade since its establishment the Fatah-run PA had become known for corruption and authoritarianism.[17] Palestinians across the oPt were outraged as they saw the sulta undermine democracy, the rule of law and civil rights.[18] Hamas drew effectively on this popular indignation, in part by emphasising that it itself was suffering from PA repression; in 1996, the sulta had begun removing Hamas figures from positions of influence in mosques.[19] Asmaa al-Ghoul, a Gaza-born journalist and herself an outspoken opponent of Hamas, would later reflect, 'Why had Hamas been so convincing? Because people, including myself, were weary of the corruption of the present government.'[20] Hamas fuelled such feelings by highlighting its leaders' humility, pointing out that Ismail Haniyeh, the head of its electoral list, still lived in Shati camp while Abbas resided in a villa. It also emphasised its own reliance on charitable donations for funding, in contrast to Fatah's dependence on patronage and rentier politics.[21]

As well as benefiting from the rising opposition to the Fatah-run PA, Hamas won support for its work in the community, where it provided food, clothing, healthcare and money to those in need.[22] The organisation supervised religious schools, managed nurseries, libraries and sports clubs, and provided student loans. These activities were a significant factor in its popular support, and Hamas cited its social work when arguing that its activities were centred around Palestinian interests, in contrast to Fatah's perceived subservience to Israel and the US.[23]

For Palestinian voters in Gaza, the aftermath of the 2005 Israeli disengagement provided further critical context to the 2006 elections. This new reality, whereby settler evacuation was juxtaposed with continuing occupation, was a boon for Hamas' electoral prospects. We have already seen how Ariel Sharon's insistence on disengaging unilaterally had enabled Hamas to claim the settlers' evacuation as a vindication of its militant tactics.[24] The day after the Israeli army's final departure, Hamas had organised a demonstration in Gaza City celebrating 'their victory' and presenting it as a foundation for further gains.[25]

At the same time, Hamas cited Israel's ongoing occupation of Gaza – whereby it retained control of the Strip's airspace, territorial waters and land boundaries – to argue that it needed to continue its armed struggle. Addressing Hamas' refusal to disarm at this time, Mahmoud Zahar asserted: 'Conditions now are that there is an occupation and nonviolent means have failed to convince [Israel] to leave, and only military means persuade it. There is no choice but to carry weapons in Gaza and Ramallah because Israel is threatening to invade any minute.'[26]

In September 2005 – immediately after the disengagement was completed – Hamas had launched twenty-nine rockets into Israel, again breaching the rules of war by indiscriminately attacking civilians.[27] In response, Israel continued to attack Gaza with air raids and bombardments. In the months between the disengagement and the Palestinian legislative elections, Israeli forces had killed thirty-seven Palestinians in Gaza.[28]

The final factor in Hamas' electoral success was its promise to end the rising lawlessness in Gaza, where inter-factional fighting had caused an increasing number of civilian abductions, injuries and fatalities.[29] With many Palestinians feeling desperate over the situation – and Fatah's failure to deal with it – Hamas drew support from its campaign's focus on providing security and re-establishing law and order.[30] When the results were announced on 29 January 2006, following elections that international observers deemed free and fair, it seemed its approach had paid off.

The post-election fallout

Hamas' electoral victory sent shockwaves around the world. The Israeli government, now headed by Ehud Olmert after Sharon had suffered a stroke and fallen into a coma,[31] liaised with the

White House to obstruct Hamas' governance. Seeking to pressure – or punish – the Palestinians into ousting Hamas, it withheld all the tax and custom duty it collected on the PA's behalf, worth around $55 million a month, in a financial blockade that amounted to collective punishment.[32] The US sharpened the impact by ceasing all its financial aid to the Palestinians. In the words of senior Israeli advisor Dov Weisglass, 'the idea is to put the Palestinians on a diet, but not to make them die of hunger.'[33] It was a chilling statement that would prove alarmingly prescient.

The new PLC was sworn in two months after the election. Hamas' Ismail Haniyeh became prime minister, with the power to appoint ministers and call cabinet meetings. Yet the new cabinet's ability to function was quickly stymied by opposition from Israel and the US. As Israel banned all Hamas parliamentarians – including Haniyeh – from travelling between Gaza and the West Bank, the PLC had to hold its first session via video link.[34]

The great irony was that in 2003, the US had pushed for the creation of the PA prime ministership and the appointment of Mahmoud Abbas to that office, demanding that powers be transferred from president to premier. Now, Abbas was president and the US wanted the exact opposite: maximum power in presidential hands and severe restrictions on the office of the prime minister, taken up by Hamas. As the PA's effective paymaster, it openly threatened to return the Islamist premier's powers to the presidency.[35]

With the blockade making it difficult for the PA to function and increasing poverty across the occupied Palestinian territories, Haniyeh began to pursue some conciliatory measures. Along with other senior Hamas figures, he made statements to the Western media about the possibility of future co-existence with Israel.[36] In April 2006, Hamas formally ended the suicide bombings for which it had become notorious, citing a 'change of belief' – although, as we shall see, it would continue to target

Israeli civilians in rocket attacks.[37] And in June, Haniyeh wrote a letter to Bush in which he requested direct negotiations, adding: 'We are so concerned about stability and security in the area that we don't mind having a Palestinian state in the 1967 borders and offering a truce for many years.'[38]

Yet the US was resolute: Hamas would not govern. Soon after the election result, it had begun a secret programme arming and training Fatah forces to go to war with Hamas. Its goal was to provoke a Palestinian civil war that would remove the latter from power and reinstate Fatah's supremacy.[39]

At the same time, Abbas was carrying out his own manoeuvres. Soon after the election, he had promoted Mohammed Dahlan, the Fatah security chief in Gaza, to his personal staff. He also asserted control by attaching the PA security forces directly to the presidency. It signalled the start of a long-running battle over the domain of 'security', which would prove the fiercest struggle between Abbas and Haniyeh.

In subsequent months, both Fatah and Hamas moved to increase their own armed forces. As Fatah deployed private militias to create disturbances and undermine its rival's governance, Hamas responded by creating a new 'Executive Force' militia reporting directly to its interior minister. Fatah countered in turn by involving the presidential guard, deploying 1,500 of its 2,600 members to Gaza.[40]

Unsurprisingly, the tensions quickly escalated. With US support, Dahlan directed Fatah fighters to wage a brutal campaign pursuing, detaining and torturing Hamas figures; with Iranian support, Hamas retaliated with its own brutality, attacking and killing even unarmed policemen who were seen as Fatah affiliates.[41] In June 2006, direct intra-Palestinian fighting culminated in a pitched battle between Hamas and Fatah in Rafah.[42]

All the while, Israeli–Palestinian violence raged. Hamas and

PIJ continued to launch rocket attacks on Israeli civilians, and Israel continued to respond with disproportionate retaliation. Now unfettered by the presence of Jewish settlers in the Strip, Israeli attacks became increasingly indiscriminate and totalising.[43] In May 2006, Israeli armoured vehicles entered Gaza for the first time since disengagement, killing three PIJ fighters.[44]

The following month, a joint force of Palestinian militants tunnelled into Israel to launch a raid on an army post, where they seized soldier Gilad Shalit, and took him back to Gaza by force. Hamas then demanded the release of all Palestinian women and children from Israeli jails in exchange for his return. Instead, Israel launched a new four-month military offensive in Gaza, which they called 'Operation Summer Rains'.

Crucially, Shalit's capture also undermined the newly announced platform for a Palestinian national unity government – an outcome that the militants had almost certainly intended – as Gaza was plunged into worsening crisis. By the end of that summer, 79 per cent of Gaza's residents were living in poverty, and those in urban areas had running water for a maximum three hours per day, as well as limited electricity after Israel had bombed Gaza's only power plant.[45] In total, over the course of 2006, Israeli forces killed 526 Palestinians in Gaza (the majority during 'Summer Rains'), and Gaza rocket attacks and gunfire killed six Israelis.[46]

Meanwhile, the violence between Hamas and Fatah continued after the pitched battle of June 2006. They were now openly fighting in the streets of Gaza, carrying out shootings, kidnappings and kneecappings. Unarmed Palestinian non-combatants were caught in the crossfire, with young children getting injured or even losing their lives.[47] Asmaa al-Ghoul recalls finding an unexploded bomb on her balcony, as her housing block was located in the middle of the inter-factional fighting.[48] All this meant that in addition to the 526 Palestinians killed by Israel in Gaza in 2006, 47 were killed by other Palestinians.[49] A Fatah–Hamas ceasefire agreed towards the end of December lasted only eight days.

As 2007 dawned, the intra-Palestinian violence continued to intensify, with a death toll of seventy-four in just two weeks.[50] Appalled by the scenes coming out of Palestine – and particularly Gaza – the Arab regimes finally intervened. King Abdullah of Saudi Arabia invited Abbas, Haniyeh and Hamas leader Khaled Meshal to Mecca, where he promised to donate $1 billion in aid provided they reach an agreement to stop the violence. It worked: they agreed to form a national unity government that would be led by Haniyeh and include ministers from both Hamas and Fatah, as well as other parties, with Abbas retaining right of veto.

The new government was inaugurated in March – but did not last long. The US refused to work with it, instead helping Dahlan set up a special force of 1,400 fighters to constrain Hamas' power.[51] Inter-factional violence quickly started to escalate again, culminating in a four-day battle in Gaza in June. With Dahlan undergoing surgery in Egypt, Hamas took advantage of his absence to launch a total assault on Fatah, successfully driving it out of Gaza and taking full control of the Strip. The US plan had backfired: rather than ousting Hamas, the civil war had entrenched its control over one part of Palestine.

Abbas declined to travel to Gaza to address the crisis. Instead, he declared a state of emergency, dissolved the national unity government, and formed a new Fatah-dominated cabinet in Ramallah, appointing technocrat Salam Fayyad as PA prime minister. Just as Fatah had been forced out of Gaza, now the PA harassed and detained Islamists across the West Bank. Palestine became further divided, between Abbas' PA in the West Bank and Hamas in Gaza. Both regimes continued to operate within the overarching context of Israeli occupation, with the Israeli army directly administering more than 60 per cent of the West Bank.

Reinforcing the division, the US and Israel quickly recognised Abbas' government, lifted the blockade on the West Bank and tightened it on Gaza. Some parties in Israel actually welcomed the Hamas takeover, with head of military intelligence Amos Yadlin saying at the time that 'Israel would be happy if Hamas took over Gaza because the IDF could then deal with Gaza as a hostile state.'[52]

BLOCKADE

From this point onwards, blockade and bombardment became the twin pillars of Israeli policy in Gaza. After Hamas took over, Israel imposed a complete and indefinite blockade on the Strip that stopped people and goods from moving in and out. As we saw in previous chapters, it had been difficult for Palestinians to leave Gaza ever since Israel first imposed its closure policy in 1991; now, it became almost impossible. From 2007, hardly any Palestinians could get the Israeli-issued permits needed to leave the Strip, with matters made worse by a presidential decree from Abbas that voided all travel documents issued in Gaza.[53] Even those who did get a permit found that the Strip's three remaining crossings were typically closed anyway.[54] UN special rapporteur John Dugard stated that Israel was largely to blame for turning Gaza into 'a prison' and 'throwing away the key'.[55]

Israel and its allies imposed the blockade by land, air and sea. As a coastal territory, Gaza's waters had long been important to life in the Strip, with fishing a critical source of food and income for much of the population. But the blockade curtailed this too.

ISRAELI RESTRICTIONS ON GAZA POST-2007

No Fishing Zone 1.5 miles

6-mile fishing limit enforced from 2012

3-mile fishing limit enforced from 2009 to 2012

MEDITERRANEAN SEA

Beit Hanoun/ Erez crossing

Shati Camp

Jabalia Camp

Jabalia

Gaza City

Al Shujaiah/ Nahal Oz crossing Fuel Pipeline *Closed since Jan. 2010*

Nuseirat Camp

Bureij Camp

Al Muntar/ Qarni crossing *Closed since June 2007*

Maghazi Camp

Deir al-Balah Camp

ISRAEL

Al Karara/Kissufim crossing *Closed since 2005*

No Fishing Zone 1 mile

Khan Younis Camp

Khan Younis

- - - - Green Line today

——— No-go zone (100 metres)

——— Access permitted on foot and for farmers only (100-300 metres)

Risk zone (effective no-go zone)

Rafah Camp

Rafah

N

Rafah border crossing

Al Awdah/Sufa crossing *Closed since Sept. 2008*

Gaza International Airport *(Destroyed/non-operational since 2002)*

Karem Abu Salem/Kerem Shalom crossing *Mainly goods-only*

EGYPT

0   5 Miles

0   10 Km

Under Oslo, Israel had agreed to allow Palestinian fishing boats to sail out 20 nautical miles from the Strip; in practice, it restricted them to 12 nautical miles and after 'disengagement' it reduced this further to 6. Once the blockade came into full force, Israeli forces restricted Gaza's fishermen to a mere 3 nautical miles off the coast. Palestinians who exceeded the limit could be fired at by Israeli patrols, and even those who didn't were sometimes harassed, detained, forcibly undressed or assaulted.[56]

In previous decades, Israel had relied on manpower to police the Strip; now, it increasingly used high-tech tools that both cheapened the cost of the occupation and minimised the human contact between occupier and occupied. In the years after 'disengagement', and even more so from 2007, Israel's closure of Gaza took a digital form, imposed not only by razor-wire fences, concrete walls and military watchtowers, but also by drones, CCTV, radar sensors, spy balloons, sonic imagery, and remote-controlled machine guns, bulldozers and boats.[57]

When it came to Gaza's southern land border, Israel had further help from its Egyptian allies. After the Hamas takeover in Gaza, the Cairo government had shut down the Rafah border crossing.[58] When Hamas used explosives to demolish 125 miles of the Egyptian border wall in 2008 – allowing as many as 700,000 Palestinians to cross into Egypt to buy food, medicine and other essentials – Israel demanded that President Hosni Mubarak immediately reseal it.[59] He agreed to do so after keeping it open for a brief period for humanitarian reasons. Like all the Arab regimes, the Egyptian government spouted the rhetoric of solidarity with the Palestinians – but its actions told another story entirely.

Israel claimed that the blockade was a necessary security measure to prevent Hamas and other militant groups from acquiring any materials that could be used for weaponry. Yet in addition to metal containers, razors, pipes and cement, the list of banned items at times also included jam, hummus, newspapers, shampoo, instant coffee, coriander, pasta, crayons and tomato paste.[60] Human rights activists pointed out that the blockade seemed designed with a view to collective punishment rather than security. After Israel eased some of the restrictions in 2010, the Israeli NGO Gisha responded sarcastically in a statement on its website that it was 'pleased to learn that coriander no longer presents a threat to Israeli security'.[61]

As it turned out, Dov Weisglass' quip about 'putting the Palestinians on a diet' had been literal. In 2008, Israel calculated the minimum number of calories on which a person could survive, a figure that it based on the Israeli average consumption and then 'adjusted to [Palestinian] culture and experience'.[62] On this basis, foods deemed 'non-essential' were banned, meaning that Palestinians in Gaza were denied apricots, grapes, plums and avocados, among other items.[63] Israel also restricted imports of seeds, fertiliser and agricultural material, making it difficult for Palestinians to grow their own food in the Strip.[64] As a result, the World Health Organization reported worsening child malnutrition in Gaza, with rates doubling between 2006 and 2008.[65]

With the official crossings closed, Palestinians became increasingly reliant on their network of tunnels for essential supplies. Palestinians had first tunnelled out of Gaza in the 1980s, after the Camp David Accords divided Rafah's families between Egyptian- and Israeli-controlled zones. Over the following two decades, several tunnels were established across the Rafah border, used mostly by families seeking reunion or individuals looking for work in Egypt. During the second intifada, Hamas began digging more tunnels for militant purposes, and after the blockade came into full force in 2007, they became critical to life in Gaza. By some estimates, Hamas dug as many as 1,500 tunnels out of the Strip in subsequent years, mostly into Egypt.[66]

In the Western and Israeli media, the tunnels were associated almost entirely with arms-smuggling, which was undeniably one of their functions at this time. Yet they also provided a (literal) underground economy that was often the only way to get hold of essential items, including food, fuel and medicines. They sometimes offered the only route for Palestinians to access necessary medical treatment, or to reunite with their husbands, wives, parents, siblings or children.[67] Tunnel activity was so varied that it occasionally had elements of absurdity: in 2008, Palestinian zookeeper Shadi Fayez smuggled gazelles, monkeys and a lion through the tunnels to populate his zoo in Rafah.[68]

For the tiny minority of Palestinians granted Israeli permits, leaving Gaza was still a humiliating and time-consuming ordeal. Izzeldin Abuelaish, whom we met in Chapter Three when Sharon's forces demolished his childhood home, was in that minority. As the only Gaza-born doctor working in Israel, he regularly made the journey back and forth across the Gaza fence. He describes the experience of crossing through Erez:

There are precisely twenty different checks at different gates and in separate locked rooms with whirring X-ray machines and cameras. Instructions, issued sometimes impersonally, sometimes with hostility, rarely reluctantly, include 'spread your legs, put your feet on the designated spots, raise your arms above your head' . . . You trek first across an open field, then down a cement corridor, and finally into the stainless steel building, obeying red and green lights that tell you to stop or to go, passing into consecutive locked cubicles with more stop-and-go instructions. Disembodied voices bark from loudspeakers . . . It used to take an hour's drive over paved goat trails to get from Gaza to Jerusalem. Now it's a half-day journey if you're lucky.[69]

In Abuelaish's view, 'The message of Erez is clear: don't live in Gaza, don't go to Gaza'.[70] (In fact, among Israelis the expression 'go to Gaza' was slang for 'go to hell' – a pun first coined in a 1970s Israeli song that played on the two words' similarity in Hebrew).[71]

Palestinians' confinement to the Gaza Strip was compounded by the constant violence they had to endure. Since entering government, Hamas had not stopped its attacks on civilian targets inside Israel, and Israel continued to launch dispropor-tionate reprisals, with its advanced weaponry and Iron Dome missile defence system creating a stark asymmetry in the Israeli and Palestinian death tolls. All the while, Israel continued to violently enforce its blockade of Gaza, while reconnaissance drones (known among Palestinians as *al-zanana*) buzzed cease-lessly over people's heads.[72]

A bilateral ceasefire, brokered by Egypt in June 2008, came to an abrupt end in November when Israel launched a raid that killed six Hamas gunmen.[73] The violence escalated quickly after Hamas retaliated with rocket fire that wounded an Israeli civil-ian.[74] In December, Israel launched its biggest assault on the Gaza Strip since disengagement: a 23-day war it dubbed 'Cast Lead' that involved a ground operation as well as air raids.

Over the course of 'Cast Lead', Israeli forces killed 1,391 Palestinians in Gaza – more than in any prior war[75] – while Palestinians killed eight Israelis.[76] Despite the significant Palestinian death toll, the Israeli assault failed to deliver a major blow to the Qassam Brigades.[77] The operation also made no difference to Gilad Shalit, whom Hamas continued to hold captive. He was eventually released in 2011 in exchange for 1,027 Palestinians from Israeli jails – among them the senior Hamas figure Yahya Sinwar.[78]

The operation did, however, cause immense pain and suffering to thousands of Palestinian civilians, including many children. It emerged that Israel was applying the so-called 'Dahiyeh doctrine', which was developed during its 2006 war in Lebanon and denotes the use of massive, disproportionate force in deliberately targeting civilians and civilian infrastructure.[79] Gadi Eizenkot, chief of Israel's Northern Command, had confirmed the use of this strategy in Lebanon to an Israeli newspaper: 'What happened in the Dahiyeh* quarter of Beirut in 2006 will happen in every village from which Israel is fired on . . . We will apply disproportionate force on [Lebanese villages that fire on Israel] and cause great damage and destruction there. From our standpoint, these are not civilian villages, these are military bases . . . This is not a recommendation. This is a plan. And it has been approved.'[80] The use of this strategy in Gaza goes some way to explaining the major Palestinian death toll, which included more than 300 children and as many as a thousand non-combatants overall.[81]

Among the fatalities were three of Izzeldin Abuelaish's daughters: 21-year-old Bessan, 15-year-old Mayar and 13-year-old Aya, as well as his 17-year-old niece Noor. When the war began, Abuelaish had decided to keep his family at home, assuming that as an employee at an Israeli hospital, with clearance to regularly cross through Erez, he would not be targeted. Yet on 18 January 2009, an Israeli tank shelled the family home and instantly killed the four girls, as well as seriously injuring Abuelaish's other daughter Shatha and other niece Ghaida. Calling on his Israeli contacts, he was able to arrange an emergency medical evacuation for Shatha and Ghaida to hospital in Israel, where they recovered. But it was too late for Bessan, Mayar, Aya and Noor.[82]

The UN later ordered a commission of inquiry into the war,

---

* Dahiyeh is a suburb in southern Beirut, with a predominantly Shi'a population. It is governed by Hizbollah and therefore often targeted by Israel.

led by South African judge Richard Goldstone. Goldstone found that both Israel and Hamas had committed war crimes and possible crimes against humanity by the targeted and arbitrary killing of civilians – Israel in its operations in Gaza and Hamas by firing rockets into civilian areas in southern Israel. His report also condemned Hamas for carrying out extrajudicial violence, including torture, against Palestinian political opponents and suspected collaborators, and condemned the Israeli military for 'systematic and deliberate violations' of the Fourth Geneva Convention, through what he described as a 'carefully planned' assault designed to 'punish, humiliate and terrorise [Gaza's] civilian population'.[83]

Goldstone's judgment was corroborated by a report from the Israeli NGO Breaking the Silence, published six months after the war. Based on the testimonies of Israeli soldiers who had fought in Gaza, it provided extensive evidence of Israeli war crimes. The soldiers described receiving orders to treat all Palestinians as the enemy ('no innocents'), using Palestinian civilians as human shields, demolishing houses without cause and deploying white phosphorus against civilians – all in violation of international law.[84]

No one in Gaza was unaffected by the war. More than 2,000 children were orphaned and more than 100,000 people made homeless, leading some Palestinians to call it 'the Nakba of 2009'.[85] By the end of the war, nearly 90 per cent of the population were entirely dependent on food aid. Israeli bombardment had destroyed or damaged beyond repair 6,400 homes, as well as 214 schools (mostly run by UNRWA) and 34 hospitals and clinics. With the total damage estimated at up to $1.9 billion, Palestinians faced a new level of catastrophe in the ongoing Nakba. Unsurprisingly, an international NGO found that 96 per cent of the population felt depressed or despondent as a result of the war.[86] And with the blockade continuing alongside constant low-level violence and drones, the people of Gaza had little chance of fully recovering and moving forward.

'MOWING THE LAWN'

Shortly after 'Cast Lead', Israeli elections returned Likud to power and Benjamin Netanyahu began his second premiership a decade after his first had ended. Employing his trademark hardline rhetoric, Netanyahu regularly named Hamas as Israel's sworn enemy and declared that his government could not recognise or negotiate with it. Yet behind the scenes things were very different. We saw in Chapter Three how Israeli intelligence services had originally aided Palestinian Islamists in Gaza as a useful rival to Fatah and the PLO. In the twenty-first century, Netanyahu took a similar approach. In his view, Hamas' governance of Gaza actually suited Israeli interests because it divided the Palestinians, gave him cover for avoiding negotiations and fuelled the aggressive discourse that empowered his premiership. At a Likud meeting in 2019, he said: 'Anyone who wants to thwart the establishment of a Palestinian state has to support bolstering Hamas and transferring money to Hamas. This is part of our strategy – to isolate the Palestinians in Gaza from those in Judea and Samaria [the West Bank].'[87]

With this in mind, Netanyahu's government continually pursued secret negotiations and deals with Hamas, seeking not to destroy the organisation but rather to keep it in power.[88] Through back channels, he requested that the Qatari regime provide funds to keep the Hamas government afloat. What's more, he enabled this financial transfer to the regime while simultaneously enforcing a blockade that prevented essential food and medicine from reaching the Strip's isolated population.[89]

In an Israeli newspaper op-ed, researchers Efraim Inbar and Eitan Shamir dubbed the government strategy in Gaza 'mowing the lawn'.[90] This meant launching regular military attacks on Gaza, designed to weaken the forces of Hamas, PIJ and other militias without overturning the status quo. Crucially, the strategy avoided any political solution or fundamental change; as such, it was aligned with Netanyahu's behind-the-scenes support for Hamas' governance in Gaza, as well as the longer-term Israeli policy of collective punishment.[91] Yet it was grounded in a series of flawed assumptions: that the deteriorating situation in Gaza was sustainable, that Palestinians and Arabs elsewhere would forget about it, and that all Palestinian grievances were fundamentally illegitimate.

In accordance with this strategy, Israel periodically launched intensive attacks in the vein of 'Cast Lead'. It defended these operations as necessary self-defence against the rocket attacks that Hamas, PIJ and other militants continued to fire into Israel, killing three civilians in the three years after the 2009 war. Among the victims was sixteen-year-old Daniel Viflic, who lost his life in 2011 when Gaza militants fired a missile that hit his school bus.[92] In the same three-year period, Israeli forces killed 216 Palestinians in Gaza, including Imad Muhammad Issa Frajallah, also sixteen, who was killed by army gunfire near Gaza City.[93]

Periodic escalations became the new norm, as Israel and Hamas observed a modus operandi that served both parties' interests – but not those of either the Palestinian people or the vast majority of Israelis.[94] And as the years went on it became increasingly clear that the blockade was doing nothing to unseat Hamas. In fact, with Gaza's residents increasingly reliant on the tunnels to survive, Hamas was actually benefiting from the situation. Having set up a 'Tunnels Department' to collect tax on all goods entering Gaza in this way, it gained a vital source of revenue. By the mid-2010s, there were estimated to be more than a thousand tunnels connecting Gaza to the outside world. Hamas took advantage of the blockade to position itself as the key supplier of essential resources in the Strip.[95] This was the true meaning of the blockade: while the Palestinian people suffered, war profiteers benefited and corruption grew.[96]

'Mowing the lawn' went hand in hand with the growing virulent dehumanisation of the Palestinians in mainstream Israeli discourse. Defending Israel's approach to Gaza in a newspaper op-ed, David Weinberg, Jerusalem Institute for Strategic Studies vice president, drew on the phrase when he wrote, 'Just like mowing your front lawn, this is constant, hard work. If you fail to do so, weeds grow wild and snakes begin to slither around in the brush.'[97] This rhetoric was fuelled by the blockade, which prevented Israelis from interacting with Palestinians from Gaza except in a military capacity; as a result, both populations increasingly came to see each other as alien.[98]

With the blockade in place, the idea took hold in Israel that nobody in Gaza was an innocent civilian. In 2012, Qadima activist Gilad Sharon (son of Ariel) openly stated as much in a newspaper op-ed: 'The desire to prevent harm to innocent civilians in Gaza will ultimately lead to harming the truly innocent: the residents of southern Israel. The residents of Gaza are not innocent, they elected Hamas. The Gazans aren't hostages; they chose this freely and must live with the consequences.'[99]

Sharon's argument was of course belied by the facts. The majority of Gaza's population – around half of whom were children – had never voted for Hamas. By 2012 the group's electoral mandate had long expired anyway, but calls for new elections repeatedly hit the stumbling blocks of Israeli obstruction, lack of international support and the stalemate of the

Hamas–Fatah divide. Regardless, Sharon's rhetoric started to become increasingly mainstream as Israeli politics moved further and further to the right.

The denial of civilian status to anyone in Gaza was reflected in Israel's military strategy in the Strip. A few months after Sharon published his op-ed, Israel launched an eight-week operation in Gaza called 'Pillar of Defence'. During this time, Israeli forces killed 173 Palestinians, including 113 civilians and 38 children, and Palestinian rockets killed four Israeli civilians and two soldiers. Two years later, Israel responded to the kidnapping of three teenagers from a settlement in the West Bank by launching its deadliest military operation in Gaza thus far; over seven weeks in the summer of 2014, the Israeli air and ground assault of 'Protective Edge' killed 2,251 Palestinians, 1,462 of whom were civilians, while Palestinians killed seventy-two Israelis, five of whom were civilians, as well as one Thai national.[100] Again, Israeli discourse blamed the Palestinians for this; writing in a newspaper op-ed, retired major general Giora Eiland echoed Sharon's argument from two years earlier: '[Gaza's residents] are to blame for this situation just like Germany's residents were to blame for electing Hitler as their leader and paid a heavy price for that, and rightfully so. Hamas is not a terror organization which came from afar and forcibly occupied Gaza. It's the authentic representation of the population there.'[101]

As the weeks of 'Protective Edge' went on, Israel faced mounting international criticism for the high civilian death toll in Gaza.[102] Some legal analysts spoke of the phenomenon of the 'shrinking civilian', whereby Israel kept expanding the definition of a 'legitimate target' until hardly anyone was left with the protections of civilian status.[103] Other analysts described the Israeli policy as *politicide*: the deliberate destruction of a community with the aim of denying them self-determination.[104]

One news story in particular caused shock and outrage around the world: on 16 July 2014, Israeli naval missiles killed four boys from the same family – Ahed, Zakaria, Ismail and Mohammed, all aged between nine and eleven – as they played football on a Gaza beach. The same attack wounded six other civilians, including four children from the same extended family as the slain boys.[105] An internal Israeli military investigation later found that the attack had targeted a Hamas compound, but international journalists who attended the scene said it was only the site of a fishermen's hut.[106]

A few days later, the focus turned to Gaza City's Shuja'iyya neighbourhood, which came under intense Israeli shelling amid clashes between the Qassam Brigades and Israeli ground forces. The Israeli bombardment killed more than seventy Palestinians, the majority of them civilians.[107] While the PA condemned the attack as a massacre, Israel argued that it had forewarned civilians to evacuate the area through leaflets, text messages and automated phone calls.[108] Yet with the entire Strip besieged and bombarded, there was nowhere safe for people to flee to. As Gaza resident Haidar Eid put it, 'it is the Israelis who want the borders closed, but it is also the Israelis who say "run away".'[109]

The high civilian death toll, and the arguments over culpability, made Shuja'iyya symbolic of the wider war on Gaza. Many legal experts, humanitarians and human rights activists argued that Israeli forces were breaching international law with their indiscriminate attacks. Israel countered that Hamas was responsible for the high death toll because it deliberately embedded itself among civilians.[110] Criticising both parties, the UN high commissioner for human rights condemned Hamas for violating international humanitarian law by firing rockets from civilian areas – but also accused Israel of failing to respect civilian status in Gaza.[111] Other analysts argued that proximity to militants made no legal difference to civilian status in wartime.[112]

Amid the decisive rightward shift in Israeli politics and society, anti-occupation activists found themselves increasingly marginalised. In 1982, the organisation Peace Now had brought 400,000 Israelis – 10 per cent of the population – to the streets of Tel Aviv to protest against the Sabra-Shatila massacre. In 2014, only 5,000 Israelis demonstrated against the Gaza war.[113] By 2021, similar public demonstrations would attract fewer than 3,000 people, many of whom were Palestinian citizens of Israel.[114] Oded Lifshitz, the anti-occupation activist we met in Chapter Three, was left in a tiny minority of Jewish Israelis, as he and his wife Yocheved campaigned against Israeli policy and helped Palestinians from the Strip access medical care in Israel.[115]

Meanwhile, Palestinians in Gaza were enduring new levels of deprivation in the years after 'Protective Edge'. As many as half a million Palestinians had been displaced, and one fifth of Gaza's buildings and infrastructure had been damaged or destroyed.[116] There were now Palestinian children under ten who had already lived through three wars, and communities in Gaza that had been displaced more than twenty times in three years.[117] Once again, the blockade made it impossible to rebuild effectively. In its report on the war, the UN Office of Human Rights called on Israel to lift the blockade 'immediately and unconditionally' – but to no avail.[118]

With its infrastructure now on the brink of collapse, Gaza entered a public health emergency. Its deteriorating waste-water treatment facilities posed a particular danger. By 2017, the equivalent of forty-three Olympic-size swimming pools of untreated sewage was being dumped into Gaza's seas every day.[119] The following year, INGOs reported that 97 per cent of Gaza's water was undrinkable.[120] At the same time, the population was increasingly malnourished, with 72 per cent of households facing food insecurity after 'Protective Edge'.[121] The effects were most evident on the most vulnerable: one in ten children in Gaza was now stunted by malnutrition.[122]

Gaza's medical system was also struggling to cope as it contended with the blockade, blackouts and repeated bombardments. And with most of the population denied the right to leave Gaza, they had little chance of accessing medical treatment elsewhere. Medical exit permits were only granted to those with 'life threatening' conditions, and over the years the odds of getting such a permit had worsened significantly, almost halving between 2012 and 2017.[123]

When Israel announced further power cuts in Gaza in 2017, it triggered fresh warnings of a looming catastrophe.[124] Gaza appeared to be breaking down irreparably. Yet its people had not given up.

SUMUD AND SURVIVAL

For decades, the Palestinians had spoken of *sumud*: an Arabic concept that loosely translates as 'steadfastness', which manifested as non-violent everyday resistance against the occupation. Palestinians enacted sumud by staying on their land; by rebuilding the homes that the military destroyed; by investing in local and national economic projects; by participating in cultural activities, including national art and music; by coming together to celebrate weddings and family occasions; and much more besides. Arguably sumud was never needed more than in 21st-century Gaza.[125]

Many Palestinians in Gaza also enacted sumud by remaining dedicated to their education. From the early aftermath of the Nakba, the Palestinian people had placed a strong emphasis on the importance of education, compelling UNRWA to increase its investment in schools and training centres.[126] In subsequent decades, they gained a reputation as the world's 'most educated refugees', with strikingly high literacy rates and educational attainment despite impoverishment and instability.[127] We saw in Chapter Two how educators like Yusra al-Barbari and Mu'in Bseiso played a leading role in Palestinian civil society and activism from as early as the 1950s in Gaza. In the twenty-first century, Gaza was the site of eleven universities, colleges and training centres, where students could study subjects ranging from English literature to biochemistry to economics.

The tragedy, of course, was that the majority of Gaza's graduates were unable to find jobs and pursue careers in which they could put their education to use. This lost potential becomes clear if we look at the stunning degree of resourcefulness shown by young people in Gaza even amid the impossible conditions of blockade and war. During the Israeli invasion of 2008–9, for instance, Izzeldin Abuelaish's teenage daughter Shatha and niece Ghaida used batteries to rig up a homemade charger, meaning the family could continue using their phones after the electricity was cut off. After the tragic shelling of the house killed three of his other daughters and another niece, it was the rigged-up charger that enabled Abuelaish to call his Israeli contacts and arrange for Shatha and Ghaida to be taken out of Gaza for emergency medical treatment.[128]

Other youths in Gaza displayed similar innovation. In 2015, civil engineer Majd Mashharawi created the startup GreenCake, which tackled the urgent need for construction material in Gaza by creating environmentally friendly bricks from ash and rubble. Two years later she developed the SunBox, a device providing solar electricity to counter the Strip's frequent blackouts.[129] And during the COVID-19 pandemic, electrical engineer Farouq Sharaf devised a ventilator that could be locally produced at low cost, as the blockade continued to inhibit Gaza's medical system, but not its people's creativity.[130]

Nor did the blockade put a stop to Palestinian cultural output from Gaza. In 2017, poet Mosab Abu Toha set up the Strip's first English-language public library.[131] Gaining international acclaim for his poetry, he went on to win a visiting fellowship at Harvard. Four years earlier, Khan Younis' Mohammad Assaf had taken the Arab world by storm on *Arab Idol* – the region's version of the reality TV singing competition. To enter the competition, Assaf had spent two days at the Rafah crossing, eventually bribing an Egyptian border guard so that he could reach the auditions in Cairo. He went on to win the show's second series and become a superstar across the Arab world, with Oscar-nominated Palestinian-Dutch film director Hany Abu-Assad making the biopic *The Idol* about him.

Earlier in this book we met Saleem al-Naffar, whose family had first sought refuge in Gaza after being displaced from their homes in Jaffa during the Nakba. Born in Shati camp in 1963, he had been exiled from Palestine as a young child before returning to the Strip during the Oslo years. By the twenty-first century, he was a renowned poet who had published more than a dozen books. Yet like virtually all his neighbours in Gaza, he remained confined to the Strip, unable to visit his ancestral hometown or meet his compatriots on the other side of the fence.

These compatriots included another branch of the al-Naffar family, who had been dispersed elsewhere after being displaced from Jaffa in 1948. This branch of the family had sought refuge in the town of Askalan (now Ashkelon in Israel), before eventually settling in the central town of Lyd (Lod). As citizens of Israel, they were cut off from Saleem and their other relatives in Gaza. By the twenty-first century, however, technological developments created new possibilities for remote connection. Tamer Nafer, who had grown up in Lod and formed the first Palestinian hip-hop group, recalls how his father reached Saleem via MSN messenger in the mid-2000s, chatting virtually across the Gaza fence. Despite their physical separation, the relatives were able to connect online.[132]

As well as using the internet to transcend their isolation, many Palestinians also used it to organise.[133] In 2011, Palestinian youths across Gaza and the West Bank launched a campaign on Facebook calling for reconciliation and an end to the Hamas–Fatah split that continued to separate the two territories. As people across the Arab world rose up that year to demand democracy, the Palestinians demanded a national resolution. In March 2011, tens of thousands in Gaza marched for this, adapting the iconic Arab revolutionary slogan 'The people want the fall of the regime' to become 'The people want an end to disunity'.[134] As protestor Asmaa al-Ghoul put it, 'We can't join the other Arab nations in demanding "the fall of the regime" because we have two regimes – and we won't get anywhere as long as the split between Fatah and Hamas persists.'[135]

Yet despite repeated attempts and agreements – including the formation of a new unity government in 2014 – full reconciliation was never achieved. This was due in part to failures and mistakes by both Hamas and Fatah, and in part to Israel's staunch refusal to work with any Palestinian government that included Hamas – while disingenuously propping up the Hamas regime in Gaza behind the scenes. To enforce this position, Israel withheld the PA's tax revenues from the unity government, severely limiting its ability to function.[136]

Throughout this period, Palestinians continued to seek alternatives to the deadlock of blockade, bombardment and disunity. As the seventieth anniversary of the Nakba approached in 2018, Palestinians planned a mass march to the Gaza fence, which they called the Great March of Return. Intended as a 45-day event, it would involve setting up camps 700–1,000 yards from the fence – outside the Israeli military's unilaterally imposed buffer zone, where anyone entering could be shot on sight – and slowly moving closer to it in weekly non-violent demonstrations, culminating on Nakba Day, 15 May.[137]

In an interview beforehand, Hasan al-Kurd, one of the twenty organisers, spoke about their rationale: 'The situation in Gaza has become unbearable and we absolutely can't live in Gaza anymore – that's what prompted us to plan this march . . . The whole idea is based on UN Security Council Resolution 194 [the right of return] . . . It is actually a peaceful act. We want to ask the Israelis to welcome [us] as if we were visitors from another country – though we're not actually visitors here.'[138] Al-Kurd emphasised that the march had been arranged by civilians – not Hamas – and that it was organised as a non-violent demonstration.

Yet in the event, the march became highly dangerous. Invoking the same language that Israel had used after the original Nakba (as we saw in Chapter Two), Benjamin Netanyahu described the demonstrations as 'terrorist infiltrations' and ordered that they be treated as such.[139] Demonstrators moved nearer to the fence sooner than the organisers had intended – and while the majority were non-violent, Israel nonetheless met them with lethal force.[140] On the very first day of the protests, Israeli troops killed fourteen Palestinians. With the original plan derailed, demonstrations lasted months – during which time Israeli forces killed at least 206 Palestinians and wounded more than 33,000.[141] Meanwhile, Hamas used this Israeli violence as cover for infiltrating and taking control of the protest movement, in turn enabling Israel to paint it as a militant attack.[142] In the end, Palestinian violence killed two Israeli soldiers and wounded six.[143]

Among the fatalities was twenty-year-old Palestinian paramedic Razan al-Najjar, whom the Israeli military shot dead on 1 June 2018. Born shortly before the second intifada, al-Najjar had grown up next to the Gaza fence. During the demonstrations, she gained a high profile as images of her tending to wounded protestors were shared across Palestine and the wider world. One month before her death, she told international journalists, 'We have one goal, to save lives and evacuate people. And to send a message to the world: Without weapons, we can do anything.'[144] Her tragically short life became a symbol of the greater tragedy in Palestine. A subsequent investigation by the Israeli human rights organisation B'Tselem found that Israeli forces had shot al-Najjar deliberately.[145]

The Return March of 2018 wasn't the first demonstration of its kind. During the 2011 Arab uprisings, Palestinians in Gaza had joined with their compatriots in the West Bank, Lebanon and Syria to march to Israel's borders and demand the right of return.[146] Palestinians in Lebanon had organised similar demonstrations further back in 2000, as did Palestinian communities in both Lebanon and Jordan in 2021.[147] With the Great March of Return, then, Palestinians in Gaza affirmed their membership of a bigger national community and challenged the isolation that the blockade imposed on them.[148]

ESCALATION

In 2006, the Palestinians had voted for change. Fed up with Fatah's corruption and inefficacy, they had overwhelmingly cast their ballots for other parties – most prominently Hamas, whose platform of 'Change and Reform' had promised effective governance, transparency and support for civil society. On all counts, Hamas failed the Palestinian people decisively. Two decades into the twenty-first century, oPt Palestinians were living under a regime divided between Gaza and the West Bank, with rising poverty, failing infrastructure and political impasse. Hanging over everything, of course, was the continuing Israeli occupation, the longest-running in modern history. As the Israeli government moved further and further rightwards, the occupation was becoming fiercer, with intensifying violence everywhere alongside settler expansionism and attacks on Palestinians in the West Bank.

Having originally gained support for its opposition to Fatah's repressive rule, Hamas was now guilty of many of the same things. It had failed to honour its electoral pledges of transparent democratic governance; instead, like the Fatah-led PA, it clamped down on political opponents and civil society activists, sometimes detaining and even torturing them. Asmaa al-Ghoul found herself a target and was repeatedly harassed, as well as being arrested and beaten for her role in organising the 'Palestinian Spring' protests in 2011.[149] Other journalists critical of Hamas had similar experiences: in 2016, for example, the regime held and tortured Mohamed Ahmed Othman in an attempt to force him to reveal his sources.[150] Palestinian and international human rights organisations, including Amnesty International and Human Rights Watch, condemned the two regimes – the Fatah-led PA in the West Bank and Hamas in Gaza – for restricting freedom of expression and punishing dissent.[151]

Both Fatah and Hamas had started out as insurrectionist groups, but both had now become elements of the status quo that – in different ways – served Israeli interests. We saw in Chapter Five how the Fatah leadership collaborated with Israel to suppress Palestinian opposition to the occupation, including non-violent resistance. In post-2007 Gaza, the Hamas regime periodically policed other militias in exchange for Israel temporarily easing the blockade.[152] In 2019, it stood aside when Israel fought PIJ in the Strip.[153]

What's more, both Hamas and Fatah facilitated the Israeli occupation by repeatedly failing to deliver on the Palestinian people's continuous demand since 2007: political unity. In 2017, there was potential progress on this front when Hamas released a new political programme, the Document of General Principles and Policies, which reduced some of the policy distance between itself and Fatah. Taking a far more pragmatic and nuanced approach than its notorious antisemitic Charter of 1988, the Document distinguished Zionism from Judaism and codified Hamas' willingness to accept a Palestinian state on the 1967 lines, without officially recognising the state of Israel.

The 2017 programme signalled the ongoing internal tensions between Hamas' hardline, moderate and pragmatic factions.[154] The moderates and pragmatists, including Ismail Haniyeh, had long favoured political participation and pushed forward the new programme to try to break the Palestinian impasse, now in its tenth year. The hardliners were sceptical that moderation would make any positive difference, arguing that it had only weakened the PLO and that Israel and the US had ignored all of Hamas' previous overtures. To prevent internal fissures, Hamas issued the new programme without repudiating its original Charter – which it actually attached to the 2017 Document as an appendix.[155]

In the event, the 2017 Document may have been the pragmatists' last gasp. When both the US and Israel rejected it – Netanyahu doing so even before its full publication – Hamas' hardliners claimed vindication.[156] Shortly afterwards, Hamas concluded its drawn-out internal election process. Haniyeh became the new chair of the Political Bureau, relocating to Qatar, while the Gaza regime came under the new leadership of Yahya Sinwar. As a hardliner who had helped found the Qassam Brigades, Sinwar's ascendance signalled the militant wing's growing power within Hamas. Having been freed from twenty-two years' Israeli imprisonment as part of the 2011 Shalit deal, Sinwar believed that only violent tactics would engender results;

he contrasted the release of 1,027 Palestinians in exchange for Gilad Shalit with the failed impact of diplomatic initiatives like the 2017 programme.[157]

Under Sinwar's leadership, the Hamas regime in Gaza continued in both its militant attacks on Israeli civilians and its clampdown on Palestinian dissent. In 2019, it violently repressed the We Want to Live (*bidna na'ish*) movement, whose protestors were campaigning for economic reform and workers' rights. Footage showed Hamas forces beating peaceful demonstrators and firing bullets into the air.[158]

Appearing to echo Israeli rhetoric, Hamas claimed that its forceful repression was necessary because the protestors were violent subversives. And in another striking parallel, some observers noticed a correlation between protests within Palestine and Hamas rocket fire into Israel: in the words of Hasan al-Kurd, Hamas sought to 'redirect the crisis toward the occupation' by firing rockets that would distract from its own failings and refocus attention on Israel.[159] Netanyahu had long done the same thing in reverse, launching attacks on Gaza whenever he faced dissent at home.[160]

These dynamics became especially noticeable from 2019, when Netanyahu was indicted on corruption charges and confronted rising domestic protests as a result. At this time, criticism of the Israeli government increasingly came to focus on Netanyahu, with both domestic and international opponents censuring his abuse of power, duplicity and deliberate sabotage of peace talks. Yet the condemnation of Netanyahu, while entirely deserved, masked a bigger reality: as we have seen throughout this book, Israel's displacement of the Palestinians and occupation of their land long preceded Netanyahu's premiership. The problem did not begin when he became prime minister for the second time in 2009, or the first time in 1996, and it would not end if he left office.

In fact, even Netanyahu's domestic political opponents were often broadly aligned with his policy on Palestine. From 2019 to 2021, Netanyahu's main political rival was Benny Gantz, a former army chief of staff who boasted in a campaign video that he had 'sent parts of Gaza back to the Stone Age' in 2014.[161] After joining a coalition government in 2020, he continued to endorse the collective punishment of the Palestinians; calling for the return of two soldiers' bodies from Gaza as defence minister in February 2021, he said, 'We will not stop working to bring [them] home … Without this happening, Gaza will not be able to develop. We will not act like them, like Hamas, as human animals – we will not withhold medicine and food. But we will not allow real, long-term development in the Strip until our sons return to their borders.'[162]

With rising internal tensions in Israel, intensifying occupation in the West Bank, and continuing crisis in Gaza, the entire region was at boiling point once again – and it soon boiled over. Three months after Gantz made these comments, huge waves of violence erupted across the whole of Israel and Palestine, in what some Palestinians would call the third intifada.

As with the second intifada, it was born in Jerusalem. Israeli efforts to expel a group of families from their homes in the East Jerusalem neighbourhood of Sheikh Jarrah sparked Palestinian protests, which intensified in May when Israeli forces seized control of the Haram al-Sharif compound, the third holiest site in Islam and a place out of bounds to almost every Palestinian in Gaza (those in the West Bank also needed a permit to go to Jerusalem). In response, Hamas fired rockets into Israel and Israel retaliated with a new eleven-day assault on Gaza.

Unlike the wars of 2009, 2012 and 2014, the violence of 2021 engulfed not just Gaza and southern Israel but the whole of Palestine and Israel, where widespread inter-communal violence took hold.[163] And yet, once again, it was Palestinians in

Gaza who bore the brunt: by the end of 2021, a total of eleven Israelis, three foreign nationals and 319 Palestinians had been killed, including 261 in Gaza during the eleven-day May war.[164] This time, however, the Palestinians in Gaza were part of a much bigger movement that transcended the Green Line and placed them alongside their compatriots inside Israel and the West Bank. The agitation even included a general strike among Palestinians on all sides of the Green Line that harked back to the 1936 revolt in Mandate Palestine. For this reason, many Palestinians described the unrest as the 'unity intifada' and spoke of a movement for Palestinian liberation on multiple fronts.[165]

The resulting morale boost was especially important because earlier that year, Mahmoud Abbas had postponed long-awaited PA elections. After years of false starts, all factions had finally agreed on them, with Abbas pledging not to run for re-election and Hamas promising not to field a presidential candidate. Yet in April, Abbas reneged on his commitment and announced that the elections would be postponed indefinitely, meaning that he was effectively now president for life. He may have inadvertently done his rivals a favour in the process – opinion polls showed that Hamas' popularity was at an all-time low.[166]

The Israeli media later reported that Abbas had come under external pressure to cancel the elections. Nadav Argaman, the chief of Israel's internal intelligence agency, Shin Bet, had paid two separate visits to Abbas demanding that he abandon the agreed plan (and around the same time, Israel had worked to sabotage the elections by arresting candidates in the West Bank).[167] Yet the PA president's own record showed he was hardly averse to such actions: Abbas had previously tried to postpone the 2006 elections, fearing Hamas would win. On that occasion, the Bush administration had intervened to force him to proceed; in 2021, the Biden administration did the opposite.[168]

The eruption of a 'third intifada' in 2021 — thirty-four years after the first — was a true indictment of almost every political actor involved. It signalled the failures of Hamas to deliver on its promises of 2006; of the Abbas-led PA to honour its people's will; of the Arab states, notably Egypt, to act on their stated solidarity with Palestine; of Israel to respect international law and human rights; and of the international community to enforce the latter. It also signalled once again the unsustainability of the status quo, and the alarming dehumanisation that increasingly characterised Israeli–Palestinian relations — as well as the impossibility of treating the Gaza crisis as a separate issue from the rest of Palestine.

In 2012, the UN had warned that Gaza would soon become 'unliveable' without drastic change.[169] Its warning went unheeded, and a decade later the Strip was still under an Israeli blockade that isolated Gaza's people, strangled its economy and destroyed its infrastructure. In the same period, Palestinians and Israelis had lived through intensifying violence, with those in Gaza at its sharpest end as they suffered through repeated Israeli bombardments amid the blockade. Nor was there much encouragement to be drawn from Palestinian politics, with the oPt still split between two different regimes while Israel benefited from the division. A survey in early 2023 found that 63 per cent of oPt Palestinians felt unrepresented by either regime, with only 19 per cent endorsing Fatah and just 11 per cent supporting Hamas.[170]

At the end of 2022, Israel's elections had resulted in its most hardline and openly racist government ever, speaking openly about land seizure and the expulsion of Palestinians. Returning as prime minister after a brief period out of office, Netanyahu now headed a cabinet that included several extremist settlers from the far right. Among them was Finance Minister Belazel

Smotrich, who called for the Palestinian village of Huwara to be 'wiped out' when it suffered a pogrom in February 2023; National Security Minister Itamar Ben-Gvir, who regularly encouraged settler violence and openly celebrated the 1994 Hebron massacre; and Minister of National Missions Orit Strook, who demanded that Palestinian homes be demolished to make way for Jewish settlements. Collectively, they called for further expulsions of Palestinians, with Smotrich even lamenting that David Ben-Gurion hadn't 'finished the job' in 1948.[171]

As 2023 dawned, Palestinians looked set to commemorate the seventy-fifth anniversary of the Nakba amid deepening political impasse and humanitarian crisis. Hope was in short supply as the whole of Palestine-Israel looked to be on the brink – with both the Israeli and the Hamas regime driving to escalate the violence even further.

EPILOGUE

On 7 October 2023, Hamas' Nukhba forces – the Qassam's elite fighting unit – broke through the fence surrounding the Gaza Strip and launched what would become the worst attack on Israel in its history. Over the course of the day, Palestinians killed 1,195 Israelis, 815 of whom were civilians, and injured thousands more.[1] Amira Hass, a daughter of Holocaust survivors and veteran Israeli journalist who had lived in Gaza in the 1990s, remarked afterwards:

> atrocities were committed [on 7 October]. And I know that it's not the time to tell Palestinians to pay attention to this, because Israel's revenge is a hundred times more bloodier, but still there were atrocities . . . I verified about many details and the atrocities were there . . . [and that] tells me how the pressure has built up, how monstrous it was, to create these monstrous attacks in one day.[2]

Details emerged of the atrocities that Hass refers to here as the day's timeline became clear. International analysts, along with the International Criminal Court (ICC) and the Israeli military itself, would later describe the attack on 7 October in terms of a series of 'waves'.[3] The first 'wave' occurred when the Nukhba forces breached the Gaza barrier and began targeting Israeli military sites – as well as attacking some civilians – as stage one of a long-planned offensive against Israel. Once news spread in Gaza that the fence was open, further 'waves' of attacks broke out as other Palestinians began crossing spontaneously from Gaza into Israel – some from Hamas' other (non-Nakhba) units, some from PIJ and five other armed factions, some from criminal gangs, and some unaffiliated.[4]

These later waves were notably more disorderly and chaotic, carrying out the widespread indiscriminate killing of men, women and children across southern Israel.[5] At the open-air Supernova Sukkot Gathering (also known as the Nova Music Festival) alone, Palestinian attackers massacred 364 people and wounded many others; some survivors recounted sexual assault.[6] In targeting civilians, including the very young and very old, they undoubtedly committed war crimes.

As part of the assault, Palestinian militants also abducted 251 people from Israel, including Jewish citizens, foreign nationals and Bedouin, and forcibly took them to Gaza. The oldest was 85-year-old Shlomo Mantzur, the youngest nine-month-old Kfir Bibas. According to Israeli Defence Minister Yoav Gallant, Kfir's parents Yarden and Shiri had tried to fight the attackers with a pistol, but were seized – along with Kfir and his four-year-old brother Ariel – by a Gaza militia 'more radical than Hamas'.[7] Video footage filmed by a local journalist moments later showed a terrified Shiri Bibas clutching her two young sons as they were taken to Gaza, with the journalist asking the gunmen not to harm them.[8]

Militants also abducted the Bibas family's Nir Oz neighbours, Oded and Yocheved Lifshitz, the long-time anti-occupation activists we met in Chapters Three and Six. They pulled 85-year-old Yocheved from her bed, shot 83-year-old Oded in the hand,

and then separated the two. Yocheved later recounted how she was 'laid on a motorbike and sped through a thicket' while being beaten with sticks. On arrival in Gaza, she was made to walk for miles through dirt tunnels.[9]

The Lifshitzes and the Bibas family were not the only ones from their kibbutz who were seized on 7 October; in total, one in four Nir Oz residents was killed or kidnapped that day. The Israeli state largely abandoned the kibbutz as militants ravaged it; first Hamas, and then PIJ and other militias along with unaffiliated individuals from Gaza. Israeli forces took seven hours to arrive, by which time the attackers had left. Only six houses in the kibbutz remained untouched.[10]

Nir Oz had long been embedded in Israeli and Palestinian geopolitics. Located just over a mile and a half from the Gaza fence, it was built on land that had belonged to the Palestinian village of Ma'in Abu Sitta before the Nakba. In May 1948, the Haganah attacked the village, killing its residents and destroying its buildings as part of the ethnic cleansing of Palestine. Survivors in the Abu Sitta family, like thousands of others, were expelled to Gaza, where some of them became prominent politicians (in Chapter Three, we met Ibrahim Abu Sitta, the former mayor of Khan Younis).[11]

Although the land was originally part of the Egyptian-controlled Palestinian territory, it was taken by Israel under the 1950 addendum agreement. A group of secular Israeli leftists, among them Oded Lifshitz, later established the Nir Oz kibbutz there, and used it as a base for their peace activism. For decades, Lifshitz and his allies campaigned against Israeli settlements and expansionism, standing with Palestinians at risk of expulsion. In a newspaper op-ed published four years before the 7 October attacks, Lifshitz had condemned the Netanyahu government and warned, 'When our Gazan neighbours have nothing to lose, we lose big time.'[12]

For seventy-five years, then, the territory of Nir Oz had been entangled with issues of land seizure, expulsion, civilian residence and tensions between those Israelis who wanted a peace agreement with the Palestinians and those who favoured further Zionist expansionism. Now, on 7 October 2023, it was one of the worst-hit kibbutzim during the worst-ever attack on Israel. In total, attackers kidnapped seventy-seven Nir Oz residents, who made up almost one third of the 251 captives.[13]

Back in Gaza, they were held variously by Hamas, PIJ and other groups, with the militias sometimes passing captives between them. In a clear violation of international law, the Hamas leadership announced that all Israeli captives were being held hostage – along with two Israeli civilians who had crossed into Gaza in 2014 and 2015 respectively[14] – until Israel released Palestinian prisoners from its jails.

The hostage-taking operation had been masterminded by Yahya Sinwar, who in recent years had taken control of Hamas' political and military wings in Gaza.[15] Released himself from an Israeli prison as part of the Gilad Shalit swap in 2011, Sinwar had determined that hostage-taking was the best way to obtain leverage against Israel; he contrasted the 1,027 Palestinian prisoners freed in 2011 with the minimal gains of Abbas' negotiating strategy, which had been met with further Israeli settlement expansion and land grab.[16] Despite allegedly saying that 'things went out of control' on 7 October, and that the kidnapping of civilian women and children 'should not have happened', Sinwar chose not to engineer the latter's immediate release.[17] Instead, on 9 October Hamas offered to release all civilian hostages in exchange for the Israeli military not entering Gaza; in mid-October, it offered the same if Israel ceased its bombing of the Strip.[18] The Israeli government rejected both proposals, and Human Rights Watch criticised Hamas and other militias for the war crime of 'treating civilians as bargaining chips'.[19]

At the time of the 7 October attack, Israel was holding more than 6,100 Palestinians in detention and prisons, including 1,300 without charge or trial and 190 minors.[20] Those numbers would soon increase dramatically, as Israel set about seizing thousands more Palestinians in sweeping raids.

The atrocities of 7 October 2023 comprised the deadliest attack on Israel in the state's seventy-five years. They came exactly fifty years and one day after the beginning of the 1973 war, when Egypt and Syria launched a surprise attack on Israel that shook the country's sense of invincibility after its huge military victory six years earlier. Yet the death toll of 7 October dwarfed any single day of the 1973 war, or any other war that Israel had fought. It was, by a significant margin, the bloodiest day in Israeli history.

It was also the first time since 1948 that Israeli forces had lost control of territory, albeit briefly. Despite the heavy militarisation of the Gaza fence, the Israeli army was tied down protecting military installations and settlements in the West Bank, where extremist Jewish settlers had been emboldened by the far-right government elected in 2022. As a result, it was slow to react, and the state failed to protect its southern communities, most notably Nir Oz.[21] The unprecedented scale of the attack – and the military's failure to prevent it – sent shockwaves across Israeli society. For seventy-five years, Jewish Israelis had relied on a social contract whereby they carried out mandatory military service on the understanding that the army would protect them; on 7 October, that contract was broken.

The Israeli response inside Gaza, by contrast, was swift and brutal. Immediately launching air raids, Benjamin Netanyahu declared that Israel would rescue the hostages and obliterate Hamas. He ordered the military to destroy 5,000 targets in Gaza; when the Chief of Staff reported that they did not have 5,000 approved targets so had attacked 1,500, Netanyahu responded with fury. 'I don't care about targets,' he exclaimed, 'take down houses, bomb with everything we have!'[22]

In the first two days, Israeli airstrikes killed 560 Palestinians in Gaza and displaced more than 185,000.[23] There was far worse to come. On 9 October, Gallant ordered a complete siege of the Gaza Strip, shutting off all water, food, fuel and electricity. Defending the order, which international human rights groups condemned as a war crime, he stated, 'We are fighting human animals and we are acting accordingly' – an echo of the language used by his predecessor Benny Gantz in 2021, as we saw in Chapter Six.[24] In a speech to Israeli soldiers, Gallant similarly advised, 'We will end things inside Gaza, I have removed all restraints . . . Gaza will not return to what it was. Hamas won't be here. We will destroy everything.'[25] Shortly afterwards, Israeli forces invaded Gaza on the ground. Army spokesperson Daniel Hagari said they were 'focused on what causes maximum damage'.[26]

After an intervention from US President Biden, Israel resumed the water supply to Gaza. But many Israeli ministers were quick to echo Gallant's rhetoric. The head of Israel's Coordination of Government Activities in the Palestinian Territories said, 'There will only be destruction [in Gaza]. You wanted hell, you will get hell.' The heritage minister called for an atomic bomb to be dropped on Gaza to 'eliminate everybody there'. We saw in

Chapter Six that pro-Nakba statements had become increasingly mainstream in Israeli politics in the years before 7 October; afterwards, they were virtually the norm. The Knesset deputy speaker asserted, 'Nakba? Expel them all!' and the minister of agriculture said that Israeli forces were 'now actually rolling out the Gaza Nakba'.[27]

Doubling down on the 'no innocents' line that had often characterised Israeli discourse about Gaza since 2007, Israeli politicians commonly held all Palestinians culpable for 7 October.[28] Two days afterwards, President Isaac Herzog told a press conference, 'The entire nation is responsible. This rhetoric of "unaware, uninvolved civilians" is not true.' The following month, Giora Eiland – the retired major general we met in Chapter Six – declared in an op-ed that Gaza's entire population was a legitimate target, comparing it to Nazi Germany and writing that 'the "poor" women of Gaza are all the mothers, sisters or wives of Hamas murderers'.[29] And in subsequent months, the Israeli government shared a video on its social media accounts proclaiming 'there are no innocent civilians in Gaza'.[30] Palestinian and international observers, along with a very small number of Israeli human rights activists, identified such statements as genocidal.[31]

Nor were these statements mere rhetoric. Within just a few weeks, Israeli forces had destroyed huge swathes of the territory. By the end of 2023, it had displaced more than 90 per cent of the Strip's population.[32] Acting on Hagari's pledge of 'causing maximum damage', Israel demolished Gaza's infrastructure, bombed clinics and hospitals, blocked the population from accessing essential aid, and repeatedly forced people to evacuate to areas it subsequently bombed. By the time a tenuous cease-fire came into effect in January 2025, the UN confirmed that Israeli forces had killed more than 47,000 Palestinians – meaning one in fifty of the Strip's population.[33] At the time of writing in late March 2025, Israel has now broken the ceasefire and resumed airstrikes on Gaza, meaning the death toll is drastically rising again.

Most people on the ground in Gaza judged that the UN-confirmed death toll was likely to be an underestimate. With Israeli bombing so constant and indiscriminate, Gaza hospital morgues were sometimes left simply to weigh body parts to try to assess how many individuals have been killed.[34] In May 2024, the UN estimated that an additional 10,000 people were buried under the rubble.[35] Many more died from disease and malnutrition brought on by the combination of war and blockade, leading some medical researchers to estimate that the total death toll by late 2024 was at least 186,000 people – nearly 8 per cent of Gaza's population.[36] The majority were civilians, including at least 14,500 children.[37]

Establishing the true figures is made more difficult by the fact that Israel hasn't allowed independent foreign press to report from Gaza. Israel's denial of access to journalists is a core element of its closure of Gaza, creating opacity around the reality inside the Strip. The work of Gaza-based Palestinian reporters has become even more vital as a result, with individuals such as Motaz Azaiza, Plestia Alaqad, Bisan Owda and Hind Khoudary among those sharing footage, stories and testimonies later picked up by international media outlets. Yet this work comes with extraordinary risk: Israel has frequently killed Palestinian reporters in Gaza, which Reporters Without Borders named the world's most dangerous place for journalists in 2024 – more than half of journalists killed worldwide that year were in Gaza.[38] In early 2025, a research team at Brown University found that more journalists have been killed in Gaza since October 2023 than in the American Civil War, both world wars, the Korean War, the

Vietnam War, the Yugoslavian wars and the post-9/11 US war in Afghanistan combined.[39]

There is, of course, a huge emotional and psychological toll as well. After an Israeli drone strike killed Al Jazeera correspondent Ismail al-Ghoul in July 2024, a colleague shared a message al-Ghoul had sent not long before:

> I no longer know the taste of sleep. The bodies of children and the screams of the injured and their blood-soaked images never leave my sight. The cries of mothers and the wailing of men who are missing their loved ones never fade from my hearing. I can no longer bear the sound of children's voices from beneath the rubble, nor can I forget the energy and power that reverberates at every moment . . . I am tired, my friend. . .[40]

From early on, Palestinians understood the war on Gaza within the longer history of the ongoing Nakba. Many called it simply *harb al-ibada* ('the war of genocide'). In a joint statement in December 2023, five human rights organisations alleged that Israel was carrying out war crimes, crimes against humanity and genocide.[41] Israel denied such accusations, calling them antisemitic – although several Jewish observers, including some Holocaust survivors, concurred that it was genocide.[42]

As the months went on, these voices were joined by a rising number of international bodies. In January 2024, the International Court of Justice ruled it 'plausible' that Israel's attack on Gaza could amount to genocide.[43] Two months later, the UN Special Rapporteur on Human Rights in the Palestinian Territory argued that Israel's military operations met the threshold for declaring a genocide.[44] The UN Special Committee, Amnesty International, Human Rights Watch and the Center for

Constitutional Rights have all since said the same.[45] They point to the mass indiscriminate killings; the total destruction of Gaza, including the demolition of vital civilian infrastructure; the siege and deprivation of resources essential to survival; the repeated displacements to areas then bombed; and the genocidal state rhetoric outlined above. In May 2024, the ICC prosecutor applied for arrest warrants for Netanyahu, Gallant, Sinwar, Haniyeh and Qassam Brigades leader Mohammad Deif for war crimes and crimes against humanity; in November, the ICC issued them.[46]

By that time, international attention was focused in particular on northern Gaza, where Israel had imposed a siege in early October 2024 and expelled civilians under threat of death after launching a renewed invasion of Jabalia camp. Allegations of ethnic cleansing were confirmed when the Israeli military stated that the Palestinians evacuated from the area wouldn't be allowed to return.[47] Israeli actions bore strong parallels with the so-called 'Generals' Plan', a proposal presented to the Knesset earlier in the year by Eiland and a group of his peers advocating the ethnic cleansing of northern Gaza – dubbed 'surrender or starve' by critics.[48] Palestinians' intensive suffering also aligned with Eiland's rhetoric, after he had argued that Israel 'must not shy away' from causing humanitarian crisis, including 'severe epidemics'.[49] The Israeli government and its defenders claimed that all civilians had the chance to safely evacuate northern Gaza; those present on the ground, including international aid workers, countered that troops were shooting at anyone who tried to leave Jabalia.[50]

The Israeli government consistently claimed that it took measures to protect civilians, and that its military tactics were necessary in order to secure the hostages' release. Yet its actions suggested otherwise. In late October 2023, Israel and Hamas had agreed to a temporary ceasefire, with terms including the release of 150 Palestinian women and children from Israeli detention, and 50 Israeli women and children from captivity in Gaza – including Yocheved Lifshitz, whom Hamas freed after 16 days, along with fellow hostage Nurit Cooper, on account of the two women's ill health.[51] Lifshitz later recounted that Netanyahu had refused earlier offers for her release.[52] And repeated subsequent attempts at a further deal fell flat, largely because Netanyahu refused to agree to a permanent ceasefire. Reliant on his far-right coalition partners, facing a corruption trial, and with opinion polls showing that most Israelis wanted him to resign as soon as the war ended, he saw ongoing war as vital to his political survival.[53]

Nor did Netanyahu limit Israeli belligerence to Gaza. As we saw in Chapter Six, in the months and years prior to October 2023, West Bank Palestinians had endured mounting aggression from Israeli settlers, sometimes erupting into vicious pogroms, with protection or even outright support from soldiers. Even before 7 October, 2023 had been the deadliest year for Palestinians since the second intifada.[54] After 7 October, these dynamics intensified as Israel conducted sweeping raids across the West Bank; it carried out mass arrests, detained thousands of people, ramped up pre-existing policies around restriction of movement and house demolitions, and continued to enable settler violence. The twelve months from October 2023 saw more than 1,400 settler attacks on West Bank Palestinians, directly facilitated by the distribution of at least 120,000 guns from the Israeli government.[55] In that period, Israeli soldiers and settlers killed 732 West Bank Palestinians, while the latter killed 39 Israelis.[56] In this way, the world's attention on Gaza and reaction to the 7 October attacks provided cover for Israel to escalate its long-running aggressive expansionism in the West Bank.

The rising regional violence also spilled over the borders of Palestine and Israel. Longstanding conflict on the Israeli–Lebanese frontier heightened after 7 October as Hizbollah fired across the border onto communities in northern Israel and Israel intensified its drone strikes on Lebanon's southern communities. In September 2024, with mounting anti-government protests at home, Netanyahu declared war on Lebanon. Critics observed that the declaration of war came shortly after a one-day general strike that had shut down Israel. The protests duly diminished – although they didn't stop altogether – as Israeli attention turned to the war in the north.

Israel's massive aerial bombing campaign on Lebanon included a targeted airstrike that killed Hizbollah leader Hassan Nasrallah at the end of September, as well as a ground invasion at the beginning of October. In total the Israeli invasion killed more than 3,500 people and displaced 1.2 million, while Hizbollah attacks killed 72 Israelis and displaced 68,000.[57] A ceasefire agreement came into effect in late November 2024, although lower-level conflict continues at the time of writing. In February 2025, Israel announced that it would keep its military at five sites inside Lebanon, in breach of the ceasefire.[58]

Amid ongoing conflict with its regional arch-enemy Iran – Hizbollah's primary backer – Israel also exchanged fire with the Tehran regime and its Yemeni proxy Ansar Allah (also known as the Houthis). And after rebel forces in neighbouring Syria toppled Bashar al-Assad's brutal regime at the end of 2024, Israel launched airstrikes on some of the country's military facilities and sent ground troops into the buffer zone beyond the Golan Heights, in breach of international agreements.[59] Across Syria and Lebanon, Palestinian communities – refugees from 1948 and their descendants – had to endure more bloodshed, displacement and terror.

Israel has only been able to launch such intensive military activity on multiple fronts because of unflinching support from the US. In the fifteen months after October 2023, the Biden administration provided the Netanyahu government with unprecedented political, military, financial and diplomatic support – standing against the international judgments outlined above, including the findings of genocide. It was not until January 2025, under pressure from the incoming second Trump administration, that Israel and Hamas reached a staged agreement to end the war. Speculation was rife as to what Donald Trump promised Netanyahu in exchange for agreeing to his 'deal'; in subsequent weeks, the president said that the US would 'own' Gaza and expel the Palestinians from it.

The terms of the January 2025 ceasefire agreement included Israeli troops' withdrawal from populated areas of Gaza (including the northern Strip), the return of displaced Palestinians to their neighbourhoods, the admission of humanitarian aid to Gaza, and the release of the remaining Israeli citizens and foreign nationals held there in exchange for 1,900 Palestinians held by Israel. Among the latter were a thousand Palestinians whom Israel had arrested on 8 October 2023 despite their non-involvement in the previous day's attacks; many argued that they were also hostages, having been taken by Israel as bargaining chips for negotiations with Hamas.[60] They came out in poor physical condition, bearing signs of the abuse, beatings, assault and torture that had characterised the treatment of Palestinians in Israeli jails for decades.[61] In subsequent rounds of exchanges, some freed Palestinians were unable to walk and were immediately hospitalised in critical condition; one man had dropped from 95 to 45 kilograms.[62]

By mid-March 2025, the ceasefire agreement had led to the release of 1,731 Palestinians, twenty-five Israelis and five Thais from Gaza, as well as the bodies of eight dead Israeli captives.

The latter included Oded Lifshitz, Shiri Bibas and Bibas' two young sons Ariel and Kfir – all of whom, it emerged, had been killed in Gaza in late 2023 after being kidnapped from their homes.[63] On release, Hamas forced the captives to participate in grotesque celebratory ceremonies – and originally released the wrong body for Shiri Bibas. Its actions caused international condemnation, including from the Red Cross, which was mediating the release.[64]

Shortly afterwards, Gallant disclosed that the Israeli government had known of the Bibas children's deaths back in November 2023; they had maintained the pretence they were alive as a rallying cry for continuing the war.[65] Meanwhile, Yarden Bibas, who had been held separately from his wife and children, had been released alive shortly beforehand, having lost 15 kilograms during his captivity.[66] Along with some of the other released Israeli hostages, he recounted continuous abuse and starvation over more than a year in Gaza; some had been kept in chains and behind bars, or imprisoned alone underground, and came out emaciated, frail and gaunt.[67]

Although the ceasefire held for eight weeks in early 2025, the violence never ended completely. Between 22 January and 11 March, the death toll in Gaza rose by more than 700 – a combination of Palestinians who were killed by the Israeli military at this time and those who bodies were retrieved from areas previously closed off.[68] The same period saw one Israeli fatality: a Defence Ministry contractor killed by Israeli army gunfire in central Gaza.[69] Then, on 18 March, Israel definitively broke the ceasefire and resumed its large-scale bombing of Gaza. Many pointed out that the timing enabled the Israeli prime minister to avoid appearing in court at his corruption trial, while also keeping him in power by shoring up his coalition with the far right.[70]

Within just two days of breaking the ceasefire, Israel had killed more than 500 Palestinians in Gaza, including at least 200 children. In response, Hamas resumed its rocket launches into Israel, with no Israeli casualties at the time of writing in late March 2025.[71] As the Israeli army began issuing evacuation orders once again, more than 124,000 Palestinians were displaced in just a few days – some having only recently returned to their neighbourhoods.[72] Palestinians' desperate calls to revive the ceasefire went unheeded by the Israeli government, which was fully supported by the Trump administration.

Even the two-month ceasefire had come too late for thousands of people trapped in Gaza. It had also highlighted how Israel had failed in both its stated war aims: rescuing the hostages and destroying Hamas. The surviving hostages who were freed were returned not by military action but by negotiation; and while Israel assassinated Ismail Haniyeh in Tehran in July 2024, and Yahya Sinwar in Gaza three months later, it did not destroy Hamas. Indeed, the fact that Israel found itself agreeing terms with Hamas in early 2025 shows that the group remained the dominant authority in Gaza.

The accounts that have come out of Gaza since October 2023 are beyond comprehension. Satellite images of the Strip show near-total devastation. More than 70 per cent of homes have been damaged or destroyed; more than 80 per cent of roads no longer function. The UN has recorded close to 2 million displaced people – almost the entire population of Gaza, which stands at around 2.1 million.[73] The majority have been displaced more than once, forced out variously by Israeli evacuation orders, airstrikes and overcrowding. Israel has repeatedly hit areas that it previously designated as safe zones, meaning there is no refuge anywhere in Gaza. At the same time, Israel has tightened the blockade, forcing the vast majority of the Strip's population to remain inside the tiny territory. Denied the right to safety either within or beyond the Gaza Strip, the Palestinian people trapped there must constantly move from place to place to try to survive.[74]

With much of Gaza uninhabitable, nearly two million Palestinians have been forced into smaller and smaller areas – again, with striking echoes of the original Nakba in 1948. One year into the war, 1.8 million people were sheltering in 20 square miles in al-Mawasi, designated a 'humanitarian area' by Israel.[75] During the January–March 2025 ceasefire, international headlines reported that Palestinians in Gaza were returning to their homes – a statement belied by images showing people walking through endless miles of rubble. With no homes to return to, many have been left to survive in tents or makeshift shelters, or simply live outside in the open. And with the Strip's infrastructure destroyed and severe overcrowding in the shelters, disease is rife. Polio, dysentery, pneumonia and acute respiratory infections all run rampant.[76]

Widespread malnutrition makes matters even worse. More than 90 per cent of Gaza's children, and 95 per cent of pregnant and breastfeeding women, face severe food shortages.[77] In November 2024, global food security experts warned of 'imminent famine' in the Strip.[78] Some newborn babies are too weak even to cry out for milk.[79] A study in December 2024 found that 96 per cent of children in Gaza feel death is close.[80] It is impossible to capture the full extent of the horrors in words.

This suffering is not only the result of bombardment. Throughout the war, Israel has severely restricted the entry of humanitarian aid into Gaza.[81] Having created a situation prior to October 2023 in which the majority of Gaza's population relied on food aid, Israel then proceeded to block 83 per cent of aid from reaching people in the Strip.[82] In October 2024, the

Knesset voted to ban UNRWA, the backbone of aid in Gaza and the main service provider to most of the population there. On top of this, more aid workers have been killed in Gaza since October 2023 than in any other war, conflict or crisis in recorded history.[83] When the aid workers are Western, their deaths occasionally make headlines: in April 2024, there was widespread outrage when an Israeli airstrike killed seven international aid workers from the World Central Kitchen.[84] The same attention is not given to the many Palestinian aid workers killed.

With such a staggering death toll, it is important not to lose sight of the people behind the numbers. They include some of those we have met in this book: Saleem al-Naffar, the Gaza-based Palestinian poet, was killed by an Israeli airstrike on his home on 7 December 2023, along with his wife, son, daughters, sister, brother-in-law and nephews.[85] Al-Naffar's life encapsulated much of the Palestinian experience: born in Shati camp in 1963, he spent much of his youth in exile before returning to the Strip during the Oslo years. One of many writers killed in Gaza since October 2023, the sumud of his poetry has lived on.

Occasionally, an individual death makes world news. In January 2024, an Israeli tank shot at the car of the Rajab family as they fled Gaza City, immediately killing five people inside. Fifteen-year-old Layan Hamadeh, who survived, phoned for help for herself and her five-year-old cousin Hind – the one other survivor – only to be shot dead by further gunfire. Hind picked up the phone and spoke to the Palestinian Red Crescent Society (PRCS) team for three hours, as they tried to send paramedics. The line then went dead, and twelve days later the family were finally able to reach the site where they discovered the bodies of Hind, Layan and their other relatives along with two PRCS paramedics.[86] Although Israel initially denied responsibility, independent media investigations found that an Israeli tank had probably shelled the vehicles and that operators would have been able to see children were present.[87]

The tragedy of Hind's killing was far from an isolated incident. In July, Mohammad Bahar, a severely disabled 24-year-old who could not move without assistance, was mauled by an Israeli military dog in his home. Israeli troops forced Bahar's family to leave the house, assuring them that he would receive medical assistance. Instead, when they were able to return a week later, they found that the troops had abandoned his dead body and left it to rot.[88]

Three months later, in October 2024, Israel bombed a group of makeshift tents near al-Aqsa Hospital in central Gaza, killing at least four people. The death of one of them, nineteen-year-old Sha'ban al-Dalou, made international headlines as footage showed him burning alive while connected to an IV drip. Al-Dalou was a software engineering student who had been displaced five times with his family since the start of the war, and was trying to raise money to evacuate them to Egypt. His mother died with him, leaving behind four children.[89]

Palestinians who have survived the airstrikes, gunfire and other fatal Israeli attacks in Gaza have been subjected to other horrors. Since October 2023, Israeli forces have detained Palestinians in numbers so large that prisons have overflowed. Prisoners are routinely kept in inhumane conditions, constantly handcuffed by all four limbs, blindfolded and fed through straws. In a letter to the government, an Israeli doctor based at the Sde Teiman detention centre – where Israel has held hundreds of Palestinians from Gaza since October 2023 – wrote that prisoners' legs are amputated as a 'routine event' due to handcuff injuries.[90]

Meanwhile, Israeli forces on the ground in Gaza have carried out human rights abuses and war crimes across the Strip, including firing on children and other civilians who are carrying white flags, sexual abuse, torture and looting.[91] Much of the evidence of these crimes comes in the form of videos taken by Israeli soldiers themselves and posted on their social media accounts.[92] In other cases, Palestinians have provided testimonies directly to the world online, particularly when it comes to their experiences of sexual assault and harassment.[93]

Mounting evidence shows Israeli forces using Palestinian civilians as human shields in operations across Gaza – something that, as we have seen, dates back to Israel's first occupation of the Strip in 1956. According to the testimonies of both Palestinians and Israeli soldiers, the army's so-called 'mosquito protocol' means that the military never enters a house in Gaza without first forcing a Palestinian to search and 'clear' it. Israeli forces also use civilians, including teenagers, as 'bait' to lure militants, or make them perform life-threatening tasks at gunpoint; Israeli soldiers have reported being told that 'our lives are more important than theirs'.[94] The post-2023 war has not created such practices anew; rather, it has intensified them to new levels of horror.

Amid such unspeakable horrors, why read – or indeed write – a history of the Gaza Strip? To do so in such a context may seem futile, a case of intellectual navel-gazing while thousands of people perish in real time. But history matters, especially in Palestine. And with an abundance of misinformation circulating, understanding this history has never been more essential.

The death toll and destruction in Israel's post-2023 war on Gaza have reached unprecedented levels. But many of the war's themes can be found throughout the history of Palestine and Israel since 1948, particularly – but not exclusively – in Gaza. The Strip came into being as a result of the original Nakba: an act of ethnic cleansing that established the state of Israel and turned the Palestinians into a dispossessed, stateless people. It became home to a majority refugee population from all over Palestine, and has served as the hub of the Palestinian national movement from then to now. Since 1948, Israel has made repeated further attempts to expel and displace Palestinians from Gaza: during its first occupation of the Strip in 1956–7, throughout its second occupation from 1967, and most overtly since October 2023. Other long-running historical themes – collective punishment, asymmetrical violence and dehumanisation – are once again playing out in Gaza today.

History also reminds us that, even if it were possible, a return to the status quo ante from before 7 October cannot be the goal – and wouldn't bring security for either Palestinians or Israelis. Before October 2023, Palestinians in the Strip were living what Gaza-born writer and analyst Muhammad Shehada describes in this book's foreword as 'a permanent state of non-life'. Most had never been able to leave the Strip's 141 square miles and were forced to survive under a suffocating blockade with regular bombardments and the constant noise of drones buzzing overhead. Israel frequently blames Hamas for Gaza's suffering. But Hamas didn't come to power in Gaza until 2006–7 – and history shows us that the closure of Gaza started much earlier than this, as did the violence, expulsions, human rights abuses and collective punishment.

Finally, and perhaps most importantly, reaching back into history reveals the long-running threads of contemporary plans for ethnic cleansing, stretching back to the original Nakba itself. Just two weeks after 7 October, Israel's Ministry of Intelligence prepared a white paper recommending the expulsion of all Palestinians from Gaza into Sinai.[95] Shortly afterwards, two members of the Knesset penned an op-ed in the *Wall Street*

Journal calling for Gaza's population to be permanently resettled outside the Strip.[96] In subsequent months, ethnic cleansing – sometimes described euphemistically as 'transfer' or 'relocation' – became a dominant theme in the Israeli public discourse about Gaza, promoted by policymakers, journalists, commentators and lobbyists.[97]

We have seen throughout this book how such ideas never went away after 1948; they retain an alarming salience today. Soon after taking office for his second presidency, Trump proposed that the US seize Gaza and expel the Palestinians to Indonesia, Sudan or Somalia (all plans he is openly touting at the time of writing in March 2025, with the support of the Israeli government).[98] There are clear echoes of Israel's post-1967 programmes to 'transfer' the Strip's population to Brazil, Canada or Australia (discussed in Chapter Three).

Supporters of the expulsion plans have claimed they are necessary for Israelis' security, arguing that the Palestinians of Gaza are an extension of Hamas. Such claims were undermined in March 2025, when large-scale anti-Hamas protests broke out in Gaza, in a revival of the 2019 'we want to live' movement discussed in Chapter Six.[99] In response, Israel simply doubled down on its expulsion plans, with Defence Minister Israel Katz suggesting that the Palestinians' 'reward' for ousting Hamas would be to 'leav[e] for other places in the world.'[100] Netanyahu was even more explicit, stating in a meeting that if Hamas laid down its weapons, Israel would 'enable the implementation of the Trump plan, the voluntary immigration plan.'[101] In other words, the Hamas regime is not – and never has been – the real reason for the expulsion efforts.

Yet as the future of Gaza remains uncertain, political players would do well to remember that previous plans ultimately failed due to the resistance of the Palestinian people themselves. The belief that Palestinians might agree to mass expulsion after decades of resisting it shows staggering historical illiteracy. The reality is best summed up by an original Nakba survivor, Abu Samir, in words spoken to a Palestinian journalist from his shelter in Khan Younis in February 2025: 'I was a child when we were forced from our village [during the Nakba]. We thought it was temporary. Now I am an old man and we are still refugees. They talk of taking Gaza like we are nothing. But we are still here. We are still Palestinians.'[102]

Further Reading: Voices from Gaza

A Short History of the Gaza Strip traces Gaza's history from 1948 to present through six key junctures. It does not and cannot speak for Palestinians in and from Gaza, whose own accounts are indispensable for understanding historical and contemporary realities in Palestine. Many Gaza-born Palestinians, including some of this book's protagonists, have published memoirs and testimonies in English, a selection of which is listed here:

Atef Abu Saif, *Don't Look Left: A Diary of Genocide* (Pluto, 2024)

Izzeldin Abuelaish, *I Shall Not Hate* (Bloomsbury, 2012)

Sahbaa Al-Barbari, *Light the Road of Freedom* (Alberta, 2021)

Madeeha Hafez Albatta, *A White Lie* (Alberta, 2020)

Asmaa al-Ghoul, *A Rebel in Gaza* (Doppelhouse Press, 2018)

Ahmed Alnaouq and Pam Bailey, *We Are Not Numbers* (Penguin, 2025)

Hekmat Al-Taweel, *Come My Children* (Alberta, 2023)

Abdel Bari Atwan, *A Country of Words: A Palestinian Journey from the Refugee Camp to the Front Page* (Saqi, 2007)

Ramzy Baroud, *My Father Was a Freedom Fighter: Gaza's Untold Story* (Pluto, 2010)

Yousef Bashir, *The Words of My Father: Love and Pain in Palestine* (Haus, 2024)

Muin Bseiso, *Descent into the Water* (Medina, 1980)

Haidar Eid, *Banging on the Walls of the Tank: Dispatches from Gaza* (BTL Books, 2025)

Mahmoud Muna, Matthew Teller, Juliette Touma and Jayyab Abusafia (eds), *Daybreak in Gaza: Stories of Palestinian Lives and Culture* (Saqi, 2024)

Rana Shubeir, *In Gaza I Dare to Dream* (SkyLimit, 2016)

In addition, the following are just some of the many journalists and writers in and from Gaza who provide vital reporting. Their words can be found online via Substack, Instagram, Bluesky and Twitter/X:

Abubaker Abed

Plestia Alaqad

Wael Al-Dahdouh

Nidal al-Mughrabi

Motaz Azaiza

Ahmed Hijazi

Hind Khoudary

Mohammad Mhawish

Mahmoud Mushtaha

Bisan Owda

Muhammad Shehada

In this book's foreword, Muhammad Shehada writes about his friend Ali, who was killed by Israel in January 2024. You can read some of Ali Adam's articles online at *Middle East Eye*, *Al Jazeera* and *Al Monitor*.

Supporting Gaza

The Palestinian people are currently enduring the worst crisis in their history due to Israel's continuing genocidal destruction and blockade of the Gaza Strip and the failures of the international community to protect human rights. In early 2025, the UN estimated that it could take more than fifteen years to rebuild Gaza; in the meantime, more than two million people continue to suffer through a public health crisis, food scarcity, homelessness, insecurity and trauma. In response to this man-made catastrophe, several organisations are doing important humanitarian work on the ground in Gaza. Two of them are highlighted here, both of which focus on providing essential services to Palestinians in partnership with local communities.

Gaza Infant Nutrition Alliance (GINA) was created in 2024 to raise awareness regarding the importance of breastfeeding as a lifesaving practice for infants, particularly in emergencies. GINA has trained a team of healthcare professionals in Gaza in lactation support, allowing mothers to receive skilled care when they need it most. GINA facilitates remote expert lactation consultations for challenging cases through an international team of volunteer lactation consultants and healthcare professionals. Aid to meet the urgent needs of mothers is provided via GINA's local NGO partners. Donate at www.gina.org.uk

Medical Aid for Palestinians (MAP) was first set up in the aftermath of the Sabra-Shatila massacre, by a group of medics who had worked in the Palestinian refugee camps in Lebanon. Today, it has permanent offices in Gaza City, Ramallah, East Jerusalem and Beirut, working with local partners to provide essential healthcare to Palestinians living under occupation and as refugees. MAP also advocates internationally for Palestinian rights and justice, and campaigns for Palestinian voices to be heard at the highest level. Donate at www.map.org.uk

The organisations and individuals named here are listed for information and have no affiliation with the author.

NOTES

INTRODUCTION: WHY GAZA MATTERS

1   Sahbaa al-Barbari, *Light the Road of Freedom* (University of Alberta Press, 2021), 90.

2   Figures sourced from the UN Office for the Coordination of Humanitarian Affairs (OCHA), https://www.ochaopt.org, accessed 22 November 2024.

3   Rasha Khatib, Martin McKee and Salim Yusuf, 'Counting the dead in Gaza: difficult but essential', *The Lancet* 404:10449 (2024), 237–8.

4   Figures sourced from OCHA. See 'Humanitarian situation update #263: Gaza Strip', https://www.unocha.org/publications/report/occupied-palestinian-territory/humanitarian-situation-update-263-gaza-strip-enarhe, accessed 13 March 2025.

5   See for example 'What is happening in Gaza? Aid urgently needed as thousands return to their homes', British Red Cross, 13 February 2025, https://www.redcross.org.uk/stories/disasters-and-emergencies/world/whats-happening-in-gaza-humanitarian-crisis-grows, accessed 13 March 2025; '"Strong likelihood" of imminent famine in northern Gaza, food experts warn, as Israel continues siege', *The Guardian*, 9 November 2024, https://www.theguardian.com/world/2024/nov/09/strong-likelihood-of-imminent-famine-in-northern-gaza-food-experts-warn-as-israel-continues-siege, accessed 13 March 2025; 'Over 1.8 million in Gaza face extreme hunger', UN News, 17 October 2024, https://news.un.org/en/story/2024/10/1155836, accessed 13 March 2025.

6   Michel Guillot, Mohammed Draidi, Valeria Cetorelli, José H. C. Monteiro Da Silva and Ismail Lubbad, 'Life expectancy losses in the Gaza Strip during the period October, 2023 to September, 2024', *The Lancet* 405:10477 (2025), 478–85.

7   See for example Report of the Special Committee to Investigate Israeli Practices Affecting the Human Rights of the Palestinian People and Other Arabs of the Occupied Territories, A/79/363, 20 September 2024; International Court of Justice, Order of 26 January 2024, Document 192-20240126-ORD-01-00-EN, https://www.icj-cij.org/node/203447, accessed 13 March 2025; Report of the Special Rapporteur on the Situation of Human Rights in the Palestinian Territory Occupied since 1967 to Human Rights Council, A/HRC/55/73, 24 March 2024; Al-Haq, Palestinian Centre for Human Rights and Al Mezan Center for Human Rights, 'As Israel's genocide in Gaza passes the one-year mark, international inaction fuels renewed wave of genocidal violence against Palestinians', 12 October 2024; 'Extermination and acts of genocide: Israel deliberately depriving Palestinians in Gaza of water', Human Rights Watch, 19 December 2024, http://hrw.org/report/2024/12/19/extermination-and-acts-genocide/israel-deliberately-depriving-palestinians-gaza, accessed 13 March 2025; '"You feel like you are subhuman": Israel's genocide against Palestinians in Gaza', Amnesty International, December 2024, https://www.amnesty.org/en/documents/mde15/8668/2024/en/, accessed 13 March 2025; Nimer Sultany, 'A threshold crossed: On genocidal intent and the duty to prevent genocide in Palestine', Journal of Genocide Research (2024), doi:10.1080/14623528.2024.2351261, accessed 19 May 2025; Noura Erakat, 'Genocide and accountability in Gaza: the limits and potential of international law' (podcast), University of Oxford Podcasts, 14 February 2024, https://podcasts.ox.ac.uk/genocide-and-accountability-gaza-limits-and-potential-international-law, accessed 13 March 2025; Raz Segal, 'A textbook case of genocide', Jewish Currents, 13 October 2023, https://jewishcurrents.org/a-textbook-case-of-genocide, accessed 13 March 2025.
8   Databases compiling genocidal statements from Israeli figures can be found at https://witnessing-the-gaza-war.com/1117-2/ and https://law4palestine.org/law-for-palestine-releases-database-with-500-instances-of-israeli-incitement-to-genocide-continuously-updated/, both accessed 25 February 2025.
9   International Court of Justice, Order of 26 January 2024.
10 Atef Alshaer, 'From Gaza to the world', in Mahmoud Muna and Matthew Teller (eds), Daybreak in Gaza: Stories of Palestinian Lives and Culture (Saqi, 2024), 286.
11 Genesis 10:19.
12 Jean-Pierre Filiu, Gaza: A History (Hurst, 2015), 3–33.

13 Displacement figures are sourced from UNHCR and the
    Norwegian Refugee Council. For death tolls, see 'Hezbollah says
    Israel "cannot impose conditions" for truce', France24, 20
    November 2024, https://www.france24.com/en/live-
    news/20241120-us-envoy-presses-israel-hezbollah-truce-bid-in-
    lebanon-visit; 'Israeli attack kills 3 more Lebanese soldiers as death
    toll passes 40', Al Jazeera, 20 November 2024, https://www.
    aljazeera.com/news/2024/11/20/israeli-attack-kills-three-more-
    lebanese-soldiers-as-death-toll-passes-forty; Ido Efrati, 'Man killed
    by rocket fire from Lebanon, Israeli rescue services says', *Haaretz*,
    21 November 2024; Emanuel Fabian, 'Authorities name 802
    soldiers, 68 police officers killed in Gaza war', *Times of Israel*, 8
    October 2023, all accessed 13 March 2025; Bassem Mroue and
    Melanie Lidman, 'The death toll in Lebanon crosses 3,000 in the
    13-month Israel–Hezbollah war, Health ministry says', AP, 4
    November 2024, https://apnews.com/article/ israel-lebanon-
    hezbollah-death-toll-798b846237a24ed37490ea29bd4e3aba,
    accessed 31 March 2025.

Chapter One:
Catastrophe Creates the Strip

1 Rashid Khalidi, *The Hundred Years War on Palestine: A History of
   Settler Colonial Conquest and Resistance* (Profile, 2020), 22; John D.
   Grainger, *The Battle for Palestine, 1917* (Boydell Press, 2006), chs 2–6.
2 Jean-Pierre Filiu, *Gaza: A History* (Hurst, 2015), 37–9.
3 The nearly 4,000 graves in these cemeteries included Jewish soldiers
   whose headstones were inscribed with Hebrew writing and the Star of
   David. All were tended by the Jaradah family until 2023, when the
   Israeli bombardment and invasion of Gaza forced them to flee south.
   See Yolande Knell, 'The Gaza family tending World War One graves for
   100 years', BBC News, 25 January 2023, https://www.bbc.co.uk/news/
   world-middle-east-64344483, accessed 19 February 2025; Tim Friend
   and David Wilkes, 'Gaza cemetery containing more than 3,000 graves
   of British and Commonwealth servicemen killed during First World
   War is damaged in the latest Israel–Hamas fighting', *Mail Online*, 7
   November 2023, https://www.dailymail.co.uk/news/article-12720727/
   Gaza-cemetery-containing-3-000-graves-British-Commonwealth-
   servicemen-killed-World-War-damaged-latest-Israel-Hamas-fighting.
   html, accessed 19 February 2025. On the fate of the cemeteries during
   Israel's bombardment of Gaza, see Abubaker Abed, 'Gaza's British

cemeteries are the only ones Israel isn't destroying', *Middle East Eye*, 26 June 2024, https://www.middleeasteye.net/news/israel-british-cemeteries-gaza-destroying, accessed 19 February 2025.

4   The Palestine Mandate, 24 July 1922, https://avalon.law.yale.edu/20th_century/palmanda.asp, accessed 19 May 2025.

5   Article 22 of the Covenant of the League of Nations, 28 June 1919.

6   On the colonial dynamics of the Mandate system, see Susan Pedersen, *The Guardians: The League of Nations and the Crisis of Empire* (Oxford University Press, 2015), 29, 95–103.

7   Theodor Herzl, *Der Judenstaat. English* (Tredition, 2012 [1896]).

8   On Jewish history in Gaza, see Hadeel al-Gherbawi, 'The lost history of Gaza's Jewish quarter', *Al-Monitor*, 23 December 2021, https://www.al-monitor.com/originals/2021/12/lost-history-gazas-jewish-quarter, accessed 19 February 2025; Hekmat al-Taweel, *Come My Children* (University of Alberta Press, 2023), 55.

9   On Jewish history in Ottoman and Mandate Palestine see Menachem Klein, *Lives in Common: Arabs and Jews in Jerusalem, Jaffa and Hebron* (Hurst, 2014); Abigail Jacobson and Moshe Naor, *Oriental Neighbors: Middle Eastern Jews and Arabs in Mandatory Palestine* (Brandeis University Press, 2016); Louis A. Fishman, *Jews and Palestinians in the Late Ottoman Era, 1908–14: Claiming the Homeland* (Edinburgh University Press, 2019).

10   Avi Shlaim, *The Iron Wall: Israel and the Arab World*, new ed. (Penguin, 2014), 1–6; Ella Shohat, *On the Arab-Jew, Palestine, and Other Displacements: Selected Writings* (Pluto, 2017), 46–8; Haim Bresheeth-Žabner, *An Army Like No Other: How the Israel Defense Forces Made a Nation* (Verso, 2020), 1.

11   Balfour Declaration, 2 November 1917, https://avalon.law.yale.edu/20th_century/balfour.asp, accessed 19 February 2025.

12   *Ibid.*

13   Hussein's son Abdullah would go on to become the first king of Jordan and a major figure in Palestinian history. He was assassinated in 1951 by a Palestinian nationalist.

14   'The McMahon Correspondence of 1915–16', *Bulletin of International News* 16:5 (1939), 6–13.

15   Palestine Mandate, Article 2.

16   Noura Erakat, *Justice for Some: Law and the Question of Palestine* (Stanford University Press, 2019), 38–41.

17   Tom Segev, *One Palestine, Complete: Jews and Arabs under the British Mandate* (Abacus, 2001), 429–32, 512. See also Khalidi, *The Hundred Years War on Palestine*, 130 n58.

18   Erakat, *Justice for Some*, 39; Pedersen, *The Guardians*, 101, 370. For a

detailed comparison of the varying levels of autonomy given to Jewish and Arab education systems in Mandate Palestine, see Suzanne Schneider, *Mandatory Separation: Religion, Education, and Mass Politics in Palestine* (Stanford University Press, 2018).

19   All figures sourced from Justin McCarthy, *The Population of Palestine: Population History and Statistics of the Late Ottoman Period and the Mandate* (Columbia University Press, 1990), 65, 171.

20   *Ibid.*, 68–73.

21   Filiu, *Gaza*, 39; Ilana Feldman, *Governing Gaza: Bureaucracy, Authority, and the Work of Rule, 1917–1967* (Duke University Press, 2008), 21–2; Jacob Norris, *Land of Progress: Palestine in the Age of Colonial Development, 1905–1948* (Oxford University Press, 2013), ch. 3; Madeeha Hafez Albatta, *A White Lie* (University of Alberta Press, 2020), 44.

22   Filiu, *Gaza*, 42; Jacobson, *Oriental Neighbours*, 127.

23   McCarthy, *The Population of Palestine*, 73.

24   Alex Winder, 'The "Western Wall" riots of 1929: religious boundaries and communal violence', *Journal of Palestine Studies* 42:1 (2012), 6–23.

25   Filiu, *Gaza*, 42–3.

26   On the life and death of Izzeldin al-Qassam, see Sami Moubayed, 'Who is Izz al-Din al-Qassam, whose name inspired the military wing of Hamas?', *Al Majalla*, 10 November 2023, https://en. majalla.com/node/303991/documents-memoirs/who-izz-al-din-al-qassam-whose-name-inspired-military-wing-hamas, accessed 19 February 2025.

27   Sahbaa al-Barbari, *Light the Road of Freedom* (University of Alberta Press, 2021), 10; Albatta, *A White Lie*, 26; al-Taweel, *Come My Children*, 36.

28   Rashid Khalidi, 'The Palestinians and 1948: the underlying causes of failure', in Eugene L. Rogan and Avi Shlaim (eds), *The War for Palestine*, 2nd ed. (Cambridge University Press, 2007), 12–36.

29   Bruce Hoffman, 'The bombing of the King David Hotel, July 1946', *Small Wars and Insurgencies* 31:3 (2020), 594–611. Begin subsequently published his memoirs of the insurgency; see Menachem Begin, *The Revolt* (W. H. Allen, 1951), trans. Samuel Katz.

30   Filiu, *Gaza*, 49–51.

31   UNGA Resolution 181(III), 29 November 1947.

32   On the death tolls from 1947 to 1949, see Rashid Khalidi, *Palestinian Identity: The Construction of Modern National Consciousness* (Columbia University Press, 1997), 245 n63; Shlaim, *The Iron Wall*, 35; Ilan Pappe, *A History of Modern Palestine*, 3rd ed. (Cambridge

University Press, 2022), 132; Benny Morris, *1948: A History of the First Arab–Israeli War* (Yale University Press, 2008), 406–7.

33 The exact number of Palestinian refugees from 1948 is disputed, but the approximate figure of 750,000 is the most widely verified. See UN Economic Survey Mission for the Middle East, First Interim Report, No. 66979, 16 November 1949, https://www.un.org/unispal/document/auto-insert-194924/, accessed 19 February 2025.

34 Filiu, *Gaza*, 69–71; Ramzy Baroud, *My Father Was a Freedom Fighter: Gaza's Untold Story* (Pluto Press, 2010), 41; Ilana Feldman, 'Home as a refrain: remembering and living displacement in Gaza', *History and Memory* 18:2 (2006), 13.

35 On the ideological basis for this, see Nur Masalha, *Expulsion of the Palestinians: The Concept of 'Transfer' in Zionist Political Thought, 1882–1948* (Institute for Palestine Studies, 1992).

36 Benny Morris, *The Birth of the Palestinian Refugee Problem Revisited* (Cambridge University Press, 2003), 60.

37 Numerous Palestinian, Israeli and other historians have described the expulsions of 1947–49 as ethnic cleansing. See for example Walid Khalidi, 'The fall of Haifa revisited', *Journal of Palestine Studies* 37:3 (2008), 30–58; Nur Masalha, *The Politics of Denial: Israel and the Palestinian Refugee Problem* (Pluto Press, 2003); Walid Khalidi, 'Why did the Palestinians leave, revisited', *Journal of Palestine Studies* 34:2 (2005), 42–54; Mustafa Abbasi, 'The fall of Acre in the 1948 Palestine War', *Journal of Palestine Studies* 39:4 (2010), 6–27; Ilan Pappe, *The Ethnic Cleansing of Palestine* (Oneworld, 2006), 40, 65–6, 80–4, 99–101; Morris, *The Birth of the Palestinian Refugee Problem Revisited*, 444–8; Daniel Blatman, 'Netanyahu, this is what ethnic cleansing really looks like', *Haaretz*, 3 October 2016, https://www.haaretz.com/opinion/2016-10-03/ty-article/.premium/netanyahu-this-is-what-ethnic-cleansing-really-looks-like/0000017f-dc4b-df9c-a17f-fe5b31e60000, accessed 19 February 2025.

38 Walid Khalidi, 'Plan Dalet: master plan for the conquest of Palestine', *Journal of Palestine Studies* 18:1 (1988), 4–33.

39 Pappe, *The Ethnic Cleansing of Palestine*, 112–14; Simha Flapan, *The Birth of Israel: Myths and Realities* (Croom Helm, 1987), 94–6. See also 'Deir Yasin', *Interactive Encyclopaedia of the Palestine Question*, https://www.palquest.org/en/place/16983/deir-yasin, accessed 19 February 2025.

40 Quoted in Daniel A. McGowan and Matthew C. Hogan, *The Saga of Deir Yassin: Massacre, Revisionism, and Reality* (Deir Yassin Remembered, 1999), 29.

41 Rosemary Sayigh, *The Palestinians: From Peasants to Revolutionaries*, new ed. (Zed, 2007), 86; Frances S. Hasso, 'Modernity and gender

in Arab accounts of the 1948 and 1967 defeats', *International Journal of Middle East Studies* 32:4 (2000), 492–3; Isabelle Humphries and Laleh Khalili, 'Gender of Nakba memory', in Lila Abu-Lughod and Ahmad H. Sa'di (eds), *Nakba: Palestine, 1948, and the Claims of Memory* (Columbia University Press, 2007), 213; Abu Iyad with Eric Rouleau, *My Home, My Land: A Narrative of the Palestinian Struggle* (Times, 1981), 4, 12; Elias Shoufani, 'The fall of a village', *Journal of Palestine Studies* 1:4 (1972), 108–21; Rochelle Davis, 'Matar 'Abdelrahim: from a Palestinian village to a Syrian refugee camp', in Mark LeVine and Gershon Shafir (eds), *Struggle and Survival in Palestine/Israel* (University of California Press, 2012), 161; Baroud, *My Father Was a Freedom Fighter*, 34–5; Asmaa al-Ghoul and Selim Nassib, *A Rebel in Gaza: Behind the Lines of the Arab Spring, One Woman's Story* (DoppelHouse Press, 2018), 28.

42   Abu Iyad, *My Home, My Land*, 3–4.

43   Tamer Nafar, 'RIP the uncle I never knew: a poet, just like me, and killed by an Israeli bomb', *The Guardian,* 24 January 2024, https://www.theguardian.com/commentisfree/2024/jan/24/poetry-israel-bomb-palestine, accessed 19 February 2025.

44   Filiu, *Gaza*, 59.

45   Al-Taweel, *Come My Children*, 66.

46   See also al-Barbari, *Light the Road of Freedom*, 21–2.

47   Sayigh, *The Palestinians*, 103–7; Feldman, 'Home as a refrain', 23–8; Baroud, *My Father Was a Freedom Fighter*, 38–9; Anne Irfan, *Refuge and Resistance: Palestinians and the International Refugee System* (Columbia University Press, 2023), 29; Fawaz Turki, *Exile's Return: The Making of a Palestinian American* (Free Press, 1994), 3.

48   The Declaration of the Establishment of the State of Israel, 14 May 1948, https://www.gov.il/en/departments/general/declaration-of-establishment-state-of-israel, accessed 19 February 2025.

49   Segev, *One Palestine, Complete*, 512.

50   Yezid Sayigh, *Armed Struggle and the Search for State: The Palestinian National Movement, 1949–1993* (Clarendon Press, 1997), 3; Rashid Khalidi, *The Iron Cage: The Story of the Palestinian Struggle for Statehood* (Oneworld, 2007), 131; Morris, *The Birth of the Palestinian Refugee Problem Revisited*, 262–3. See also Khaled Elgindy, *Blind Spot: America and the Palestinians, from Balfour to Trump* (Brookings Institution Press, 2019), 47; Bresheeth-Žabner, *An Army Like No Other*, 65.

51   While five Arab states declared war on Israel, the oft-repeated claim that they all 'invaded' the new state is erroneous. The Lebanese army never crossed its international southern border. The Jordanian and Iraqi armies stayed within the areas designated to the would-be

Palestinian Arab state under the UN Partition Plan. It was only two Arab armies – Syria's and Egypt's – that crossed into the territory of the Jewish state. See Khalidi, *The Iron Cage*, xxxiii.

52   On the Jordanian–Zionist secret agreements see Avi Shlaim, *Collusion across the Jordan: King Abdullah, the Zionist Movement, and the Partition of Palestine* (Columbia University Press, 1988).

53   Pappe, *The Ethnic Cleansing of Palestine*, ch. 8.

54   Zarifa's story is recounted by her son in his autobiography. See Abdel Bari Atwan, *A Country of Words: A Palestinian Journey from the Refugee Camp to the Front Page* (Saqi, 2008), 15–24.

55   *Ibid.*

56   Abu Iyad, *My Home, My Land*, 13.

57   Alan Hart, *Arafat: Terrorist or Peacemaker?*, 3rd ed. (Sidgwick & Jackson, 1987), 75–7; Said K. Aburish, *Arafat: From Defender to Dictator* (Bloomsbury, 1999), 17–19.

58   Avi Shlaim, 'The rise and fall of the All-Palestine Government in Gaza', *Journal of Palestine Studies* 20:1 (1990), 37–53. See also Johanna Caldwell, 'Inter-Arab rivalry and the All-Palestine Government of 1948', *Jerusalem Quarterly* 62 (2015), 50–64.

59   *Ibid.*

60   Egyptian–Israeli General Armistice Agreement, 24 February 1949, https://peacemaker.un.org/en/node/9440, accessed 19 February 2025. See also Ilan Pappe, *The Biggest Prison on Earth: A History of the Occupied Territories* (Oneworld, 2017), 37.

61   Salman Abu Sitta, 'Gaza Strip: the lessons of history', in Helga Tawil-Souri and Dina Matar (eds), *Gaza as Metaphor* (Hurst, 2016), 107. See also Atef Alshaer, 'Che and Malcolm', in Mahmoud Muna and Matthew Teller (eds), *Daybreak in Gaza: Stories of Palestinian Lives and Culture* (Saqi, 2024), 289.

62   Article V of Egyptian–Israeli General Armistice Agreement.

63   Abu Sitta, 'Gaza Strip', 107.

64   Ghazi al-Sourani, 'The Gaza Strip 1948–57: a historical political and social study', https://www.ahewar.org/debat/show.art.asp?aid=364924 [Arabic], accessed 19 February 2025. The term 'Gaza Strip' (*qita' ghaza*) was first officially used in a 1955 Egyptian law.

65   Sara Roy, 'The Gaza Strip: critical effects of the occupation', *Arab Studies Quarterly* 10:1 (1988), 63–4. Around 56 per cent of refugees in the Strip came from other parts of the pre-1948 Gaza District, while 42 per cent came from Lydda District in central Palestine. See Beryl Cheal, 'Refugees in the Gaza Strip, December 1948–May 1950', *Journal of Palestine Studies* 18:1 (1988), 138–9.

66   'A Gaza Chronology, 1948–2008', *Journal of Palestine Studies* 38:3 (2009), 98–9.

67 'Where We Work: Gaza Strip', https://www.unrwa.org/where-we-work/gaza-strip, accessed 19 February 2025. Additional information provided by Matthias Schmale, UNRWA director in Gaza, and Rafiq Abed, chief of the UNRWA Infrastructure & Camp Improvement Programme in Gaza, via email, 29 May 2018.

68 https://www.unrwa.org/where-we-work/gaza-strip. On Nuseirat see also 'Refugee Reminiscences III: Nuseirat's Abu Hisham', in UNRWA, *Palestine Refugees Today*, 126 (1990), Social Sciences Library, Oxford University.

69 Donald Macintyre, *Gaza: Preparing for Dawn* (Oneworld, 2017), 22.

70 Atwan, *A Country of Words*, 15–24.

71 UNGA Resolution 194 (III).

72 Interim Report of the UNRWA Director to the UNGA, A/1451/Rev.1, 6 October 1950, Paragraph 51.

73 See for example Izzeldin Abuelaish, *I Shall Not Hate: A Gaza Doctor's Journey on the Road to Peace and Human Dignity* (Bloomsbury, 2011), 78; Atwan, *A Country of Words*, 27. See also Feldman, *Governing Gaza*, 129.

74 Al-Taweel, *Come My Children*, 67.

75 Macintyre, *Gaza*, 24.

76 Cheal, 'Refugees in the Gaza Strip' 146; Feldman, *Governing Gaza*, 22, 128–35, 148–9; Feldman, 'Home as a refrain', 27.

77 Humphries and Khalili, 'Gender of Nakba memory'; Salman Abu Sitta, *Mapping My Return: A Palestinian Memoir* (AUC Press, 2016), 69; Jana Kotaishová, *Nahr Al-Bared* (Jana Kotaishova, 2014), 82–3.

78 Lausanne Conference – Lausanne Protocol, April–June 1949, paras 16–17, 32, https://www.un.org/unispal/document/auto-insert-209249/, accessed 19 February 2025.

79 Irfan, *Refuge and Resistance*, 42.

80 Benny Morris, *Israel's Border Wars, 1949–1956: Arab Infiltration, Israeli Retaliation, and the Countdown to the Suez War* (Clarendon Press, 1992), ch. 2; Filiu, *Gaza*, 79–81; Feldman, *Governing Gaza*, 22–3; Adel Yahya, *The Palestinian Refugees, 1948–98: An Oral History* (PACE, 1999), 48–53; Jehad Abu Salim, 'From fence to fence: Gaza's story in its own words', in Tawil-Souri and Matar, *Gaza as Metaphor*, 90–1.

81 Atwan, *A Country of Words*, 24.

82 Morris, *Israel's Border Wars*, 416.

83 Feldman, 'Home as a refrain', 29–30.

84 Gene Currivan, 'Torture reports studied by Israel', *New York Times*, 8 June 1950; Gene Currivan, 'Israel is adamant over frontier ban', *New York Times*, 9 June 1950.

85 Atwan, *A Country of Words*, 44–5.

86 Abu Salim, 'From fence to fence', 88–9.

87   Figures sourced from Annual Report of the UNRWA Director, 1952, A/2171; Population and demographic developments in the West Bank and Gaza Strip until 1990: a study prepared by Wael R. Ennab, 28 June 1994, TD/JUNCTAD/ECDC/SEU/1.
88   Sayigh, *Armed Struggle and the Search for State*, 37–9.
89   Shlaim, *The Politics of Partition*, 199.

Chapter Two:
The Egyptian Era

1   On the ongoing Nakba that stemmed from this see Rabea Eghbariah, 'Toward Nakba as a legal concept', *Columbia Law Review* 124:4 (2024), 887–992.
2   Beryl Cheal, 'Refugees in the Gaza Strip, December 1948–May 1950', *Journal of Palestine Studies* 18:1 (1988), 139; Sara Roy, 'The Gaza Strip: critical effects of the occupation', *Arab Studies Quarterly* 10:1 (1988), 71.
3   'A Gaza Chronology, 1948–2008', *Journal of Palestine Studies* 38:3 (2009), 98–9. See also Sahbaa al-Barbari, *Light the Road of Freedom* (University of Alberta Press, 2021), 23.
4   Ilana Feldman, *Governing Gaza: Bureaucracy, Authority, and the Work of Rule, 1917–67* (Duke University Press, 2008), 24.
5   Sara Roy, *The Gaza Strip: The Political Economy of De-development* (Institute for Palestine Studies, 1995), 80.
6   Edward Buehrig, *The UN and the Palestinian Refugees: A Study in Nonterritorial Administration* (Indiana University Press, 1971), 130.
7   Ilana Feldman, 'Home as a refrain: remembering and living displacement in Gaza', *History and Memory* 18:2 (2006), 26–7; Cheal, 'Refugees in the Gaza Strip', 143–8.
8   UNRWA, *Palestine Refugees Today*, issue 53. See also UNRWA, 'Replacing tents with fabricated shelters', https://www.unrwa.org/content/replacing-tents-fabricated-shelters, accessed 19 February 2025.
9   Izzeldin Abuelaish, *I Shall Not Hate: A Gaza Doctor's Journey on the Road to Peace and Human Dignity* (Bloomsbury, 2011), 38–9.
10   Elizabeth F. Thompson, *Justice Interrupted: The Struggle for Constitutional Government in the Middle East* (Harvard University Press, 2013), 248. Khalaf recounts the meeting with Eric Rouleau in Abu Iyad, *My Home, My Land: A Narrative of the Palestinian Struggle* (Times, 1981), 17–21.
11   On the GUPS see Laurie Brand, 'Nasir's Egypt and the reemergence of the Palestinian national movement', *Journal of*

Palestine Studies 17:2 (1988), 30, 33–6. On the involvement of Arafat and Khalaf see Abu Iyad, *My Home, My Land*, 19–21; Alan Hart, *Arafat: Terrorist or Peacemaker?* (Sidgwick & Jackson, 1987), 87–8; Rashid Khalidi, *Palestinian Identity: The Construction of Modern National Consciousness* (Columbia University Press, 1997), 180.

12 On the expulsion of Palestinians from Lydda see Benny Morris, 'Operation Dani and the Palestinian exodus from Lydda and Ramle in 1948', *Middle East Journal* 40:1 (1986), 82–109.

13 'Ismail Shammout', *Interactive Encyclopaedia of the Palestine Question*, https://www.palquest.org/en/biography/9727/ismail-shammout, accessed 19 February 2025.

14 Islad Jad, 'From salons to the popular committees: Palestinian women, 1919–89', in Ilan Pappe (ed.), *The Israel/Palestine Question* (Psychology Press, 1999), 220.

15 Roy, 'The Gaza Strip', 64.

16 *Ibid.*

17 Yezid Sayigh, *Armed Struggle and the Search for State: The Palestinian National Movement, 1949–1993* (Clarendon Press, 1997), 59.

18 Feldman, 'Home as a refrain', 16, 29–32.

19 Benny Morris, *Israel's Border Wars, 1949–1956: Arab Infiltration, Israeli Retaliation, and the Countdown to the Suez War* (Clarendon Press, 1992), 28.

20 Ilan Pappe, *The Biggest Prison on Earth: A History of the Occupied Territories* (Oneworld, 2017), 40–1.

21 Jean-Pierre Filiu, *Gaza: A History* (Hurst, 2015), 88–9.

22 Homer Bigart, 'Soviet says "volunteers" can go to Egypt if troops of 3 powers do not leave', *New York Times*, 11 November 1956.

23 Feldman, *Governing Gaza*, 9.

24 Roy, 'The Gaza Strip', 64.

25 Filiu, *Gaza*, 77.

26 On Egyptian governance of Gaza in this period, see Tayseer Muhaisen, 'Palestinian refugees in the Gaza Strip, 1948–1967', *Interactive Encyclopaedia of the Palestine Question*, https://www.palquest.org/en/highlight/22188/palestinian-refugees-gaza-strip-1948-1967, accessed 19 February 2025; Sayigh, *Armed Struggle and the Search for State*, 41; Brand, 'Nasir's Egypt', 31.

27 On Nasser's experiences of the Palestine War, see Gamal Abdel Nasser and Walid Khalidi, 'Nasser's memoirs of the first Palestine war', *Journal of Palestine Studies* 2:2 (1973), 3–32; Gamal Abdel Nasser, *Falsafat al-thawra* (Al-Matba'ah al-'Alamiyah, 1954) [Arabic]; Gamal Abdel Nasser, 'The Egyptian Revolution', *Foreign Affairs* 33:2 (1955), 202–3. See also Saïd K. Aburish, *Nasser: The Last Arab* (Duckworth, 2004), 24–7.

28 'A Gaza Chronology', 99; Filiu, *Gaza*, 77; Brand, 'Nasir's Egypt', 32.

29 Filiu, *Gaza*, 119.
30 Feldman, *Governing Gaza*, 23.
31 *Ibid.*, 9, 23. See also Sayigh, *Armed Struggle and the Search for State*, 61; Ronen Bergman, *Rise and Kill First: The Secret History of Israel's Targeted Assassinations* (John Murray, 2019), 39–40.
32 Khalidi, *Palestinian Identity*, 183.
33 On these dynamics, see Sayigh, *Armed Struggle and the Search for State*, 59; E. L. M. Burns, *Between Arab and Israeli* (Ivan Obolensky, 1963), 63–4; Feldman, *Governing Gaza*, 22; Filiu, *Gaza*, 80; Feldman, 'Home as a refrain', 29–30.
34 Avi Shlaim, *The Iron Wall: Israel and the Arab World*, new ed. (Penguin, 2014), 54, 101–3, 125–9. On Israeli–Egyptian relations at this time, see also Pappe, *The Biggest Prison on Earth*, 39; Nasser, 'The Egyptian Revolution', 210–11.
35 Sitta, *Mapping My Return*, 113–15.
36 Anne Irfan, 'The long, bloody history of the Israel–Gaza "border"', *The Nation*, 29 November 2023, https://www.thenation.com/article/world/gaza-israel-border-history/, accessed 19 February 2025.
37 Jehad Abu Salim, 'From fence to fence: Gaza's story in its own words', in Helga Tawil-Souri and Dina Matar (eds), *Gaza as Metaphor* (Hurst, 2016), 89–91.
38 Al-Wazir recounted his family's experiences during the Nakba to journalist Alan Hart. See Hart, *Arafat*, 91–100.
39 Said K. Aburish, *Arafat: From Defender to Dictator* (Bloomsbury, 1999), 28.
40 *Ibid.*, 29–30. See also Hart, *Arafat*, 100–1.
41 Bergman, *Rise and Kill First*, 40.
42 Martin Gilbert, *The Routledge Atlas of the Arab–Israeli Conflict*, 9th ed. (Routledge, 2008), 58.
43 Filiu, *Gaza*, 80.
44 Morris, *Israel's Border Wars*, 167.
45 'A Gaza Chronology', 99.
46 Morris, *Israel's Border Wars*, 202.
47 'A Gaza Chronology', 99; Filiu, *Gaza*, 85.
48 Maher Charif, 'The March 1955 outburst in the Gaza Strip: thwarting resettlement schemes', *Interactive Encyclopaedia of the Palestine Question*, https://www.palquest.org/en/highlight/21228/march-1955-outburst-gaza-strip, accessed 19 February 2025.
49 Prevention of Infiltration (Offences and Jurisdiction) Law, 5714-1954, https://web.archive.org/web/20111006160636/http://www.israellawresourcecenter.org/emergencyregs/fulltext/preventioninfiltrationlaw.htm, accessed 19 February 2025.

50 Abu Iyad, *My Home, My Land*, 24; Hart, *Arafat*, 102–3; Filiu, *Gaza*, 84; Morris, *Israel's Border Wars*, 50.

51 Filiu, *Gaza*, 87; Shlaim, *The Iron Wall*, 131–5; Abu Sitta, *Mapping My Return*, 117–18.

52 UN Security Council Resolution 106, S/3378, 29 March 1955.

53 Nasser discusses the plan in 'The Egyptian Revolution', 205. See also Charif, 'The March 1955 outburst in the Gaza Strip'; Benjamin N. Schiff, *Refugees unto the Third Generation: UN Aid to Palestinians* (Syracuse University Press, 1996), 89.

54 Charif, 'The March 1955 outburst in the Gaza Strip'. For direct accounts of the 1955 uprising, see al-Taweel, *Come My Children*, 71–2; al-Barbari, *Light the Road of Freedom*, 37. Bseiso describes his experiences of imprisonment in *Dafatir Filistiniya* (Dar al-Farabi, 1978) [Arabic].

55 Al-Barbari, *Light the Road of Freedom*, 37.

56 Brand, 'Nasir's Egypt', 34.

57 Abu Iyad, *My Home, My Land*, 22.

58 Pappe, *The Biggest Prison on Earth*, 40–1; 'A Gaza Chronology', 99; Burns, *Between Arab and Israeli*, 18.

59 Feldman, *Governing Gaza*, 23; Jean-Pierre Filiu, 'The twelve wars on Gaza', *Journal of Palestine Studies* 44:1 (2014), 53; Feldman, 'Home as a refrain', 35–6; Filiu, *Gaza*, 89–90; Morris, *Israel's Border Wars*, 343–5.

60 Burns, *Between Arab and Israeli*, 88, 139–43, 148.

61 Filiu, *Gaza*, 90; Morris, *Israel's Border Wars*, 345–52. Madeeha Hafez Albatta recalls the attack on Khan Younis in *A White Lie* (University of Alberta Press, 2020), 49.

62 These figures were recorded by the UN Truce Supervision Organisation (UNTSO), which didn't distinguish between Egyptians and Palestinians. Burns, *Between Arab and Israeli*, 47.

63 Sayigh, *Armed Struggle and the Search for State*, 64.

64 Filiu, *Gaza*, 91; Morris, *Israel's Border Wars*, 371–3.

65 Their agreement is known as the Protocol of Sèvres. A copy can be found in the appendix of: Avi Shlaim, 'The Protocol of Sèvres, 1956: Anatomy of a war plot', *International Affairs* 73:3 (1997), 509-30.

66 For more on the machinations behind the invasion, see Shlaim, *The Iron Wall*, 173–90.

67 Sayigh, *Armed Struggle and the Search for State*, 65.

68 Filiu, *Gaza*, 96; Morris, *Israel's Border Wars*, 407–9.

69 Special Report of the Director of UNRWA, A/3212/Add.1, 15 December 1956. Joe Sacco draws on oral history testimonies to depict the Khan Younis and Rafah massacres in *Footnotes in Gaza* (Jonathan Cape, 2009).

70 Albatta, *A White Lie*, 52–4.

71 Filiu, *Gaza*, 96–8; Morris, *Israel's Border Wars*, 408; Special Report of the Director of UNRWA, A/3212/Add.1, 15 December 1956. Eedson Burns, who served as chief of staff of the UN Truce Supervision Organisation (UNTSO) in Gaza from 1954 to 1956, later wrote of Israeli forces' 'severe repressive measures against Arab civilians'. See Burns, *Between Arab and Israeli*, 191.

72 Filiu, *Gaza*, 97–101.

73 See Convention (IV) relative to the Protection of Civilian Persons in Time of War, Geneva, 12 August 1949.

74 Filiu, *Gaza*, 98.

75 Albatta, *A White Lie*, 55.

76 Abdel Bari Atwan, *A Country of Words: A Palestinian Journey from the Refugee Camp to the Front Page* (Saqi, 2008), 29–30.

77 Filiu, 'The twelve wars on Gaza', 53.

78 Filiu, *Gaza*, 96–7; Morris, *Israel's Border Wars*, 408.

79 Agence France-Press, 'Suez crisis triggered Israel's first occupation of Gaza', France 24, 2 November 2021, https://www.france24.com/en/live-news/20211102-suez-crisis-triggered-israel-s-first-occupation-of-gaza, accessed 20 February 2025. See also Filiu, *Gaza*, 29–30.

80 Al-Barbari, *Light the Road of Freedom*, 19.

81 Filiu, *Gaza*, 100–1.

82 Al-Barbari, *Light the Road of Freedom*, 38.

83 *Ibid.*, 45.

84 Atwan, *A Country of Words*, 32–3.

85 Abu Iyad, *My Home, My Land*, 23.

86 Brand, 'Nasir's Egypt', 34.

87 Abu Iyad, *My Home, My Land*, 23–7. See also Thompson, *Justice Interrupted*, 248; Filiu, *Gaza*, 82–4.

88 Thompson, *Justice Interrupted*, 248.

89 Abu Iyad, *My Home, My Land*, 28.

90 Thompson, *Justice Interrupted*, 248.

91 Hussein Agha and Ahmad Samih Khalidi, 'Yasser Arafat: why he still matters', *The Guardian*, 13 November 2014, https://www.theguardian.com/news/2014/nov/13/-sp-yasser-arafat-why-he-still-matters, accessed 20 February 2025.

92 In Arabic custom an adult is often referred to by their *kunya*, meaning the name of their eldest son preceded by *father of* (abu) or *mother of* (umm). Khalaf and al-Wazir followed this custom in their respective *kunyas* here. As Arafat didn't have any sons, and remained childless until the birth of his daughter in 1995, he went by Abu Ammar, in reference to one of the Prophet Muhammad's early companions.

93 Filiu, *Gaza*, 113.

94 *Ibid.*, 112; al-Barbari, *Light the Road of Freedom*, 40–3.

95 Mu'in Basisu, 'Palestinian notes from Cairo's military prison', *Arab Studies Quarterly* 1:4 (1979), 288.

96 Al-Barbari, *Light the Road of Freedom*, 49.

97 Bseiso, *Dafatir Filistiniya*. See also Basisu, 'Palestinian notes from Cairo's military prison'.

98 Filiu, *Gaza*, 114–16.

99 Brand, 'Nasir's Egypt', 41–2; Aburish, *Nasser*, 222–4.

100 Filiu, *Gaza*, 116–20.

101 Maya Angelou, *Singin' and Swingin' and Gettin' Merry like Christmas* (Virago, 2008 [1976]), 258.

102 Alex White, 'The caged bird sings of freedom: Maya Angelou's anti-colonial journalism in the United Arab Republic and Ghana, 1961–1965', *Journal of Global History* 19:3 (2024), 421–38.

103 On these various visits see Atef Alshaer, 'Che and Malcolm', in Mahmoud Muna and Matthew Teller (eds), *Daybreak in Gaza: Stories of Palestinian Lives and Culture* (Saqi, 2024), 289–91; Filiu, *Gaza*, 112, 120; Michael R. Fischbach, *Black Power and Palestine: Transnational Countries of Color* (Stanford University Press, 2018), 16–17; Adam Shatz, 'One day I'll tell you what I think', *London Review of Books*, 22 November 2018, https://www.lrb.co.uk/the-paper/v40/n22/adam-shatz/one-day-i-ll-tell-you-what-i-think, accessed 20 February 2025; Reda Merida, 'On Jean-Paul Sartre and Palestine', *Middle East Eye*, 20 May 2020, https://www.middleeasteye.net/opinion/jean-paul-sartre-and-palestine, accessed 20 February 2025. Footage of Nehru's visit to Gaza can be viewed at https://www.britishpathe.com/asset/256966/, accessed 20 February 2025.

104 On the international dynamics of Palestinian politics see Fischbach, *Black Power and Palestine*; Steven Salaita, *Inter/Nationalism: Decolonizing Native America and Palestine* (University of Minnesota Press, 2016); Anne Irfan, *Refuge and Resistance: Palestinians and the International Refugee System* (Columbia University Press, 2023); Miryam Aouragh, *Palestine Online: Transnationalism, the Internet and the Construction of Identity* (I. B. Tauris, 2011); Paul Thomas Chamberlin, *The Global Offensive: The United States, the Palestine Liberation Organization, and the Making of the Post-Cold War Order* (Oxford University Press, 2012); Waziyatawin, 'Malice enough in their hearts and courage enough in ours: reflection on US Indigenous and Palestinian experiences under occupation', *Settler Colonial Studies* 2:1 (2012), 172–89.

105 Nathan Thrall, 'BDS: How a controversial non-violent movement has transformed the Israeli–Palestinian debate', *The Guardian*, 14 August 2018, https://www.theguardian.com/news/2018/aug/14/bds-boycott-divestment-sanctions-movement-transformed-israeli-palestinian-debate, accessed 20 February 2025.

Chapter Three:
Israeli Occupation

1   Figure sourced from Janet L. Abu-Lughod, 'Demographic consequences of the occupation', *MERIP Reports* 115 (1983), 13–17.

2   Avi Raz, *The Bride and the Dowry: Israel, Jordan, and the Palestinians in the Aftermath of the June 1967 War* (Yale University Press, 2012), 3.

3   Ilan Pappe, *The Biggest Prison on Earth: A History of the Occupied Territories* (Oneworld, 2017), 20–1.

4   From 1948 to 1967, Jerusalem had been divided between the Israeli-controlled west and the Jordanian-controlled east. This was contrary to the UN Partition Plan, which had envisaged a separate international administration for Jerusalem. On 8 June 1967, before the war was even over, Eshkol declared that a unified Jerusalem would serve as Israel's eternal capital. See Anne Irfan, 'Is Jerusalem international or Palestinian? Rethinking UNGA Resolution 181', *Jerusalem Quarterly* 70 (2017), 52–60; Noura Erakat, *Justice for Some: Law and the Question of Palestine* (Stanford University Press, 2019), 71–5.

5   Palestine National Council, Fourth Session: Political Resolutions, 10–17 July 1968, https://www.palquest.org/en/historictext/16256/palestine-national-council-4th-session-political-resolutions, accessed 20 February 2025.

6   Letter from R. E. Skinner, director of UNRWA Operations, West Bank, to Chief Relief Operations Division HQ, 1 February 1971, OP/RE/223, File RE210/03(WB) II, Box RE7, UNRWA Central Registry Archive, Amman, Jordan (UCRA). UNRWA, *Palestine Refugees Today* 125, February 1990, Box GP3 PALESTINE, Social Sciences Library, University of Oxford (SSL). See also Ilana Feldman, *Governing Gaza: Bureaucracy, Authority and the Work of Rule, 1917–1967* (Duke University Press, 2008), 227–8; Sara Roy, *The Gaza Strip: The Political Economy of De-development* (Institute for Palestine Studies, 2016), 105; Tom Segev, 'The June 1967 War and the Palestinian refugee problem', *Journal of Palestine Studies* 36:3 (2007), 6–22; Tareq Baconi, *Hamas Contained: The Rise and Pacification of Palestinian Resistance* (Stanford University Press: 2018), 11, 65; Anne Irfan, *Refuge and Resistance: Palestinians and the International Refugee System* (Columbia University Press, 2023), 85–8.

7   Quoted in Segev, 'The June 1967 War and the Palestinian refugee problem', 12.

8   Ilan Pappe, 'Israel's Message', *London Review of Books*, 1 January 2009, https://www.lrb.co.uk/the-paper/v31/n01/ilan-pappe/israel-s-message, accessed 2 May 2025.

9   Tom Segev, *1967: Israel, the War and the Year that Transformed the Middle East* (Little, Brown, 2007), trans. Jessica Cohen, 325.

10   Jean-Pierre Filiu, *Gaza: A History* (Hurst, 2015), 126–7, 134–5, 150.

11   Figure sourced from Report of the UNRWA Commissioner General, A/7213, 1 July 1967–30 June 1968. On fears stemming from 1956, see Abdel Bari Atwan, *A Country of Words: A Palestinian Journey from the Refugee Camp to the Front Page* (Saqi, 2008), 49; Madeeha Hafez Albatta, *A White Lie* (University of Alberta Press, 2020), 80; Hekmat al-Taweel, *Come My Children* (University of Alberta Press, 2023), 77.

12   Filiu, *Gaza*, 127. See also Tayseer Muhaisen, 'Palestinian refugees in the Gaza Strip since 1967: incubators of resistance', *Interactive Encyclopaedia of the Palestine Question*, https://www.palquest.org/en/highlight/22192/palestinian-refugees-gaza-strip-1967, accessed 20 February 2025.

13   Albatta, *A White Lie*, 75.

14   Sahbaa al-Barbari, *Light the Road of Freedom* (University of Alberta Press, 2021), 57.

15   Pappe, *The Biggest Prison on Earth*, 84.

16   Omri Shafer Raviv, 'Israeli emigration policies in the Gaza Strip: crafting demography and forming control in the aftermath of the 1967 War', *Middle Eastern Studies* 57:2 (2021), 349. On the situation of 'ex-Gazans' in Jordan, see Oroub El Abed, 'Immobile Palestinians: ongoing plight of Gazans in Jordan', *Forced Migration Review* 26 (2006), 17–18.

17   Filiu, *Gaza*, 144; Roy, *The Gaza Strip*, 139.

18   Segev, 'The June 1967 War and the Palestinian refugee problem', 17–18.

19   Shafer Raviv, 'Israeli emigration policies in the Gaza Strip', 342, 350.

20   Segev, *1967*, 627.

21   Shafer Raviv, 'Israeli emigration policies in the Gaza Strip', 347; Pappe, *The Biggest Prison on Earth*, 157–8. On US support for Israel see Rashid Khalidi, *Brokers of Deceit: How the US Has Undermined Peace in the Middle East* (Beacon Press, 2013).

22   Segev, 'The June 1967 War and the Palestinian refugee problem', 11.

23   Shafer Raviv, 'Israeli emigration policies in the Gaza Strip', 344, 348.

24   Segev, 'The June 1967 War and the Palestinian refugee problem', 7, 15–16.

25   *Ibid.*, 15.

26   Al-Barbari, *Light the Road of Freedom*, 14. Madeeha Hafez Albatta recalls her own activities in the Women's Union in *A White Lie*, 77.

27 Jamil Hilal, 'Class transformation in the West Bank and Gaza', *Journal of Palestine Studies* 6:2 (1977), 171–2. See also Paul Cossali and Clive Robson, *Stateless in Gaza* (Zed, 1986), 126.

28 Filiu, *Gaza*, 157.

29 'Yusra al-Barbari', *Interactive Encyclopaedia of the Palestine Question*, https://www.palquest.org/en/biography/14291/yusra-al-barbari, accessed 20 February 2025.

30 Filiu, *Gaza*, 132, 154–6.

31 'Appeal addressed by representatives of municipalities, religious bodies and labour and professional unions of the West Bank and the Gaza Strip to the President of the Security Council and the Secretary-General of the United Nations, July 1973', *Journal of Palestine Studies* 3:1 (1973), 187–9.

32 Filiu, *Gaza*, 136; Cossali and Robson, *Stateless in Gaza*, 62, 132–4.

33 Albatta, *A White Lie*, 85–6.

34 Filiu, *Gaza*, 136, 138.

35 *Ibid.*, 155; 'Yusra al-Barbari'.

36 Albatta, *A White Lie*, 86–92, 106.

37 Roy, *The Gaza Strip*, 104; Sara Roy, 'The Gaza Strip: critical effects of the occupation', *Arab Studies Quarterly* 10:1 (1988), 67; Filiu, *Gaza*, 129, 135; Cossali and Robson, *Stateless in Gaza*, 61.

38 Abu Karim quoted in Cossali and Robson, *Stateless in Gaza*, 125.

39 Cossali and Robson, *Stateless in Gaza*, 125; Filiu, *Gaza*, 127–8, 138.

40 Cossali and Robson, *Stateless in Gaza*, 125.

41 Anne Irfan, 'An unusual revolution: the Palestinian *thawra* in Lebanon, c.1969–82', *Durham Middle East Papers* 103 (2020), 1–43.

42 Filiu, *Gaza*, 136–7.

43 Sara Roy, *Hamas and Civil Society in Gaza: Engaging the Islamist Social Sector* (Princeton University Press, 2011), 23–4, 71, 73, 75. On the Israeli perspective on this, see Ronen Bergman, *Rise and Kill First: The Secret History of Israel's Targeted Assassinations* (John Murray, 2019), 411.

44 Jean-Pierre Filiu, 'The twelve wars on Gaza', *Journal of Palestine Studies* 44:1 (2014), 54.

45 Ramzy Baroud, *My Father Was a Freedom Fighter: Gaza's Untold Story* (Pluto Press, 2010), 84; Cossali and Robson, *Stateless in Gaza*, 61.

46 Albatta, *A White Lie*, 83; Roy, *The Gaza Strip*, 105.

47 Filiu, *Gaza*, 139–40.

48 Abu Hassan, quoted in Cossali and Robson, *Stateless in Gaza*, 64.

49 Roy, *The Gaza Strip*, 105.

50 Filiu, *Gaza*, 141.

51 Bergman, *Rise and Kill First*, 123, 134–5.

52 'Peres: We will aid the refugees, but cannot solve entire problem', *Jerusalem Post*, 19 February 1970; Acting DUO/Gaza, Note for the

Record, October 19, 1971; both File OR215(IS)I, Box OR59, UCRA. See also Feldman, *Governing Gaza*, 171, 228.

53 Irfan, *Refuge and Resistance*, 87–8.

54 Filiu, *Gaza*, 141–5, 389.

55 Ramzy Baroud, 'Fighting another day: Gaza's unrelenting resistance', in Helga Tawil-Souri and Dina Matar (eds), *Gaza as Metaphor* (Hurst, 2016), 139.

56 Baroud, *My Father Was a Freedom Fighter*, 91.

57 'Palestine refugees in the Gaza Strip, report of the Secretary-General', DC/OR/UNR/PR/5, File DC/OR/UNR/ICI/IPU/IPR, Box UNR 1, Cooper Archive, SSL.

58 Izzeldin Abuelaish, *I Shall Not Hate: A Gaza Doctor's Journey on the Road to Peace and Human Dignity* (Bloomsbury, 2011), 59–60.

59 *Ibid.*, 31, 59.

60 Baroud, 'Fighting another day', 139.

61 Roy, *The Gaza Strip*, 105.

62 Bergman, *Rise and Kill First*, 131.

63 Filiu, *Gaza*, 141–3, 389.

64 Stackhouse/US Embassy Israel to Sisco/US State Dept, Confidential Memo, 16 August 1971, File POL 28, Box 21, Entry A1-5632, RG59, US National Archives, College Park, MD (USNA).

65 'Roomy new housing for Gaza refugees', *Jerusalem Post*, 31 December 1974, File OR215(IS) II, Box OR59, UCRA.

66 'Liquidation and resettlement', *Al Quds*, 14 December 1972, File OR215(IS) II, Box OR59, UCRA; Rafah Refugee Services Officer, memo to DUO/Gaza, 20 June 1971, UCRA. See also Irfan, *Refuge and Resistance*, 88–9; Filiu, *Gaza*, 141–3, 389.

67 Pappe, *The Biggest Prison on Earth*, 176.

68 See Chapter One on Said Shawwa's intervention to protect Gaza's Jewish communities in 1929.

69 On Shawwa's mayoralty and Israel's experiments with indirect rule in Gaza, see Filiu, *Gaza*, 146, 148, 152, 163; Feldman, *Governing Gaza*, 171, 228; Roy, *The Gaza Strip*, 100, 106–7; Pappe, *The Biggest Prison on Earth*, 182, 206–7.

70 Filiu, *Gaza*, 144, 147; Roy, 'The Gaza Strip', 96.

71 Shafer Raviv, 'Israeli emigration policies in the Gaza Strip', 342, 350; Irfan, *Refuge and Resistance*, 75.

72 Rashid Khalidi, *The Iron Cage: The Story of the Palestinian Struggle for Statehood* (Oneworld, 2007), 164.

73 See for example Abuelaish, *I Shall Not Hate*, 65–6.

74 Gershom Gorenberg, *The Accidental Empire: Israel and the Birth of the Settlements, 1967–1977* (Times, 2006), Kindle loc. 2514; Yusif Sayigh, 'The Palestinian economy under occupation: Dependency

and pauperization', *Journal of Palestine Studies* 15:4 (1986), 56; Cossali and Robson, *Stateless in Gaza*, 97–100; Roy, 'The Gaza Strip', 62, 68.

75 Pappe, *The Biggest Prison on Earth*, 14, 217.

76 Cossali and Robson, *Stateless in Gaza*, 63, 137.

77 Filiu, *Gaza*, 135–6.

78 Cossali and Robson, *Stateless in Gaza*, 61, 64–70, 140–5.

79 Baroud, *My Father Was a Freedom Fighter*, 85.

80 Yezid Sayigh, *Armed Struggle and the Search for State: The Palestinian National Movement, 1949–1993* (Clarendon Press, 1997), 287.

81 Andrew Ross, *Stone Men: The Palestinians Who Built Israel* (Verso, 2019), 140.

82 For accounts of living through this, see Albatta, *A White Lie*, 83; al-Taweel, *Come My Children*, 76–8.

83 Sayigh, 'The Palestinian economy', 56; Segev, 'The June 1967 War and the Palestinian refugee problem', 16–17.

84 Idith Zertal and Akiva Eldar, *Lords of the Land: The War over Israel's Settlements in the Occupied Territories*, trans. Vivian Eden (Bold Type, 2007), 4–6.

85 Gorenberg, *The Accidental Empire*, locs 2625–78, 2732–2894. Hebron remains home to some of the most extremist settlers who regularly commit anti-Palestinian violence. See Badia Dwaik and Gilbert Ramsay, 'Who is observing the occupation in Hebron?', openDemocracy, 22 February 2019, https://www.opendemocracy.net/en/north-africa-west-asia/who-is-observing-occupation-in-hebron/, accessed 21 February 2025; Imad Abu Hawash, '"If you don't leave, we'll kill you": hundreds flee Israeli settler violence in Hebron area', +972, 22 November 2023, https://www.972mag.com/hebron-area-settler-violence-expulsions/, accessed 21 February 2025.

86 Zertal and Eldar, *Lords of the Land*, 345.

87 Ariel Sharon with David Chanoff, *Warrior: The Autobiography of Ariel Sharon*, 2nd ed. (Simon & Schuster, 2001), 554.

88 Roy, *The Gaza Strip*, 150; Filiu, *Gaza*, 161–2.

89 Quoted in Zertal and Eldar, *Lords of the Land*, 281.

90 *Ibid.*

91 See Chapter One.

92 Baroud, *My Father Was a Freedom Fighter*, 98–9; Gorenberg, *The Accidental Empire*, locs 4216–20.

93 The settlements' illegality was confirmed in writing by the Israeli Foreign Ministry's own legal advisor Theodor Meron, later president of the International Criminal Tribunal for the Former Yugoslavia. In 2007, he reaffirmed this position. See Donald Macintyre, *Gaza: Preparing for Dawn* (Oneworld, 2017), 31–2.

94 Convention (IV) relative to the Protection of Civilian Persons in Time of War. Geneva, 12 August 1949, https://ihl-databases.icrc.org/en/ihl-treaties/gciv-1949, accessed 21 February 2025.

95 Nimer Sultany, 'Activism and legitimacy in Israel's jurisprudence of occupation', *Social & Legal Studies* 23:3 (2014), 320–1.

96 Roy, *The Gaza Strip*, 106. The exact number is disputed. Israel stated that it was less than 5,000, while the Bedouin sheikhs said that the Israeli army forced more than 20,000 people from their homes. See Baroud, *My Father Was a Freedom Fighter*, 98; Gorenberg, *The Accidental Empire*, locs 4177, 4181. On the case more generally, see Zertal and Eldar, *Lords of the Land*, 281–2; Pappe, *The Biggest Prison on Earth*, 166.

97 Zertal and Eldar, *Lords of the Land*, 347–8. See also Khalidi, *Brokers of Deceit*.

98 Seth Anziska, *Preventing Palestine: A Political History from Camp David to Oslo* (Princeton University Press, 2018), 49–51.

99 Pappe, *The Biggest Prison on Earth*, 200.

100 Filiu, *Gaza*, 166.

101 *Ibid.*, 165.

102 Macintyre, *Gaza*, 30–1.

103 These roads had been part of Allon's original settlement plans. Gorenberg, *The Accidental Empire*, locs 3302, 3306.

104 Cossali and Robson, *Stateless in Gaza*, 74.

105 Pappe, *The Biggest Prison on Earth*, 201–2.

106 Filiu, *Gaza*, 196; Roy, 'The Gaza Strip', 60, 75.

107 Pappe, *The Biggest Prison on Earth*, 14.

108 Zertal and Eldar, *Lords of the Land*, 372–3.

109 Sayigh, 'The Palestinian economy: critical effects of the occupation', 57.

110 Roy, 'The Gaza Strip', 82.

111 Cossali and Robson, *Stateless in Gaza*, 74–5.

112 In 1981, Israel unilaterally annexed the Golan Heights in a move that was largely regarded as illegitimate. The US recognised the Golan as Israeli in 2019.

113 Roy, *The Gaza Strip*, 106.

114 Abuelaish, *I Shall Not Hate*, 73.

115 James J. Zogby, 'What we choose to ignore about the 1967 war', *+972*, 17 June 2017, https://www.972mag.com/what-we-choose-to-ignore-about-the-1967-war/, accessed 21 February 2025.

116 The Khartoum Resolutions, 1 September 1967, https://avalon.law.yale.edu/20th_century/khartoum.asp, accessed 21 February 2025.

117 Camp David Accords: Framework for the Conclusion of a Peace Treaty between Egypt and Israel, 17 September 1978, https://www.jimmycarterlibrary.gov/research/additional-resources/camp-david-

accords/framework-for-the-conclusion-of-a-peace-treaty, accessed 21 February 2025.

118 Peace Treaty Between the State of Israel and the Arab Republic of Egypt, 26 March 1979, https://peacemaker.un.org/en/node/9427, accessed 21 February 2025.

119 Rob Geist Pinfold, *Understanding Territorial Withdrawal: Israeli Occupations and Exits* (Oxford University Press, 2023), 33.

120 Camp David Accords: The Framework for Peace in the Middle East, 17 September 1978, https://www.jimmycarterlibrary.gov/research/additional-resources/camp-david-accords/framework-for-peace-in-the-middle-east, accessed 21 February 2025.

121 Roy, 'The Gaza Strip', 69.

122 'Resolutions passed at the Gaza National Conference which met at Gaza, 16 and 18 October 1978', *Journal of Palestine Studies* 8:2 (1979), 199–200. See also Filiu, *Gaza*, 169–70.

123 In 1981, Sadat was assassinated in Cairo by the Egyptian Islamic Jihad. Among other things, they opposed his agreement with Israel.

124 Baroud, *My Father Was a Freedom Fighter*, 110.

125 *Ibid.*, 177–8. The pacification of Israel's southern border also facilitated its expansionism in the north. The same year that the settlers left Sinai, Israel invaded Lebanon, ultimately occupying the country's southern region until 2000. Geist Pinfold, *Understanding Territorial Withdrawal*, 65; see ch. 3 on Israel's eventual withdrawal from southern Lebanon.

126 See Chapter Two.

127 Partly in response, the Jeddah-based Organisation of the Islamic Conference (OIC) – which, like the Arab League, had expelled Egypt following its peace agreement with Israel – provided $150,000 to aid the establishment of Gaza's first higher education institution, the Islamic University. Filiu, *Gaza*, 167, 171. For Palestinian views on the Islamic University, see Cossali and Robson, *Stateless in Gaza*, 41–3.

128 Toufic Haddad, 'Insurgent infrastructure: tunnels of the Gaza Strip', *Middle East – Topics & Arguments* 10 (2018), 78.

129 Atef Alshaer, 'Carving positive spaces', in Mahmoud Muna and Matthew Teller (eds), *Daybreak in Gaza: Stories of Palestinian Lives and Culture* (Saqi, 2024), 282.

130 Filiu, *Gaza*, 126, 147.

131 Shafer Raviv, 'Israeli emigration policies in the Gaza Strip', 345.

132 Ilan Pappe, *The Forgotten Palestinians: A History of the Palestinians in Israel* (Yale University Press, 2011), 97, 103, 111–14.

133 Ilana Feldman, 'Home as a refrain: remembering and living displacement in Gaza', *History and Memory* 18:2 (2006), 23. See also

Amjad Iraqi, 'How Palestinian resistance tore down the Green Line long ago', +972, 10 August 2022, https://www.972mag.com/green-line-palestinian-resistance/, accessed 21 February 2025.

134 Al-Taweel, *Come My Children*, 79–83.

135 Leila Farsakh, 'Independence, cantons, or Bantustans: Whither the Palestinian State?', *Middle East Journal* 59:2 (2005), 230–45. See also Sayigh, 'The Palestinian economy', 53.

136 Cossali and Robson, *Stateless in Gaza*, 83–4; Pappe, *The Biggest Prison on Earth*, 215.

137 Filiu, *Gaza*, 162.

138 Cossali and Robson, *Stateless in Gaza*, 83–8.

139 Filiu, *Gaza*, 163.

140 Baroud, *My Father Was a Freedom Fighter*, 86–7; Atwan, *A Country of Words*, 51.

141 Abuelaish, *I Shall Not Hate*, 57–8, 71–2, 87–8.

142 Cossali and Robson, *Stateless in Gaza*, 36–7, 52–3, 83–7.

143 Macintyre, *Gaza*, 27. See also Atwan, *A Country of Words*, 51.

144 Filiu, *Gaza*, 139, 162.

145 Sayigh, 'The Palestinian economy', 49, 63.

146 Filiu, *Gaza*, 162.

147 Roy, 'The Gaza Strip', 88, 91.

148 Sayigh, 'The Palestinian economy', 47–8.

149 Roy, 'The Gaza Strip', 60.

150 Cossali and Robson, *Stateless in Gaza*, 76–80.

151 Roy, 'The Gaza Strip', 78, 86.

152 Sayigh, 'The Palestinian economy', 50; Baroud, *My Father Was a Freedom Fighter*, 87; Roy, 'The Gaza Strip', 69, 78–9; Cossali and Robson, *Stateless in Gaza*, 77–81, 135–6.

153 Roy, 'The Gaza Strip', 81, 82, 86.

154 Roy, *The Gaza Strip*, 137–8. See also Sara Roy, 'The Gaza Strip: a case of economic de-development', *Journal of Palestine Studies* 17:1 (1987), 56–88.

155 Sayigh, 'The Palestinian economy', 58–63; Pappe, *The Biggest Prison on Earth*, 216; Roy, *The Gaza Strip*, 132.

156 Cossali and Robson, *Stateless in Gaza*, 95–6; Roy, 'The Gaza Strip: critical effects of the occupation', 61, 73.

157 Roy, 'The Gaza Strip: critical effects of the occupation', 91.

158 Sayigh, 'The Palestinian economy', 51.

159 On UNRWA see Irfan, *Refugee and Resistance*; UNRWA annual reports, available via https://www.un.org/unispal/data-collection/

160 Roy, 'The Gaza Strip: critical effects of the occupation', 93.

161 Roy, *The Gaza Strip*, 143–4; Gorenberg, *The Accidental Empire*, loc. 2501; Roy, 'The Gaza Strip: critical effects of the occupation', 74–5.

162 Rebecca L. Stein, '#StolenHomes: Israeli tourism and/as military occupation in historical perspective', *American Quarterly* 68:3 (2016), 546–9.

163 Mark Tessler, 'The intifada and political discourse in Israel', *Journal of Palestine Studies* 19:2 (1990), 44.

164 Abuelaish, *I Shall Not Hate*, 54.

165 Gorenberg, *The Accidental Empire*, locs 4203-4208, 6022-6,034.

Chapter Four:
The First Intifada

1 Jean-Pierre Filiu, *Gaza: A History* (Hurst, 2015), 195.

2 Rashid Khalidi, *The Hundred Years War on Palestine: A History of Settler Colonial Conquest and Resistance* (Profile, 2020), 79–80.

3 Avi Shlaim, *The Iron Wall: Israel and the Arab World*, new ed. (Penguin, 2014), 406–8.

4 Khalidi, *The Hundred Years War on Palestine*, 142–3.

5 *Ibid.*, 142.

6 Rashid Khalidi, *Under Siege: PLO Decisionmaking during the 1982 War* (Columbia University Press, 2014 ed.), 168–71.

7 Filiu, *Gaza*, 180.

8 Sahbaa al-Barbari, *Light the Road of Freedom* (University of Alberta Press, 2021), 68–71.

9 On US culpability for the Sabra-Shatila massacre, see Seth Anziska, 'A preventable massacre', *New York Times*, 16 September 2012, https://www.nytimes.com/2012/09/17/opinion/a-preventable-massacre.html, accessed 21 February 2025. The documents revealing Israeli and American culpability for the massacre can be found at https://archive.nytimes.com/www.nytimes.com/interactive/2012/09/16/opinion/20120916_lebanondoc.html?ref=opinion, accessed 21 February 2025.

10 The true number is likely to be higher, as many victims were never found. See Bayan Nuwayhed al-Hout, *Sabra and Shatila, September 1982* (Pluto Press, 2004), 276–8.

11 The surgeon Swee Chai Ang was volunteering in Gaza Hospital at the time. She recounts the massacre in her memoir *From Beirut to Jerusalem*, 2nd ed. (Other Press, 2002), ch. 6. See also Madeline Edwards, 'The ghosts of war haunting Beirut's Gaza Hospital', *Inkstick*, 21 January 2025, https://inkstickmedia.com/the-ghosts-of-war-haunting-beiruts-gaza-hospital/, accessed 21 February 2025.

12 The Lebanese perpetrators of the massacre were acquitted as part of

a general amnesty at the end of the Lebanese war. Some of them spoke anonymously about their actions in the 2005 documentary *Massaker*, dir. Monika Borgmann, Nina Menkes, Lokman Slim and Hermann Theissen. See 'Film of the week #29', PFP, 14 April 2021, https://www.palestinefilminstitute.org/en/pfp/archive/massacre, accessed 21 February 2025.

13   Al-Barbari, *Light the Road of Freedom*, 73–5; Filiu, *Gaza*, 180.

14   Filiu, *Gaza*, 179.

15   On these protests see: Efraim Davidi, 'Protest Amid Confusion', *Middle East Report*, 217 (Winter 2000). For contemporaneous coverage see: William E. Farrell, 'Israelis, at huge rally in Tel Aviv, demand Begin and Sharon resign', *New York Times*, 26 September 1982, https://www.nytimes.com/1982/09/26/world/israelis-at-huge-rally-in-tel-aviv-demand-begin-and-sharon-resign.html, accessed 15 May 2025.

16   The Kahan Commission's report is available at https://www.jewishvirtuallibrary.org/the-kahan-commission-of-inquiry, accessed 21 February 2025. The report's secret appendices are available at https://www.palestine-studies.org/en/node/232060, accessed 21 February 2025.

17   Shlaim, *The Iron Wall*, 429.

18   Filiu, *Gaza*, 181.

19   Arab League Resolution on Palestine, 28 October 1974, https://www.un.org/unispal/document/auto-insert-194621/, accessed 21 February 2025. UN General Assembly Resolution 3236(XXIX) on the Question of Palestine, A/RES/3236(XXIX), 22 November 1974.

20   UN General Assembly Resolution 3237(XXIX) Observer Status for the Palestine Liberation Organization, A/RES/3237(XXIX), 22 November 1974.

21   Ramzy Baroud, *My Father Was a Freedom Fighter: Gaza's Untold Story* (Pluto Press, 2010), 129.

22   Filiu, *Gaza*, 188–9.

23   Gershom Gorenberg, *The Accidental Empire: Israel and the Birth of the Settlements, 1967–1977* (Times, 2006), Kindle loc. 6870.

24   Sara Roy, 'The Gaza Strip: critical effects of the occupation', *Arab Studies Quarterly* 10:1 (1988), 59.

25   Sara Roy, *The Gaza Strip: The Political Economy of De-development* (Institute for Palestine Studies, 2016), 110.

26   Lisa Taraki, 'The Islamic Resistance Movement in the Palestinian Uprising', *Middle East Report* 156 (1989), 30–2.

27   Loren D. Lybarger, *Identity and Religion in Palestine: The Struggle between Islamism and Secularism in the Occupied Territories* (Princeton University Press, 2007), 83–4.

28 Tareq Baconi, *Hamas Contained: The Rise and Pacification of Palestinian Resistance* (Stanford University Press, 2018), 44.

29 Paul Cossali and Clive Robson, *Stateless in Gaza* (Zed, 1986), 150–6.

30 Joost R. Hiltermann, 'The women's movement during the uprising', *Journal of Palestine Studies* 20:3 (1991), 49.

31 Cossali and Robson, *Stateless in Gaza*, 135–6.

32 Filiu, *Gaza*, 188–93.

33 As we saw in Chapter Three, Jabalia had been a major target of Sharon's campaign against the fedayeen in the early 1970s. On the camp's reputation, see Cossali and Robson, *Stateless in Gaza*, 61, 137–8.

34 Baroud, *My Father Was a Freedom Fighter*, 131.

35 Filiu, *Gaza*, 193–4.

36 Izzeldin Abuelaish, *I Shall Not Hate: A Gaza Doctor's Journey on the Road to Peace and Human Dignity* (Bloomsbury, 2011), 80.

37 On participation in the first intifada among Palestinian citizens of Israel, see Ilan Pappe, *The Forgotten Palestinians: A History of the Palestinians in Israel* (Yale University Press, 2011), 174–5.

38 Quoted in Amira Hass, *Drinking the Sea at Gaza: Days and Nights in a Land under Siege*, trans. Elana Wesley and Maxine Kaufman-Lacusta (Henry Holt, 1999), 33.

39 Filiu, *Gaza*, 200.

40 Many of these leaflets are reprinted in Shaul Mishal and Reuben Aharoni (eds), *Speaking Stones: Communiqués from the Intifada Underground* (Syracuse University Press, 1994).

41 Edward Said, 'Intifada and independence', *Social Text* 22 (1989), 37–8.

42 Hiltermann, 'The women's movement during the uprising', 50–1.

43 Said, 'Intifada and independence', 38.

44 Hiltermann, 'The women's movement during the uprising', 51–3.

45 *Ibid*. See also Eileen S. Kuttab, 'Palestinian women in the "intifada": fighting on two fronts', *Arab Studies Quarterly* 15:2 (1993), 75–6.

46 Ayesh's story is told in the documentary *Naila and the Uprising* (dir. Julia Bacha, 2017). See also Zahra Hankir, '"My story is one of many": the Palestinian women behind the First Intifada', *Middle East Eye*, 15 March 2018, https://www.middleeasteye.net/features/my-story-one-many-palestinian-women-behind-first-intifada, accessed 21 February 2025; Khelil Bouarrouj, 'Naila and the Uprising: Women of the First Intifada', Institute for Palestine Studies blog, 21 January 2018, https://www.palestine-studies.org/en/node/232097, accessed 21 February 2025.

47 *Ibid*.

48 Audrey Kurth Cronin, 'How fighting ends: asymmetric wars, terrorism, and suicide bombing', in Holger Afflerbach and Hew

Strachan (eds), *How Fighting Ends: A History of Surrender* (Oxford University Press, 2012), 436.

49 Baroud, *My Father Was a Freedom Fighter*, 135.

50 *Ibid.*, 131–2.

51 Yezid Sayigh, *Armed Struggle and the Search for State: The Palestinian National Movement, 1949–1993* (Clarendon Press, 1997), 635–6.

52 Ronen Bergman, *Rise and Kill First: The Secret History of Israel's Targeted Assassinations* (John Murray, 2019), 311–12.

53 Baconi, *Hamas Contained*, 27, 46.

54 Hamas' first official communiqué is available in Mishal and Aharoni, *Speaking Stones*, 201–3. The previous month, it had issued a leaflet that endorsed the intifada as an Islamic uprising but didn't yet use the name Hamas. See Baconi, *Hamas Contained*, 27; Khaled Hroub, *Hamas: Political Thought and Practice* (Institute for Palestine Studies, 2002), 265–6.

55 Lisa Hajjar, 'The Islamist movements in the Occupied Territories: an interview with Iyad Barghouti', *Middle East Report* 183 (1993), 9–12.

56 Filiu, *Gaza*, 204.

57 Hamas' Charter is reprinted in Hroub, *Hamas*, 267–91.

58 *Ibid.*

59 Filiu, *Gaza*, 205; Baconi, *Hamas Contained*, 52.

60 In the end Hamas issued more *bayans* (statements) than the UNC. See Mishal and Aharoni, *Speaking Stones*.

61 Baconi, *Hamas Contained*, 53.

62 Chloé Benoist, 'Palestinian women haunted by abuse in Israeli jails', *Middle East Eye*, 8 February 2018, https://www.middleeasteye.net/features/palestinian-women-haunted-abuse-israeli-jails, accessed 24 February 2025. See also 'Documenting the plight of Palestinian female prisoners', *Al-Monitor*, March 2013, https://www.al-monitor.com/originals/2013/03/palestinian-female-prisoners.html, accessed 24 February 2025.

63 Rema Hammami, 'Women, the hijab and the intifada,' *Middle East Report* 164/165 (1990), 24–8, 71, 78. See also Kuttab, 'Palestinian women in the "intifada"', 83; Hiltermann, 'The women's movement during the uprising', 54–5.

64 Hroub, *Hamas*, 74.

65 Sara Roy, *Hamas and Civil Society in Gaza: Engaging the Islamist Social Sector* (Princeton University Press, 2011), 29.

66 Baconi, *Hamas Contained*, 53–4.

67 Roy, *Hamas and Civil Society in Gaza*, 31.

68 Baconi, *Hamas Contained*, 56.

69 Filiu, *Gaza*, 210–11; Roy, *Hamas and Civil Society in Gaza*, 32.

70 Bergman, *Rise and Kill First*, 311–22.

71 Filiu, *Gaza*, 202.

72 Bergman, *Rise and Kill First*, 323.

73 Both Shamir and Rabin had been complicit in the war crimes of 1948. Shamir was a leader of the Lehi militia, which attacked Palestinian civilians and was one of the parties responsible for the Deir Yassin massacre. Meanwhile, as a commander in the Palmach (Haganah's elite unit) Rabin gave the direct order to expel all 50,000 Palestinians from Lydda in July 1948, resulting in a forced march in which around 1,000 people died. Survivors included George Habash, who would go on to found the PFLP, and Ismail Shammout, whom we met in Chapter Two when he displayed his art at an exhibition in 1950s Gaza. See Neve Gordon, 'On human shields', *London Review of Books*, 1 December 2023, https://www.lrb.co.uk/blog/2023/december/on-human-shields, accessed 24 February 2025; Sana Hammoudi, 'Lydda, 9–13 July 1948: A city-wide massacre culminating in the death march', *Interactive Encyclopaedia of the Palestine Question*, https://www.palquest.org/en/highlight/24073/lydda-9-13-july-1948, accessed 24 February 2025; Spiro Munayyer, 'The fall of Lydda', *Journal of Palestine Studies* 27:4 (1998), 80–98.

74 Quoted in Ilan Pappe, *The Biggest Prison on Earth: A History of the Occupied Territories* (Oneworld, 2017), 224. See also Baroud, *My Father Was a Freedom Fighter*, 133.

75 Filiu, *Gaza*, 201.

76 Pappe, *The Biggest Prison on Earth*, 222. See also 'Fatalities in the first intifada', B'Tselem, https://www.btselem.org/statistics/first_intifada_tables, accessed 24 February 2025.

77 Filiu, *Gaza*, 201.

78 For contemporaneous reports on Rabin's order see John Kifner, 'Arabs recount severe beatings by Israel troops', *New York Times*, 23 January 1988; 'Colonel says Rabin ordered breaking of Palestinians' bones', *Los Angeles Times*, 22 June 1990, https://www.latimes.com/archives/la-xpm-1990-06-22-mn-431-story.html, accessed 24 February 2025. For later analyses see Amjad Iraqi, 'The myth of Rabin the peacemaker', +972, 27 September 2020, https://www.972mag.com/yitzhak-rabin-oslo-accords-aoc/, accessed 24 February 2025.

79 Baroud, *My Father Was a Freedom Fighter*, 143.

80 *Ibid.*

81 Cited in James Garbarino and Kathleen Kostelny, 'The effects of political violence on Palestinian children's behavior problems: a risk accumulation model', *Child Development* 67:1 (1996), 34.

82 Pappe, *The Biggest Prison on Earth*, 226.

83 Swedish Save the Children, *The Status of Palestinian Children during*

the Uprising, excerpted summary material, *Journal of Palestine Studies* 19:4 (1990), 136–49.

84 Sara Roy, *Failing Peace: Gaza and the Palestinian–Israeli Conflict* (Pluto Press, 2007), 52.

85 Kuttab, 'Palestinian women in the "intifada"', 78–9.

86 Jennifer Creery, 'A life in resistance: Naila Ayesh and the women of the First Palestinian Intifada', *Hong Kong Free Press*, 30 March 2019, https://hongkongfp.com/2019/03/30/life-resistance-naila-ayesh-women-first-palestinian-intifada/, accessed 24 February 2025.

87 Pappe, *The Biggest Prison on Earth*, 235; Filiu, *Gaza*, 202.

88 Filiu, *Gaza*, 216. The deportations led to the first ever joint UNC–Hamas communiqué, calling for the deportees' unconditional repatriation.

89 Pappe, *The Biggest Prison on Earth*, 231.

90 Asmaa al-Ghoul and Selim Nassib, *A Rebel in Gaza: Behind the Lines of the Arab Spring, One Woman's Story* (DoppelHouse Press, 2018), 20.

91 Filiu, *Gaza*, 208.

92 Collective punishment is illegal under international law: see Article 50, Convention (IV) respecting the Laws and Customs of War on Land and its annex: Regulations concerning the Laws and Customs of War on Land, The Hague, 18 October 1907; Article 33, Convention (IV) relative to the Protection of Civilian Persons in Time of War. Geneva, 12 August 1949.

93 Pappe, *The Biggest Prison on Earth*, 237.

94 Madeeha Hafez Albatta, *A White Lie* (University of Alberta Press, 2020), 118; Pappe, *The Biggest Prison on Earth*, 231.

95 Filiu, *Gaza*, 208.

96 Baroud, *My Father Was a Freedom Fighter*, 137.

97 'Divide and rule: prohibition on passage between the Gaza Strip and the West Bank', B'Tselem, May 1998, https://www.btselem.org/sites/default/files/sites/default/files2/publication/199805_divide_and_rule_eng.pdf, accessed 24 February 2025.

98 *Ibid.*

99 Pappe, *The Biggest Prison on Earth*, 237.

100 Baroud, *My Father Was a Freedom Fighter*, 150.

101 Roy, *Failing Peace*, 43–5.

102 Filiu, *Gaza*, 206, 222.

103 For Palestinian population statistics, see Population and demographic developments in the West Bank and Gaza Strip until 1990: a study prepared by Wael R. Ennab, 28 June 1994, TD/JUNCTAD/ECDC/SEU/1.

104 Pappe, *The Biggest Prison on Earth*, 241.

105 Filiu, *Gaza*, 208.

106 Mark Tessler, *A History of the Israeli–Palestinian Conflict*, 2nd ed. (Indiana University Press, 2009), 749.

107 Roy, *Hamas and Civil Society in Gaza*, 32.

108 Pappe, *The Biggest Prison on Earth*, 238.

109 Al-Barbari, *Light the Road of Freedom*, 78–9.

110 Kurth Cronin, 'How fighting ends', 426.

111 Filiu, *Gaza*, 201.

112 Roni C. Rabin, 'Israeli TV's editing brings harsh questions', *New York Times*, 3 March 1988, https://www.nytimes.com/1988/03/03/world/israeli-tv-s-editing-brings-harsh-questions.html, accessed 24 February 2025.

113 Country Reports on Human Rights Practices for 1988: Report submitted to the Committee on Foreign Affairs, US House of Representatives and Committee on Foreign Relations, US Senate by the Department of State.

114 UN Security Council Resolution 605, S/RES/605, 22 December 1987.

115 UN Security Council Resolution 799, S/RES/799, 18 December 1992.

116 Address to the nation, Amman, 31 July 1988, http://www.kinghussein.gov.jo/88_july31.html, accessed 24 February 2025.

117 Filiu, *Gaza*, 199.

118 Palestinian Declaration of Independence, 15 November 1988, https://www.palquest.org/en/historictext/9673/palestinian-declaration-independence, accessed 24 February 2025.

119 Edward Said, 'From intifadah to independence', *Middle East Report* 158 (1989), 12–16.

120 Filiu, *Gaza*, 215.

121 Roy, *Hamas and Civil Society in Gaza*, 27–8.

122 Seth Anziska, *Preventing Palestine: A Political History from Camp David to Oslo* (Princeton University Press, 2018), 263–5.

123 Filiu, *Gaza*, 199.

124 Tessler, *A History of the Israeli–Palestinian Conflict*, 747.

125 Idith Zertal and Akiva Eldar, *Lords of the Land: The War over Israel's Settlements in the Occupied Territories*, trans. Vivian Eden (Bold Type, 2007), 104–14.

126 Quoted in Mark Tessler, 'The intifada and political discourse in Israel', *Journal of Palestine Studies* 19:2 (1990), 45.

127 'Fatalities in the first intifada'.

128 Itamar Rabinovich, *Yitzhak Rabin: Soldier, Leader, Statesman* (Yale University Press, 2017), 157–8.

129 Filiu, *Gaza*, 218.

130 Donald Macintyre, *Gaza: Preparing for Dawn* (Oneworld, 2017), 36.

131 Rashid Khalidi, *Brokers of Deceit: How the US Has Undermined Peace in the Middle East* (Beacon Press, 2013), 49–50.

132 Filiu, *Gaza*, 213.

133 Excerpt from speech of Haidar Abd al-Shafi at the Madrid Conference, 31 October 1991, https://www.palquest.org/en/historictext/23288/speech-haydar-abd-al-shafi-madrid-conference, accessed 24 February 2025.

134 Sayigh, *Armed Struggle and the Search for State*, 651–2.

135 Anne Irfan, 'Palestine in exile: blurring the boundaries and recreating the homeland', in Tamar Mayer and Trin Tranh (eds), *Displacement, Belonging, and Migrant Agency in the Face of Power* (Routledge, 2022), 202.

136 Roy, *Failing Peace*, 43–5.

137 Khalidi, *The Hundred Years War on Palestine*, 184.

138 For detailed discussion and analysis of the negotiations in the early 1990s, see Noura Erakat, *Justice for Some: Law and the Question of Palestine* (Stanford University Press, 2019), 144–66.

139 Khalidi, *The Hundred Years War on Palestine*, 100.

140 Erakat, *Justice for Some*, 164.

141 Declaration of Principles on Interim Self-Government Arrangements (The Oslo Agreement), https://www.un.org/unispal/document/auto-insert-180015/, accessed 24 February 2025.

142 Filiu, *Gaza*, 219.

Chapter Five:
The Oslo Years

1 Said K. Aburish, *Arafat: From Defender to Dictator* (Bloomsbury, 1999), 275–6.

2 'Yasser Arafat: facts', Nobel Prize, https://www.nobelprize.org/prizes/peace/1994/arafat/facts/, accessed 24 February 2025.

3 Sara Roy, '"The seed of chaos, and of night": the Gaza Strip after the agreement', *Journal of Palestine Studies* 23:3 (1994), 85–98.

4 On the parallels between Camp David and Oslo, see Seth Anziska, *Preventing Palestine: A Political History from Camp David to Oslo* (Princeton University Press, 2018).

5 Agreement on the Gaza Strip and the Jericho Area, Cairo, 4 May 1994.

6 Hussein Agha and Ahmed Samih Khalidi, 'Yasser Arafat: why he still matters', *The Guardian*, 13 November 2014, https://www.theguardian.com/news/2014/nov/13/-sp-yasser-arafat-why-he-still-matters, accessed 20 February 2025.

7   Jean-Pierre Filiu, *Gaza: A History* (Hurst, 2015), 225.

8   Quoted in: Aburish, *Arafat*, 268.

9   Rashid Khalidi, *The Hundred Years War on Palestine: A History of Settler Colonial Conquest and Resistance* (Profile, 2020), 204.

10 Filiu, *Gaza*, 223.

11 Zahra Hankir, '"My story is one of many": the Palestinian women behind the first intifada', *Middle East Eye*, 15 March 2018, https://www.middleeasteye.net/features/my-story-one-many-palestinian-women-behind-first-intifada, accessed 24 February 2025.

12 Edward Said, 'The morning after', *London Review of Books*, 21 October 1993, https://www.lrb.co.uk/the-paper/v15/n20/edward-said/the-morning-after, accessed 24 February 2025.

13 On opposition to Oslo in the refugee camps, see Julie Peteet, *Landscape of Hope and Despair: Palestinian Refugee Camps* (University of Pennsylvania Press, 2011), 209–13. On the camps' centrality to the Palestinian struggle in earlier decades, see Anne Irfan, *Refuge and Resistance: Palestinians and the International Refugee System* (Columbia University Press, 2023), ch. 2.

14 Ilan Pappe, *The Biggest Prison on Earth: A History of the Occupied Territories* (Oneworld, 2017), 253.

15 Hermann and Ephraim Yuchtman-Yaar, 'Divided yet united: Israeli-Jewish attitudes toward the Oslo process', *Journal of Peace Research* 39:5 (2002), 602.

16 Nur Masalha, *Imperial Israel and the Palestinians: The Politics of Expansion* (Pluto Press, 2000), 99.

17 Joshua Leifer, 'The Netanyahu doctrine: how Israel's longest-serving leader reshaped the country in his image', *The Guardian*, 21 November 2023, https://www.theguardian.com/world/2023/nov/21/the-netanyahu-doctrine-how-israels-longest-serving-leader-reshaped-the-country-in-his-image, accessed 24 February 2025.

18 The Ibrahimi mosque is part of the Cave of the Patriarchs, which had long been a point of contention. It was shared as a place of worship between Israelis and Palestinians on an unequal basis, with the time and space allocated to around 120,000 local Muslims curtailed in favour of fewer than 3,000 Jewish settlers.

19 Edward Said, 'Reflections on the Hebron massacre', *London Review of Books*, 7 April 1994, https://www.lrb.co.uk/the-paper/v16/n07/edward-said/diary, accessed 24 February 2025.

20 Itamar Ben-Gvir, who was elected to the Knesset in 2021 and became Israel's national security minister the following year, is an open supporter of Goldstein, whose framed photo hung on his wall until political pressure forced him to take it down in 2020. In 2023,

Ben-Gvir spoke at a memorial event for Goldstein, whom he described as a 'martyr'.

21 Amira Hass, *Drinking the Sea at Gaza: Days and Nights in a Land under Siege*, trans. Elana Wesley and Maxine Kaufman-Lacusta (Henry Holt, 1999), 23–4.

22 Filiu, *Gaza*, 234.

23 Idith Zertal and Akiva Eldar, *Lords of the Land: The War over Israel's Settlements in the Occupied Territories*, trans. Vivian Eden (Bold Type, 2007), 122.

24 Mia Bloom, *Dying to Kill: The Allure of Suicide Terror* (Columbia University Press, 2005), 20.

25 Tareq Baconi, *Hamas Contained: The Rise and Pacification of Palestinian Resistance* (Stanford University Press, 2018), 57–8.

26 Khalidi, *The Hundred Years War on Palestine*, 214. On Palestinian opposition to suicide bombings, see Bloom, *Dying to Kill*, 25; Lori Allen, 'There are many reasons why: suicide bombers and martyrs in Palestine', *Middle East Report* 223 (2002), 34–7.

27 Zertal and Eldar, *Lords of the Land*, 122–3.

28 'Israeli Election Results – May 1996', https://embassies.gov.il/MFA/AboutIsrael/history/Pages/Israeli%20Election%20Results-%20May%201996.aspx , accessed 24 February 2025.

29 Ahmad S. Khalidi, 'The Palestinians' first excursion into democracy', *Journal of Palestine Studies* 25:4 (1996), 25; Baconi, *Hamas Contained*, 61. See Aburish, *Arafat*, 263.

30 As'ad Ghanem, 'Founding elections in a transitional period: the first Palestinian general elections', *Middle East Journal* 50:4 (1996), 525.

31 *Ibid.*, 527.

32 Hass, *Drinking the Sea at Gaza*, 27.

33 Filiu, *Gaza*, 237.

34 *The January 20, 1996 Palestinian Elections* (National Democratic Institute for International Affairs / Carter Center, 1997), https://www.cartercenter.org/documents/electionreports/democracy/FinalReportPalestine1996.pdf, accessed 24 February 2025.

35 Sara Roy, 'Palestinian society and economy: the continued denial of possibility', *Journal of Palestine Studies* 30:4 (2001), 5–6.

36 Hass, *Drinking the Sea at Gaza*, 18–24.

37 Marcello Di Cintio, 'A climate of sorrow', PEN Canada, 8 April 2024, https://pencanada.ca/blog/a-climate-of-sorrow/, accessed 24 February 2025.

38 David Hirst, 'Shameless in Gaza', *The Guardian*, 19 May 1997.

39 Sahbaa al-Barbari, *Light the Road of Freedom* (University of Alberta Press, 2021), 90.

40 Nidal al-Mughrabi, 'Travel agency in isolated Gaza recalls the "golden" 1950s', Reuters, 5 February 2016, https://www.reuters.com/article/lifestyle/travel-agency-in-isolated-gaza-recalls-the-golden-1950s-idUSKCN0VE17Q/, accessed 24 February 2025; Donald Macintyre, 'Who'd be a travel agent in Gaza?', *The Independent*, 16 July 2010, https://www.independent.co.uk/news/world/middle-east/who-d-be-a-travel-agent-in-gaza-2027723.html., accessed 24 February 2025. See also Donald Macintyre, *Gaza: Preparing for Dawn* (Oneworld, 2017), 260–2.

41 Deborah Sontag, 'Palestinians walking on air at opening of Gaza airport', *New York Times*, 25 November 1998.

42 Al-Barbari, *Light the Road of Freedom*, 87–9.

43 Aburish, *Arafat*, 268, 285.

44 Roy, 'Palestinian society and economy', 7.

45 Roy, '"The seed of chaos, and of night"', 86.

46 Sharif Elmusa, 'When the wellsprings of identity dry up: reflections on Fawaz Turki's *Exile's Return*', *Journal of Palestine Studies* 25:1 (1995), 98.

47 Ramzy Baroud, *My Father Was a Freedom Fighter: Gaza's Untold Story* (Pluto Press, 2010), 157.

48 Hass, *Drinking the Sea at Gaza*, 53.

49 Hirst, 'Shameless in Gaza'.

50 Baroud, *My Father was a Freedom Fighter*, 157; Khalidi, *The Hundred Years War on Palestine*, 207.

51 Filiu, *Gaza*, 238.

52 Quoted *ibid.*, 219.

53 Roy, 'Palestinian society and economy', 7.

54 Filiu, *Gaza*, 231.

55 Aburish, *Arafat*, 288.

56 Filiu, *Gaza*, 236.

57 Khalidi, *The Hundred Years War on Palestine*, 205; Baconi, *Hamas Contained*, 59.

58 Filiu, *Gaza*, 230; Aburish, *Arafat*, 287.

59 Edgar O'Ballance, *The Palestinian Intifada* (Macmillan, 1998), 185.

60 Filiu, *Gaza*, 230, 241.

61 Roy, 'Palestinian society and economy', 6–7.

62 Aburish, *Arafat*, 304.

63 Roy, '"The seed of chaos, and of night"', 94–5; Roy, 'Palestinian society and economy', 12.

64 Roy, 'Palestinian society and economy', 8.

65 Aburish, *Arafat*, 289, 310–12.

66 'Palestinian Authority: Prisoner of conscience/legal concern: Fathi Subuh', Index no. MDE 21/003/1997, Amnesty International, 9 July

1997, https://www.amnesty.org/en/documents/mde21/003/1997/
en/, accessed 24 February 2025.

67   Aburish, *Arafat*, 314.

68   Khalidi, *The Hundred Years War on Palestine*, 214.

69   Aburish, *Arafat*, 312.

70   Filiu, *Gaza*, 241.

71   Baroud, *My Father Was a Freedom Fighter*, 154.

72   Said, 'The morning after'.

73   Roy, '"The seed of chaos, and of night"', 95.

74   Aburish, *Arafat*, 264.

75   Graham Usher, *Palestine in Crisis: The Struggle for Peace and Political Independence after Oslo* (Pluto Press, 1995), 15–16.

76   Hass, *Drinking the Sea at Gaza*, 58.

77   *Ibid.*, 25.

78   Baroud, *My Father Was a Freedom Fighter*, 156.

79   Roy, 'Palestinian society and economy', 68.

80   'Conquer and Divide: the Gaza perimeter fence', B'Tselem, https://conquer-and-divide.btselem.org/map-en.html, accessed 24 February 2025.

81   Khalidi, *The Hundred Years War on Palestine*, 203.

82   Baroud, *My Father Was a Freedom Fighter*, 155.

83   Amira Hass, 'Israel's closure policy: an ineffective strategy of containment and repression', *Journal of Palestine Studies* 31:3 (2002), 10.

84   Sara Roy, 'De-development revisited: Palestinian economy and society since Oslo', *Journal of Palestine Studies* 28:3 (1999), 74.

85   Hass, 'Israel's closure policy', 8.

86   Khalidi, *The Hundred Years War on Palestine*, 207–9.

87   *Ibid.*, 208.

88   Filiu, *Gaza*, 243.

89   Roy, 'De-development revisited', 69.

90   Protocol on Economic Relations between the Government of the State of Israel and the PLO, representing the Palestinian people, Annex IV of the Gaza–Jericho Agreement, 29 April 1994.

91   Roy, 'De-development revisited', 69.

92   Roy, 'Palestinian society and economy', 11–12.

93   US Department of State, 'Inverted cornucopia: worsening performance of Gaza's agricultural exports', quoted in Roy, 'De-development revisited', 75.

94   Hass, 'Israel's closure policy', 9.

95   Hass, *Drinking the Sea at Gaza*, 28.

96   Amjad Iraqi, 'The myth of Rabin the peacemaker', +972, 27 September 2020, https://www.972mag.com/yitzhak-rabin-oslo-accords-aoc/, accessed 24 February 2025.

97   Filiu, *Gaza*, 224.

98   'Construction starts in settlements by year', Peace Now, https://
peacenow.org.il/en/settlements-watch/settlements-data/construction,
accessed 24 February 2025. See also Aburish, *Arafat*, 269.

99   Aburish, *Arafat*, 299.

100   Masalha, *Imperial Israel and the Palestinians*, 101.

101   Gershom Gorenberg, *The Accidental Empire: Israel and the Birth of the
Settlements, 1967–1977* (Times, 2006), Kindle loc. 6934.

102   Ahron Bregman, *Cursed Victory: A History of Israel and the Occupied
Territories* (Allen Lane, 2014), 248.

103   Baroud, *My Father Was a Freedom Fighter*, 167.

104   Zertal and Eldar, *Lords of the Land*, 389.

105   Pappe, *The Biggest Prison on Earth*, 259.

106   The Palestine Papers, https://transparency.aljazeera.net/en/projects/
thepalestinepapers/, accessed 17 October 2024. See also Robert
Malley and Hussein Agha, 'Camp David: The Tragedy of Errors',
New York Review of Books, 9 August 2001, https://www.nybooks.
com/articles/2001/08/09/camp-david-the-tragedy-of-errors/,
accessed 25 February 2025.

107   Khalidi, *The Hundred Years War on Palestine*, 211; Pappe, *The Biggest
Prison on Earth*, 248–53. On Barak's long-running hostility to Oslo,
see Bregman, *Cursed Victory*, 217.

108   'Barak's victory speech', BBC News, 18 May 1999, http://news.bbc.
co.uk/1/hi/world/monitoring/346507.stm, accessed 25 February 2025.

109   Baconi, *Hamas Contained*, 65.

110   For a summary of Sharon's crimes against Palestinians, see Zertal
and Eldar, *Lords of the Land*, 408.

111   Baroud, *My Father Was a Freedom Fighter*, 166.

112   Suzanne Goldenberg, 'Rioting as Sharon visits Islam holy site', *The
Guardian*, 29 September 2000, https://www.theguardian.com/
world/2000/sep/29/israel, accessed 25 February 2025.

113   Baconi, *Hamas Contained*, 66.

114   Reuven Pedatzur, 'More than a million bullets', *Haaretz*, 29 June
2004, https://www.haaretz.com/2004-06-29/ty-article/more-than-a-
million-bullets/0000017f-dbb5-df62-a9ff-dff7bd500000, accessed 25
February 2025.

115   Bregman, *Cursed Victory*, 250.

116   Zertal and Eldar, *Lords of the Land*, 412.

117   Baconi, *Hamas Contained*, 67.

118   *Ibid.*, 71–5.

119   Khalidi, *The Hundred Years War on Palestine*, 214.

120   B'Tselem data on fatalities, https://statistics.btselem.org/
en/stats/before-cast-lead/by-date-of-incident?section=

overall&tab=overview&dateSensor=%22970192800000
%2C1130367599000%22, accessed 25 February 2025.

121   Zertal and Eldar, *Lords of the Land*, 420.

122   Khalidi, *The Hundred Years War on Palestine*, 216.

123   Baconi, *Hamas Contained*, 76, 80–7, 91, 94.

124   For the full contents of the API, see AFP, 'Text of Arab peace initiative adopted at Beirut summit', available at https://www.europarl.europa.eu/meetdocs/2009_2014/documents/empa/dv/1_arab-initiative-beirut_/1_arab-initiative-beirut_en.pdf, accessed 25 February 2025.

125   Baconi, *Hamas Contained*, 84.

126   B'Tselem data on fatalities, https://statistics.btselem.org/en/stats/before-cast-lead/by-date-of-incident?section=overall&tab=overview&dateSensor=%22970192800000,1130367599000%22, accessed 25 February 2025.

127   Baroud, *My Father Was a Freedom Fighter*, 171.

128   Filiu, *Gaza*, 265.

129   *Ibid.*, 259.

130   Al-Barbari, *Light the Road of Freedom*, 89.

131   Roy, 'Palestinian economy and society', 14.

132   Baroud, *My Father Was a Freedom Fighter*, 165.

133   Filiu, *Gaza*, 258.

134   OCHA report, 'Humanitarian situation update: Northern Gaza', 12 October 2004, https://www.un.org/unispal/document/auto-insert-205525/, accessed 25 February 2025.

135   'Tanks attack Palestinian refugee site', *The Guardian*, 11 April 2001, https://amp.theguardian.com/world/2001/apr/11/israel, accessed 25 February 2025.

136   Address by Prime Minister Ariel Sharon at the Fourth Herzliya Conference, 18 December 2003, CIE, https://israeled.org/resources/documents/address-by-prime-minister-ariel-sharon-at-the-fourth-herzliya-conference/, accessed 25 February 2025.

137   See for example 'Israel's unlikely dove', *The Economist*, 21 October 2004.

138   As'ad Ghanem, 'A new phase in Israel's approach to the Palestinian question', *Palestine–Israel Journal* 13:2 (2006), 35–41. See also Rob Geist Pinfold, *Understanding Territorial Withdrawal: Israeli Occupations and Exits* (Oxford University Press, 2023), ch. 4.

139   David Landau, *Arik: The Life of Ariel Sharon* (Alfred A. Knopf, 2014), 445.

140   Daphna Baram, 'Disengagement and ethnic cleansing', *The Guardian*, 16 August 2005, https://www.theguardian.com/world/2005/aug/16/comment.israelandthepalestinians, accessed 25 February 2025.

141   Address by Sharon at the Fourth Herzliya Conference.

142   Quoted in Zertal and Eldar, *Lords of the Land*, 446.

143   Ari Shavit, 'The big freeze', *Haaretz*, 7 October 2004, https://www.
      haaretz.com/2004-10-07/ty-article/the-big-freeze/0000017f-e597-
      d62c-a1ff-fdffe50c0000, accessed 25 February 2025.

144   *Ibid.*

145   *Ibid.*

146   On Israeli calculations behind the withdrawal from southern
      Lebanon, see Geist Pinfold, *Understanding Territorial Withdrawal*, ch. 3.
      On the role of Hizbollah, see Augustus Richard Norton, 'Hizballah
      and the Israeli withdrawal from Southern Lebanon', *Journal of
      Palestine Studies* 30:1 (2000), 22–35. See also Augustus R. Norton,
      Hezbollah: A Short History, new ed. (Princeton University Press,
      2014), 79–92.

147   Baconi, *Hamas Contained*, 64, 99.

148   *Ibid.*, 100–4.

149   On the assassinations of Yassin and Rantisi, see Ronen Bergman,
      Rise and Kill First: The Secret History of Israel's Targeted Assassinations
      (John Murray, 2019), 552–7.

150   On this aspect of the Yassin assassination, see Bergman, *Rise and Kill
      First*, 564–5.

151   Coby Ben-Simhon, '"Israel could have made peace with Hamas
      under Yassin"', *Haaretz*, 16 April 2009, https://www.haaretz.
      com/2009-04-16/ty-article/israel-could-have-made-peace-with-
      hamas-under-yassin/0000017f-e383-d7b2-a77f-e387ade40000,
      accessed 25 February 2025.

152   Suspicions that Arafat was poisoned have never gone away. The
      Israeli journalist Ronen Bergman gained unprecedented access to
      the records of Israel's security services for his research into their
      targeted assassinations. Discussing Arafat's death, he notes that Sharon
      saw the PA president as an irredeemable obstacle to his vision for
      the region and considered exiling him permanently. He adds that
      traces of polonium were found on Arafat's clothes and remains.
      Bergman goes on to say, 'If I knew the answer to the question of
      what killed Yasser Arafat, I wouldn't be able to write it here in this
      book, or even be able to write that I know the answer. The military
      censor in Israel forbids me from discussing this subject.' Bergman,
      Rise and Kill First, 558–63.

153   Baconi, *Hamas Contained*, 129. See also Sara Roy, *Hamas and Civil
      Society in Gaza: Engaging the Islamist Social Sector* (Princeton
      University Press, 2011), ch. 4.

154   For more on Arafat's death, see Marian Houk, 'More subtle than it
      seems: The mystery of Arafat's death', *+972*, 18 November 2013,

https://www.972mag.com/more-subtle-than-it-seems-behind-the-mystery-of-arafats-death/, accessed 25 February 2025.

155 Filiu, *Gaza*, 262–7.

156 Baconi, *Hamas Contained,* 89. See also 'Abbas gives up premiership', Al Jazeera, 7 September 2003, https://www.aljazeera.com/news/2003/9/7/abbas-gives-up-premiership, accessed 25 February 2025.

157 Filiu, *Gaza*, 224.

158 Khalidi, *The Hundred Years War on Palestine*, 217.

159 For the full results, see https://www.elections.ps/Portals/30/pdf/PE2005-ResultsSummary_AR.pdf [Arabic], accessed 25 February 2025.

160 Sharm el-Sheikh Summit – PNA President Abbas' Declaration, accessible via https://ecf.org.il/media_items/1101

161 Bregman, *Cursed Victory*, 299; Filiu, *Gaza*, 286.

162 Asmaa al-Ghoul and Selim Nassib, *A Rebel in Gaza: Behind the Lines of the Arab Spring, One Woman's Story* (DoppelHouse Press, 2018), 84.

163 Nicolas Pelham, 'Gaza's tunnel phenomenon: the unintended dynamics of Israel's siege', *Journal of Palestine Studies* 41:4 (2012), 8.

164 Baconi, *Hamas Contained*, 106.

165 Filiu, *Gaza*, 285.

166 Avi Shlaim, 'How Israel brought Gaza to the brink of humanitarian catastrophe', *The Guardian*, 7 January 2009, https://www.theguardian.com/world/2009/jan/07/gaza-israel-palestine, accessed 25 February 2025.

167 *Disengaged Occupiers: The Legal Status of Gaza*, Gisha, January 2007, https://gisha.org/en/disengaged-occupiers-the-legal-status-of-gaza/, accessed 25 February 2025.

168 Bregman, *Cursed Victory*, 302; Darryl Li, 'Gaza at the frontiers of Zionism', in Helga Tawil-Souri and Dina Matar (eds), *Gaza as Metaphor* (Hurst, 2016), 190.

169 On Israel's continuing occupation of Gaza after 2005, see Safaa Sadi Jaber and Ilias Bantekas, 'The status of Gaza as occupied territory under international law', *International & Comparative Law Quarterly* 72:4 (2023), 1069–88; Shane Darcy and John Reynolds, 'An enduring occupation: the status of the Gaza Strip from the perspective of international humanitarian law', *Journal of Conflict & Security Law* 15:2 (2010), 211–43; Iain Scobbie, 'An intimate disengagement: Israel's withdrawal from Gaza, the law of occupation, and of self-determination', *Yearbook of Islamic and Middle Eastern Law Online* 11 (2004), 3–31. See also Lisa Hajjar, 'Is Gaza still occupied and why does it matter?', *Jadaliyya*, 14 July 2014, https://www.jadaliyya.com/Details/27557/Is-Gaza-Still-Occupied-and-Why-Does-It-Matter, accessed 25 February 2025; Michael Schaeffer

Omer-Man, 'Is Gaza still occupied? New video aims to settle the debate', *+972*, 25 October 2015, https://www.972mag.com/is-gaza-still-occupied-al-jazeera-video-aims-to-settle-the-debate/, accessed 25 February 2025.

170 Roy, 'Palestinian society and economy', 6, 14.

171 B'Tselem data on fatalities, https://statistics.btselem.org/en/stats/before-cast-lead/by-date-of-incident?section=overall&tab=overview&dateSensor=%22970192800000,1130367599000%22, accessed 25 February 2025.

Chapter Six:
The Rise of Hamas

1 Jean-Pierre Filiu, *Gaza: A History* (Hurst, 2015), 283.

2 For the full list of results, see https://www.elections.ps/tabid/237/language/en-US/Default.aspx, accessed 19 May 2025.

3 The Cairo Declaration (2005), available at https://ecf.org.il/issues/issue/1165, accessed 14 March 2025.

4 Paola Caridi, *Hamas: From Resistance to Government* (Seven Stories Press, 2012), 173–4.

5 Tareq Baconi, *Hamas Contained: The Pacification of a Resistance Movement* (Stanford University Press, 2018), 118–21. See also Khaled Hroub, 'A "new Hamas" through its documents', *Journal of Palestine Studies* 35:4 (2006), 8–9; Arnon Regular, 'Hamas' Zahar: More kidnappings if Israel doesn't release political prisoners', *Haaretz*, 26 October 2005, https://www.haaretz.com/2005-10-26/ty-article/hamas-zahar-more-kidnappings-if-israel-doesnt-release-prisoners/0000017f-f44b-d5bd-a17f-f67b6c130000, accessed 14 March 2025.

6 On US overtures to Qatar about Hamas, see 'Hamad bin Jassim yakshif an dor Qatar fi aqna' Hamas balmusharaka fi al-intikhabat, Sama News, 9 March 2022, https://shorturl.at/o4CXn [Arabic], accessed 21 February 2025; 'Qatar persuaded Hamas to participate in 2006 elections, ex-PM says', *Middle East Monitor*, 10 March 2022, https://www.middleeastmonitor.com/20220310-qatar-persuaded-hamas-to-participate-in-2006-elections-ex-pm-says/, accessed 14 March 2025.

7 For example, in 2012 the Qadima activist Gilad Sharon (son of Ariel) wrote, 'The residents of Gaza are not innocent, they elected Hamas . . . they chose this freely and must live with the consequences.' See Gilad Sharon, 'A decisive conclusion is necessary', *Jerusalem Post*, 18 November 2012, https://www.jpost.com/opinion/

op-ed-contributors/a-decisive-conclusion-is-necessary, accessed 14 March 2025.

8 The full breakdown of the electoral results is available at https://www.elections.ps/Portals/0/pdf/Votes%20for%20lists%20 per%20districts.pdf, accessed 14 March 2025.

9 The equivalent figures for the West Bank were 23.6 per cent and 35.6 per cent respectively. See Jamil Hilal, 'Hamas' rise as charted in the polls, 1994–2005', *Journal of Palestine Studies* 35:3 (2006), 7.

10 Hroub, 'A "new Hamas" through its documents', 10–13.

11 'The Hamas conundrum', *The Economist*, 10 November 2005, https://www.economist.com/middle-east-and-africa/2005/11/10/ the-hamas-conundrum, accessed 14 March 2025.

12 Regular, 'Hamas' Zahar'.

13 Baconi, *Hamas Contained*, 135. See also Steven R. Weisman, 'Bush defends his goal of spreading democracy to the Mideast', *New York Times*, 27 January 2006, https://www.nytimes.com/2006/01/27/ politics/bush-defends-his-goal-of-spreading-democracy-to-the-mideast.html, accessed 14 March 2025.

14 Exit poll conducted by Near East Consulting. See https://www. neareastconsulting.com/plc2006/blmain.html, accessed 14 March 2025.

15 Graham Usher, *Palestine in Crisis: The Struggle for Peace and Political Independence after Oslo* (Pluto Press, 1995), 34.

16 Weisman, 'Bush defends his goal of spreading democracy to the Mideast'.

17 Ilan Halevi, 'Self-government, democracy, and mismanagement under the Palestinian Authority', *Journal of Palestine Studies* 27:3 (1998), 35–48.

18 Amira Hass, *Reporting from Ramallah: An Israeli Journalist in an Occupied Land* (Semiotext(e), 2003), 110, 129.

19 Amira Hass, *Drinking the Sea at Gaza: Days and Nights in a Land Under Siege*, trans. Elana Wesley and Maxine Kaufman-Lacusta (Henry Holt, 1999), 112. See also Hussein Hijazi, 'Hamas: waiting for secular nationalism to self-destruct – an interview with Mahmud Zahhar', *Journal of Palestine Studies* 24:3 (1995), 81–8.

20 Asmaa al-Ghoul and Selim Nassib, *A Rebel in Gaza: Behind the Lines of the Arab Spring, One Woman's Story* (DoppelHouse Press, 2018), 86.

21 Helga Baumgarten, 'The Three Faces/Phases of Palestinian nationalism, 1948-2005', *Journal of Palestine Studies* 34:4 (2005), 40.

22 Sara Roy, '"The seed of chaos, and of night:": the Gaza Strip after the agreement', *Journal of Palestine Studies* 23:3 (1994), 89.

23 Baconi, *Hamas Contained*, 129.

24 Mohammad Dajani, 'Lessons from the Gaza disengagement',

Palestine–Israel Journal of Politics, Economics and Culture 13:2 (2006), 13–17.

25 Filiu, *Gaza*, 279, 286–7.

26 Regular, 'Hamas' Zahar'.

27 Ahron Bregman, *Cursed Victory: A History of Israel and the Occupied Territories* (Allen Lane, 2014), 302. For human rights organisations' condemnation of the rockets, see 'Gaza: Palestinian rockets unlawfully targeted Israeli civilians', Human Rights Watch, 24 December 2012, https://www.hrw.org/news/2012/12/24/gaza-palestinian-rockets-unlawfully-targeted-israeli-civilians; 'Targeting of Israeli civilians by Palestinians', B'Tselem, 11 November 2017, https://www.btselem.org/israeli_civilians#data; both accessed 14 March 2025.

28 In the same period, two Palestinian suicide bombers from the West Bank killed twelve Israeli civilians. and Israeli forces killed forty-five Palestinians in the West Bank. Statistics taken from B'Tselem.

29 'Israel/Occupied Territories: Concerns at growing lawlessness in Gaza', Public Statement 15/046/2005, Amnesty International, 12 August 2005.

30 For Hamas' campaign platform, see 'Change and Reform List', Hamas' manifesto for the January 2006 legislative elections. See also 'Enter Hamas: The challenges of political integration', International Crisis Group, 18 January 2006, https://www.crisisgroup.org/middle-east-north-africa/eastern-mediterranean/israelpalestine/enter-hamas-challenges-political-integration, accessed 14 March 2025; Baconi, *Hamas Contained*, 131.

31 Sharon remained in a coma for eight years and eventually died in January 2014. He was buried on his family ranch, located on the former site of Huj village, from which Izzeldin Abuelaish's family had been expelled during the Nakba. See Olivia Ward, 'Palestinian history buried with Ariel Sharon', *Toronto Star*, 14 January 2014; Izzeldin Abuelaish, *I Shall Not Hate: A Gaza Doctor's Journey on the Road to Peace and Human Dignity* (Bloomsbury, 2011), 30–2.

32 Baconi, *Hamas Contained*, 136. See also Sara Roy, *Hamas and Civil Society in Gaza: Engaging the Islamist Social Sector* (Princeton University Press, 2011), 39–50; Filiu, *Gaza*, 291.

33 Conal Urquhart, 'Gaza on brink of implosion as aid cut-off starts to bite', *The Observer*, 16 April 2006, https://www.theguardian.com/world/2006/apr/16/israel, accessed 14 March 2025.

34 Filiu, *Gaza*, 291.

35 *Ibid.*

36 See for example Mousa Abu Marzook, 'What Hamas is seeking', *Washington Post*, 30 January 2006, https://www.washingtonpost.com/archive/opinions/2006/01/31/what-hamas-is-seeking/

293fce5e-00b0-4f4d-a271-e8c635c53061/; 'We do not wish to throw them into the sea', *Washington Post*, 25 February 2006, https://www.washingtonpost.com/archive/opinions/2006/02/26/we-do-not-wish-to-throw-them-into-the-sea/56c26504-1608-4d18-b118-ba89ed4ffb66/; both accessed 14 March 2025.

37 Conal Urquhart, 'Hamas in call to end suicide bombings', *The Observer*, 9 April 2006, https://www.theguardian.com/world/2006/apr/09/israel, accessed 14 March 2025.

38 Barak Ravid and Haaretz Correspondent, 'In 2006 letter to Bush, Haniyeh offered compromise with Israel', *Haaretz*, 14 November 2008, https://www.haaretz.com/2008-11-14/ty-article/in-2006-letter-to-bush-haniyeh-offered-compromise-with-israel/0000017f-f4c5-d47e-a37f-fdfd0abb0000, accessed 14 March 2025.

39 Baconi, *Hamas Contained*, 136.

40 Filiu, *Gaza*, 291–4; Baconi, *Hamas Contained*, 151–2.

41 David Rose, 'The Gaza bombshell', *Vanity Fair*, 3 March 2008, https://www.vanityfair.com/news/2008/04/gaza200804?srsltid=AfmBOor4IxUnHlxy_EbQa7fTevQcY7UXVB-tzhVe9_W7BEpPfpY1zzf3, accessed 14 March 2025.

42 Filiu, *Gaza*, 294.

43 Ilan Pappe, *The Biggest Prison on Earth: A History of the Occupied Territories* (Oneworld, 2017), 273.

44 Filiu, *Gaza*, 294.

45 Michele K. Esposito, 'Quarterly update on conflict and diplomacy', *Journal of Palestine Studies* 36:1 (2006), 124. On the bombing of the power plant, see Darryl Li, 'Gaza at the frontiers of Zionism', in Helga Tawil-Souri and Dina Matar (eds), *Gaza as Metaphor* (Hurst, 2016), 190.

46 Figures sourced from B'Tselem.

47 Rose, 'The Gaza bombshell'.

48 Al-Ghoul and Nassib, *A Rebel in Gaza*, 88–9.

49 Figures sourced from B'Tselem.

50 Filiu, *Gaza*, 300.

51 *Ibid.*, 302.

52 Yaakov Katz, 'Yadlin: Israel would be "happy" if Hamas takes over Gaza', *Jerusalem Post*, 21 December 2010, https://www.jpost.com/defense/yadlin-israel-would-be-happy-if-hamas-takes-over-gaza, accessed 14 March 2025.

53 Filiu, *Gaza*, 304.

54 Li, 'Gaza at the frontiers of Zionism', 191.

55 'UN says Gaza crisis "intolerable"', BBC News, 26 September 2006, http://news.bbc.co.uk/1/hi/world/middle_east/5382976.stm, accessed 14 March 2025.

56 'Restrictions on fishing: The Gaza Strip', B'Tselem, 1 January 2011,

https://www.btselem.org/gaza_strip/restrictions_on_fishing, accessed 14 March 2025. See also Abuelaish, *I Shall Not Hate*, 130.

57 For more on this, see Helga Tawil-Souri, 'Digital occupation: Gaza's high-tech enclosure', *Journal of Palestine Studies* 41:2 (2012), 27–43.

58 'Movement of people between Gaza and Egypt via Rafah crossing', Gisha, 26 December 2013, https://gisha.org/en/movement-of-people-via-rafah-crossing/, accessed 14 March 2025.

59 'Egypt blocks Gazans' access to the outside world', Amnesty International, 31 January 2008, http://amnesty.org/en/latest/news/2008/01/egypt-blocks-gazans-access-outside-world-20080131/, accessed 14 March 2025. See also Sarah El Deeb, 'Border breach temporary boost for Gaza', Associated Press, 28 January 2008.

60 'Partial list of items prohibited/permitted into the Gaza Strip', Gisha, 6 June 2010, https://gisha.org/en/partial-list-of-items-prohibitedpermitted-into-the-gaza-strip/, accessed 14 March 2025.

61 'Gisha response to new food items being permitted into Gaza', Gisha, 10 June 2010, https://gisha.org/en/gisha-response-to-new-food-items-being-permitted-into-gaza/, accessed 14 March 2025.

62 Amira Hass, '2,279 calories per person: how Israel made sure Gaza didn't starve', *Haaretz*, 17 October 2012, https://www.haaretz.com/2012-10-17/ty-article/.premium/israels-gaza-quota-2-279-calories-a-day/0000017f-e0f2-d7b2-a77f-e3f755550000, accessed 14 March 2025.

63 Abuelaish, *I Shall Not Hate*, 125.

64 *The Besieged Palestinian Agricultural Sector*, UN Conference on Trade and Development, 2015, https://unctad.org/system/files/official-document/gdsapp2015d1_en.pdf, accessed 14 March 2025.

65 'Worsening malnutrition among Gaza children', 21 April 2009, available at https://www.un.org/unispal/document/auto-insert-198266/, accessed 14 March 2025.

66 See Nicolas Pelham, 'Gaza's tunnel phenomenon: the unintended dynamics of Israel's siege', *Journal of Palestine Studies* 41:4 (2012), 6–31; Toufic Haddad, 'Insurgent infrastructure: tunnels of the Gaza Strip', *Middle East – Topics and Argument* 10 (2018), 71–85.

67 Khaled Hroub, 'Tunnels: love, lions and. . . absurdities', in Tawil-Souri and Matar, *Gaza as Metaphor*, 73–4.

68 'Not just guns: Gazans smuggle lions into zoo', NBC News, 9 August 2008, https://www.nbcnews.com/id/wbna26096748, accessed 14 March 2025.

69 Abuelaish, *I Shall Not Hate*, 23–5.

70 *Ibid.*, 24.

71 Israeli singer Arik Einstein first coined the pun in his 1974 song 'Sa Leat'.

72 On the use of Israeli drones in Gaza, see Mohamed Solaimane, '"It feels like another war is being waged against us": Despite the ceasefire, Israel continues to haunt Gaza with the constant buzz of drones', *New Arab*, 28 January 2025, https://www.newarab.com/features/psychological-strain-israels-drones-continue-terrorise-gaza, accessed 14 March 2025.

73 Rory McCarthy, 'Gaza truce broken as Israeli raid kills six Hamas gunmen', *The Guardian*, 5 November 2008, https://www.theguardian.com/world/2008/nov/05/israelandthepalestinians, accessed 14 March 2025. See also 'The June 2008 Gaza Ceasefire', Carter Center, https://www.cartercenter.org/resources/pdfs/peace/human_rights/conflict_resolution/gaza_movement_and_fatalities_report%20final%201%2022%2009.pdf, accessed 14 March 2025.

74 Filiu, *Gaza*, 315.

75 'Israel/Gaza: Operation "Cast Lead" – 22 days of death and destruction', Amnesty International, July 2009, https://www.amnesty.org/en/documents/mde15/015/2009/en/, accessed 14 March 2025.

76 Figures sourced from B'Tselem.

77 Filiu, *Gaza*, 317.

78 'Gilad Shalit freed in Israeli–Palestinian prisoner swap', BBC News, 18 October 2011, https://www.bbc.co.uk/news/world-middle-east-15339604, accessed 14 March 2025.

79 On the application of the Dahiyeh doctrine in Gaza, see Camille Mansour, 'Reflections on the war on Gaza', *Journal of Palestine Studies* 38:4 (2009), 95.

80 'Israel warns Hezbollah war would invite destruction', Reuters, 3 October 2008, https://www.reuters.com/article/world/israel-warns-hezbollah-war-would-invite-destruction-idUSTRE4923I0/, accessed 14 March 2025.

81 Israel argued that the non-combatant death toll was far lower than this, because it counted police officers as combatants. Human rights activists countered that under international humanitarian law, civil police carrying out duties such as ordinary internal law enforcement or traffic regulation should be afforded civilian protections. They also pointed out that the police force in Gaza were separate from Hamas' internal security forces. See '"Operation Cast Lead:" A Statistical Analysis', Al-Haq, August 2009, https://www.alhaq.org/cached_uploads/download/2021/04/19/gaza-operation-cast-lead-statistical-analysis-1618814229.pdf, accessed 14 March 2025.

82 Abuelaish recalls these events in his memoir *I Shall Not Hate*, 160–87.

83 'Human Rights in Palestine and other occupied Arab territories',

Report of the United Nations Fact-finding Mission on the Gaza Conflict, A/HRC/12/48, 25 September 2009.

84 *Soldiers' Testimonies from Operation Cast Lead, Gaza 2009*, Breaking the Silence, June 2009, https://www.breakingthesilence.org.il/wp-content/uploads/2011/02/Operation_Cast_Lead_Gaza_2009_Eng.pdf, accessed 14 March 2025.

85 'OPT: Gaza appeal total doubles overnight', CARE, 27 January 2009.

86 'Damage to Palestinian people and property during Operation Cast Lead', *Journal of Palestine Studies* 38:3 (2009), 210.

87 Gidi Weitz, 'Another concept implodes: Israel can't be managed by a criminal defendant', *Haaretz*, 9 October 2023, https://www.haaretz.com/israel-news/2023-10-09/ty-article/.premium/another-concept-implodes-israel-cant-be-managed-by-a-criminal-defendant/0000018b-1382-d2fc-a59f-d39b5dbf0000, accessed 14 March 2025.

88 Tal Schneider, 'For years, Netanyahu propped up Hamas. Now it's blown up in our faces', *Times of Israel*, 8 October 2023, https://www.timesofisrael.com/for-years-netanyahu-propped-up-hamas-now-its-blown-up-in-our-faces/, accessed 14 March 2025.

89 Joshua Leifer, 'The Netanyahu doctrine: how Israel's longest-serving leader reshaped the country in his image', *The Guardian*, 21 November 2023, https://www.theguardian.com/world/2023/nov/21/the-netanyahu-doctrine-how-israels-longest-serving-leader-reshaped-the-country-in-his-image, accessed 24 February 2025.

90 Efraim Inbar and Eitan Shamir, 'Mowing the grass in Gaza', *Jerusalem Post*, 22 July 2014, https://www.jpost.com/opinion/columnists/mowing-the-grass-in-gaza-368516, accessed 14 March 2025.

91 Efraim Inbar and Eitan Shamir, '"Mowing the grass": Israel's strategy for protracted intractable conflict', *Journal of Strategic Studies* 37:1 (2014), 65-90. See also Mouin Rabbani, 'Israel mows the lawn', *London Review of Books*, 31 July 2014, https://www.lrb.co.uk/the-paper/v36/n15/mouin-rabbani-israel-mows-the-lawn, accessed 14 March 2025.

92 'Israeli boy Daniel Viflic dies after rocket hits bus', BBC News, 18 April 2011, https://www.bbc.co.uk/news/world-middle-east-13115127, accessed 14 March 2025.

93 Information sourced from B'Tselem.

94 For more on the dynamics between Israel and Hamas in this period, see Baconi, *Hamas Contained*.

95 Jean-Pierre Filiu, *Gaza: A History*, 2nd ed. (Hurst, 2024), 441.

96 Hroub, 'Tunnels: love, lions and. . . absurdities', 76–9.

97 David M. Weinberg, 'Israel must prove it has freedom to defend itself', *Jerusalem Post*, 13 May 2021, https://www.jpost.com/opinion/israel-must-prove-it-has-freedom-to-defend-itself-opinion-668124, accessed 14 March 2025.

98 For more on this, see Baconi, *Hamas Contained*, 12–13.

99 Sharon, 'A decisive conclusion is necessary'.

100 Figures sourced from B'Tselem and Al-Haq.

101 Giora Eiland, 'In Gaza, there is no such thing as "innocent civilians"', *ynetnews*, 8 May 2014, https://www.ynetnews.com/articles/0,7340,L-4554583,00.html, accessed 14 March 2025.

102 Pappe, *The Biggest Prison on Earth*, 278.

103 Nimer Sultany, 'Repetition', in Tawil-Souri and Matar, *Gaza as Metaphor*, 203–17; Noura Erakat, 'The sovereign right to kill: a critical appraisal of Israel's shoot-to-kill policy in Gaza', *International Criminal Law Review* 19:5 (2019), 783–818.

104 Max Blumenthal, 'Politicide in Gaza: how Israel's far right won the war', *Journal of Palestine Studies* 44:1 (2014), 14–28. See also Baruch Kimmerling, *Politicide: Ariel Sharon's War Against the Palestinians*, updated ed. (Verso, 2006).

105 'The Bakr Boys: Israeli military attack in the fishing beach in Gaza in which 4 children were killed during "Operation Protective Edge"', Adalah, https://www.adalah.org/en/content/view/10514, accessed 14 March 2025.

106 Peter Beaumont, 'Israel exonerates itself over Gaza beach killings of four children last year', *The Guardian*, 11 June 2015, https://www.theguardian.com/world/2015/jun/11/israel-clears-military-gaza-beach-children, accessed 14 March 2025. For journalists' first-hand accounts of the attack, see Peter Beaumont, 'Witness to a shelling: first-hand account of deadly strike on Gaza port', *The Guardian*, 16 July 2014, https://www.theguardian.com/world/2014/jul/16/witness-gaza-shelling-first-hand-account; William Booth, 'Israeli strike kills four children on a Gaza beach', *Washington Post*, 16 July 2014, https://www.washingtonpost.com/news/worldviews/wp/2014/07/16/dispatch-israeli-strike-kills-four-children-at-a-gaza-beach/; Patrick Martin, 'Globe reporter recalls air force strike on Gaza beach that killed four boys', *Globe and Mail*, 12 June 2015, https://www.theglobeandmail.com/news/world/globe-reporter-recalls-air-force-strike-on-gaza-beach-that-killed-four-boys/article24939034/; all accessed 14 March 2025.

107 'Bureau of Committee on the Exercise of the Inalienable Rights of the Palestinian People strongly condemns ongoing Israeli military operation in Gaza', GA/PAL/1311, 21 July 2014. See also Sharif Abdel Kouddous, 'Massacre in Shejaiya', *The Nation*, 21 July 2014,

https://www.thenation.com/article/archive/massacre-shejaiya/, accessed 14 March 2025.

108 Ilana Feldman, 'Isolating Gaza', *Jadaliyya*, 29 July 2014, https://www. jadaliyya.com/Details/31014, accessed 14 March 2025.

109 Haidar Eid, 'Diary, 20 July 2014', in Tawil-Souri and Matar, *Gaza as Metaphor*, 30. For more Palestinian accounts of living through the 2014 war, see al-Ghoul and Nassib, *A Rebel in Gaza*, chs 28, 32; Atef Abu Saif, *The Drone Eats With Me* (Beacon Press, 2016).

110 Anne Barnard and Jodi Rudoren, 'Israel says that Hamas uses civilian shields, reviving debate', *New York Times*, 23 July 2014, https://www.nytimes.com/2014/07/24/world/middleeast/israel-says-hamas-is-using-civilians-as-shields-in-gaza.html, accessed 14 March 2025.

111 'Pillay condemns continuing attacks on civilians in Gaza', Office of the High Commissioner for Human Rights, 31 July 2014, https://www.ohchr.org/en/press-releases/2014/07/pillay-condemns-continuing-attacks-civilians-gaza, accessed 14 March 2025.

112 Neve Gordon and Nicola Perugini, *Human Shields: A History of People in the Line of Fire* (University of California Press, 2020), chs 16–17.

113 Noa Yachot, '"No more deaths": thousands of Israelis protest the Gaza war', +972, 26 July 2014, https://www.972mag.com/no-more-deaths-israelis-protest-the-gaza-war/, accessed 14 March 2025.

114 Ira Berkovic, 'Thousands rally for peace and equality', Workers' Liberty, 25 May 2021, https://www.workersliberty.org/story/2021-05-25/thousands-rally-peace-and-equality, last accessed 14 March 2025.

115 'Oded Lifshitz drove Gazans to hospitals', *Times of Israel*, 23 October 2023.

116 UN OCHA, Occupied Palestinian territory: Gaza Emergency, Situation Report, 25 August 2014. See also Sara Roy, *The Gaza Strip: The Political Economy of De-development* (Institute for Palestine Studies, 2016), 395.

117 UN OCHA OPT, Humanitarian bulletin: monthly report, May 2015.

118 Report of the independent commission of inquiry established pursuant to Human Rights Council resolution S-21/1, A/HRC/29/52, 24 June 2015.

119 UN Country Team in the Occupied Palestinian Territory, *Gaza: Ten Years Later*, July 2017, 20, https://unsco.unmissions.org/gaza-ten-years-later-report-july-2017, accessed 14 March 2025.

120 'Gaza's humanitarian emergency', Medical Aid for Palestinians (MAP), Autumn 2018.

121 'Report on UNCTAD assistance to the Palestinian people: developments in the economy of the occupied Palestinian territory', United Nations Conference on Trade and Development (UNCTAD), 6 July 2015.

122 'Gaza's humanitarian emergency'.

123 See 'Access to healthcare: health under occupation – chapter 1', MAP, September 2017, https://www.map.org.uk/downloads/map-ch1--access-to-healthcare.pdf, accessed 14 March 2025; 'Gaza's humanitarian emergency'; 'Monthly report: June 2018', World Health Organization, Occupied Palestinian Territory, https://www.emro.who.int/images/stories/palestine/documents/rad-june_2018.pdf, accessed 14 March 2025.

124 'Gaza: Looming humanitarian catastrophe highlights need to lift Israel's 10-year illegal blockade', Amnesty International, 14 June 2017, https://www.amnesty.org/en/latest/news/2017/06/gaza-looming-humanitarian-catastrophe-highlights-need-to-lift-israels-10-year-illegal-blockade-2/, accessed 14 March 2025.

125 Said Shehadeh, 'Ghazeh el sumud: Confronting Israeli mass torture', in Tawil-Souri and Matar, *Gaza as metaphor*, 37. See also Runa Johannessen, 'Sumud: steadfastness as everyday resistance', *Interactive Encyclopaedia of the Palestine Question*, https://www.palquest.org/en/highlight/33633/sumud, accessed 17 March 2025; Alexandra Rijke and Toine Van Teeffelen, 'To exist is to resist: sumud, heroism and the everyday', *Jerusalem Quarterly* 59 (2014), 86–99; Yousef Alhelou, 'The living spirit of Sumud: Palestinians' form of resistance and steadfastness continues to grow stronger', *New Arab*, 31 October 2019, https://www.newarab.com/analysis/sumud-palestinians-form-steadfastness-continues-grow-stronger, accessed 17 March 2025.

126 Anne E. Irfan, 'Educating Palestinian refugees: the origins of UNRWA's unique schooling system', *Journal of Refugee Studies* 34:1 (2021), 1037–59.

127 Anne Irfan, 'Why Palestinians are known as the world's "best educated refugees"', Columbia University Press blog, 23 August 2023, https://cupblog.org/2023/08/23/why-palestinians-are-known-as-the-worlds-best-educated-refugeesanne-irfan/, accessed 17 March 2025.

128 Abuelaish, *I Shall Not Hate*, 163. Footage of Abuelaish's live phone call to Israeli TV upon his daughters' deaths can be viewed at 'Gaza father on phone with Israeli TV as tank shells kill his 3 daughters', MEMO/YouTube, 25 July 2017, https://youtu.be/LodLfrMckus?si=Zd2JMzZR8XDsKvG7, accessed 17 March 2025.

129 Majd Mashharawi, 'How I'm making bricks out of ashes and rubble in Gaza', TED Talks, November 2018, https://www.ted.com/talks/majd_mashharawi_how_i_m_making_bricks_out_of_ashes_and_rubble_in_gaza/, accessed 17 March 2025.

130 Caitlin Procter, 'Coerced innovation: Gaza makes its own tools to fight against COVID-19', openDemocracy, 16 April 2020, https://www.opendemocracy.net/en/north-africa-west-asia/coerced-innovation-gaza-makes-its-own-tools-fight-against-covid-19/, accessed 17 March 2025. See also Anne Irfan, 'COVID-19 in the Palestinian refugee camps', Refugee Studies Centre, University of Oxford, 12 May 2020, https://www.rsc.ox.ac.uk/news/covid-19-in-the-palestinian-refugee-camps, accessed 17 March 2025.

131 Mersiha Gadzo, 'Meet the man crowd-funding Gaza's first English library', Al Jazeera, 10 February 2017, https://www.aljazeera.com/features/2017/2/10/meet-the-man-crowd-funding-gazas-first-english-library, accessed 17 March 2025.

132 Tamer Nafar, 'RIP the uncle I never knew: a poet, just like me, and killed by an Israeli bomb', *The Guardian*, 24 January 2024, https://www.theguardian.com/commentisfree/2024/jan/24/poetry-israel-bomb-palestine, accessed 19 February 2025.

133 On the internet as a tool for Palestinian activism, see Miriyam Aouragh, *Palestine Online: Transnationalism, the Internet and the Construction of Identity* (I. B. Tauris, 2012).

134 In Arabic, these phrases were respectively *ash-shaab yurid isqat an-nizam* and *ash-shaab yurid inha' al-inqisam*.

135 Al-Ghoul and Nassib, *A Rebel in Gaza*, 151.

136 *Israel's Retaliatory Seizure of Tax: A War Crime to Punish Palestinian ICC Membership*, Al-Haq, 2015, https://www.alhaq.org/publications/8069.html, accessed 17 March 2025.

137 Rami Younis, 'Gaza "Return March" organizer: "We'll ensure it doesn't escalate to violence – on our end"', +972, 27 March 2018, https://www.972mag.com/gaza-return-march-organizer-well-ensure-it-doesnt-escalate-to-violence-on-our-end/, accessed 17 March 2025.

138 *Ibid*.

139 Filiu, *Gaza*, 438.

140 See 'Violence on demonstrators in Gaza is "unacceptable and inhumane"', Medecins Sans Frontieres (MSF), 14 May 2018, https://www.msf.org/palestine-violence-demonstrators-gaza-unacceptable-and-inhuman; 'Israel: Gaza killings unlawful, calculated', Human Rights Watch, 3 April 2018, https://www.hrw.org/news/2018/04/03/israel-gaza-killings-unlawful-calculated; *Unwilling and Unable: Israel's Whitewashed Investigations of the Great March of Return Protests*, B'Tselem and PCHR, December 2021, https://

www.btselem.org/publications/202112_unwilling_and_unable; all accessed 17 March 2025.

141 'Humanitarian snapshot: casualties in the context of demonstrations and hostilities in Gaza, 30 March 2018–31 July 2019', UN OCHA, 31 August 2019. https://www.ochaopt.org/content/humanitarian-snapshot-casualties-context-demonstrations-and-hostilities-gaza-30-mar-2018-0, accessed 17 March 2025.

142 Rami Younis, 'Everywhere you go in Gaza, you see people wounded in the Return March', +972, 28 March 2019, https://www.972mag.com/everywhere-go-gaza-see-people-wounded-return-march/, accessed 17 March 2025.

143 'Humanitarian snapshot'.

144 Iyad Abuheweila and Isabel Kershner, 'A woman dedicated to saving lives loses hers in Gaza violence', *New York Times*, 2 June 2018, https://www.nytimes.com/2018/06/02/world/middleeast/gaza-paramedic-killed.html, accessed 17 March 2025.

145 'Israeli soldiers deliberately and fatally shot Palestinian paramedic Rozon a-Najar in the Gaza Strip', B'Tselem, 17 July 2018, https://www.btselem.org/gaza_strip/20180718_paramedic_rozan_a_najar_killed_by_deliberate_fire, accessed 17 March 2025.

146 'Deadly violence erupts on Israel's borders', France24, 15 May 2011; Ethan Bronner, 'Israeli troops fire as marchers breach borders', *New York Times*, 15 May 2011, https://www.nytimes.com/2011/05/16/world/middleeast/16mideast.html, accessed 17 March 2025.

147 'Situation in the area, July–October 2000', in 'UNIFIL Background', UNIFIL, https://unifil.unmissions.org/unifil-background#para6; Tessa Fox, 'Protests in Lebanon continue in support of Palestine', Al Jazeera, 17 May 2021, https://www.aljazeera.com/news/2021/5/17/protests-in-lebanon-continue-in-support-of-palestine; 'Protestors rush towards Israeli border in Jordan and Lebanon', *Al Monitor*, 14 May 2021, https://www.al-monitor.com/originals/2021/05/protesters-rush-toward-israeli-border-jordan-and-lebanon; all accessed 17 March 2025.

148 On these dynamics, see Anne Irfan, *Refuge and Resistance: Palestinians and the International Refugee System* (Columbia University Press, 2023), 195–6.

149 Al Ghoul, *A Rebel in Gaza*, 143–60.

150 'PCHR calls for investigating arrest and torture of journalist on grounds of freedom of expression', Palestinian Centre for Human Rights, 7 September 2016, https://pchrgaza.org/pchr-calls-for-investigating-arrest-and-torture-of-journalist-on-grounds-of-freedom-of-expression/, accessed 17 March 2025.

151 See for example 'Hamas government infringes upon the right to

freedom of expression', Al-Haq, 3 April 2014, https://www.alhaq. org/monitoring-documentation/6664.html; 'PCHR condemns dispersing a peaceful assembly in Rafah by police and Hamas activists using force', Palestinian Centre for Human Rights, 16 June 2008, https://pchrgaza.org/pchr-condemns-dispersing-a-peaceful-assembly-in-rafah-by-police-and-hamas-activists-using-force/; 'State of Palestine: alarming attack on freedom of expression', Amnesty International, 23 August 2017, https://www.amnesty.org/en/ documents/mde15/6983/2017/en/; 'Two authorities, one way, zero dissent: arbitrary arrest and torture under the Palestinian Authority and Hamas', Human Rights Watch, 23 October 2018, https://www. hrw.org/report/2018/10/23/two-authorities-one-way-zero-dissent/ arbitrary-arrest-and-torture-under; 'Human rights in Palestine (State of): Review of 2018', Amnesty International, 26 February 2019, https://www.amnesty.org/en/documents/mde21/9912/2019/en/; all accessed 17 March 2025.

152 Muhammad Shehada, 'Hamas (Palestine)', in *Guns and Governance: How Europe Should Talk with Non-state Armed Groups in the Middle East*, European Council of Foreign Relations, https://ecfr.eu/special/ mena-armed-groups/hamas-palestine/, accessed 17 March 2025.

153 Barbara Plett Usher, 'Israel–Gaza clash: why Hamas chose restraint', BBC News, 18 November 2019, https://www.bbc.co.uk/news/ world-middle-east-50458141, accessed 17 March 2025.

154 For more on these dynamics, see Shehada, 'Hamas (Palestine)'.

155 For analysis of the 2017 document, see Khaled Hroub, 'A newer Hamas? The revised Charter', *Journal of Palestine Studies* 46:4 (2017), 100–11; Tareq Baconi, 'Why now is the time to talk to Hamas', *The Guardian*, 2 May 2017, https://www.theguardian.com/ commentisfree/2017/may/02/hamas-charter-antisemitism, accessed 17 March 2025.

156 'Israel says Hamas trying to fool the world with new policy paper', Reuters, 1 May 2017, https://www.reuters.com/article/ world/israel-says-hamas-trying-to-fool-the-world-with-new-policy-paper-idUSKBN17X1SX/; Patrick Wintour, 'Hamas presents new charter accepting a Palestine based on 1967 borders', *The Guardian*, 1 May 2017, https://www.theguardian.com/world/2017/ may/01/hamas-new-charter-palestine-israel-1967-borders; both accessed 17 March 2025.

157 Shehada, 'Hamas (Palestine)'.

158 Maram Humaid, 'Gaza rights groups denounce Hamas crackdown on protests', Al Jazeera, 19 March 2019, https://www.aljazeera.com/ news/2019/3/19/gaza-rights-groups-denounce-hamas-crackdown-on-protests, accessed 17 March 2025.

159 Younis, 'Everywhere you go in Gaza, you see people wounded in the Return March'.

160 On this, see Daniel Falcone, 'Was Israel's latest attack on Gaza manufactured to divert "democracy" protests?', *truthout*, 10 June 2023, https://truthout.org/articles/was-israels-latest-attack-on-gaza-manufactured-to-divert-democracy-protests/, accessed 17 March 2025.

161 The video can be viewed at https://www.youtube.com/watch?v=PEUQId3oTNo, accessed 4 March 2025. See also: Raoul Wootliff, '"Parts of Gaza sent back to Stone Age:" Gantz videos laud his IDF bona fides', *The Times of Israel*, 20 January 2019, https://www.timesofisrael.com/only-the-strong-survive-gantzs-new-campaign-videos-laud-his-idf-bona-fides/, accessed 2 May 2025. A Palestinian media company later accused Gantz of having stolen the footage used. See Oren Ziv, 'Palestinian media company says ex-IDF chief stole footage of Gaza destruction for campaign video', *+972*, 27 January 2019, https://www.972mag.com/palestinian-company-says-former-idf-head-stole-gaza-footage-campaign-video/, accessed 17 March 2025.

162 The speech can be accessed via https://www.maariv.co.il/news/military/Article-822723, accessed 17 March 2025 [Hebrew].

163 See for example Nimer Sultany, 'Peaceful coexistence in Israel hasn't been shattered – it's always been a myth', *The Guardian*, 19 May 2021, https://www.theguardian.com/commentisfree/2021/may/19/peaceful-coexistence-israel-myth-palestinian-denied-rights; Diana Buttu, 'The myth of coexistence in Israel', *New York Times*, 25 May 2021, https://www.nytimes.com/2021/05/25/opinion/israel-palestinian-citizens-racism-discrimination.html; both accessed 17 March 2025.

164 Figures sourced from B'Tselem and UN OCHA.

165 Amjad Iraqi, Edo Konrad and Henriette Chacar, 'An uprising for Palestinian unity', podcast, *+972*, 3 June 2021, https://www.972mag.com/palestinian-citizens-israel-unity-podcast/, accessed 17 March 2025.

166 Filiu, *Gaza*, 443.

167 'Report: Shin Bet chief demanded President Abbas cancel the Palestinian elections', *Haaretz*, 31 March 2021, https://www.haaretz.com/israel-news/2021-03-31/ty-article/report-shin-bet-chief-demanded-president-abbas-cancel-the-palestinian-elections/0000017f-e50a-d9aa-afff-fd5a994e0000; 'Israeli authorities continue to intervene in the Palestinian elections, and arrest another candidate running for the legislative elections', Palestinian Centre for Human Rights, 15 April 2021, https://pchrgaza.org/israeli-authorities-continue-to-

intervene-in-the-palestinian-elections-and-arrest-another-candidate-running-for-the-legislative-elections/; both accessed 17 March 2025.

168 Fred Kaplan, 'How George W. Bush helped Hamas come to power', *Slate*, 24 October 2023, https://slate.com/news-and-politics/2023/10/was-hamas-elected-to-govern-gaza-george-w-bush-2006-palestinian-election.html, accessed 17 March 2025.

169 UN Country Team in the Occupied Palestinian Territory, 'Gaza in 2020: a liveable place?', August 2012, https://www.un.org/unispal/document/auto-insert-195081/, accessed 17 March 2025.

170 Jonathan Gornall, 'Neither Fatah nor Hamas: *Arab News*/YouGov poll shows Palestinians want nothing to do with their leadership', *Arab News*, 20 May 2023, https://arab.news/bjg3v, accessed 17 March 2025.

171 Anne Irfan, 'Why Palestinians could be facing another Nakba', *The Nation*, 17 August 2023, https://www.thenation.com/article/world/palestine-second-nakba/, accessed 17 March 2025.

Epilogue

1 Figures taken from UN Office for the Coordination of Humanitarian Affairs (OCHA), https://www.ochaopt.org/; 'October 7 crimes against humanity, war crimes by Hamas-led groups', Human Rights Watch, 17 July 2024, https://www.hrw.org/news/2024/07/17/october-7-crimes-against-humanity-war-crimes-hamas-led-groups; both accessed 31 March 2025.

2 'Israeli journalist Amira Hass, daughter of Holocaust survivors, calls for Gaza ceasefire now', *Democracy Now!*, 20 October 2023, https://www.democracynow.org/2023/10/20/israeli_journalist_amira_hass_daughter_of, accessed 2 April 2025.

3 ICC Chief Prosecutor Karim Khan spoke about this in a meeting with Israeli hostage families. The leaked recording is available via https://www.maariv.co.il/journalists/Article-1101602, accessed 2 April 2025 [Hebrew]. On the Israeli military investigation, see Yonah Jeremy Bob, 'October 7 probe: IDF only arrived in Nir Oz after Hamas terrorists left because it was "far away"', *The Jerusalem Post*, 14 March 2025, https://www.jpost.com/israel-news/article-846063, accessed 2 April 2025.

4 On the timeline of attacks on 7 October 2023, see Muhammad Shehada, 'How Palestinians look back on 7 October a year later', *New Arab*, 10 October 2024, https://www.newarab.com/analysis/how-palestinians-look-back-7-october-year-later; Bob, 'October 7

probe'. See also Israeli reporting at https://www.kan.org.il/content/kan-news/defense/866943/ and https://www.kan.org.il/content/kan-news/defense/861251/ [Hebrew]; all accessed 2 April 2025.

5 *Ibid.*

6 See 'One year on from the 7 October attacks: helping the helpers', World Health Organization, 7 October 2024, https://www.who.int/europe/news-room/07-10-2024-one-year-on-from-the-7-october-attacks-in-israel--helping-the-helpers, accessed 31 March 2025; reporting via https://www.kan.org.il/content/kan-news/defense/861251/, accessed 2 April 2025 [Hebrew]. On the sexual assaults committed on 7 October and surrounding controversies, see Anwar Mhajne, 'Understanding Sexual Violence Debates Since 7 October: Weaponization and Denial', *Journal of Genocide Research* (2024), https://doi.org/10.1080/14623528.2024.2359851, accessed 31 March 2025; Samah Salaime, 'Women's liberation mustn't stop at either side of the Gaza fence', *+972*, 22 December 2023, https://www.972mag.com/palestinian-jewish-feminists-women-liberation-gaza-fence/, accessed 31 March 2025; 'Reasonable grounds to believe conflict-related sexual violence occurred in Israel during 7 October attacks, senior UN official tells Security Council', UN 9572nd meeting, SC/15621, 11 March 2024.

7 Gallant made this comment in an interview on the *Call Me Back* podcast in February 2025, accessible via https://www.youtube.com/watch?v=aPEPztvsJGQ. See also Seth Frantzman, 'Which Palestinian terror group took the Bibas family hostage? – analysis', *The Jerusalem Post*, 21 February 2025, https://www.jpost.com/middle-east/article-843197; 'Release of two more hostages gives some hope to families of others abducted in the attack on Israel', The Associated Press, 23 October 2023, https://apnews.com/article/hostages-israel-hamas-war-what-to-know-406920c384818fa4fe3525327adf3f50; all accessed 2 April 2025.

8 The journalist was Muthana al-Najjar, who subsequently shared his footage with the *New York Times*. See Yousur Al-Hlou, 'Video images show Palestinian gunmen abducting residents of a kibbutz', *New York Times*, 9 October 2023, https://www.nytimes.com/live/2023/10/09/world/israel-gaza-war-hamas, accessed 2 April 2025.

9 '"I asked him how he isn't ashamed": 85-year-old Israeli hostage says she confronted Hamas chief Sinwar in Gaza tunnel', *Haaretz*, 29 November 2023, https://www.haaretz.com/israel-news/2023-11-29/ty-article/85-year-old-freed-israeli-hostage-confronted-hamas-chief-sinwar-in-gaza-tunnel/0000018c-1ad5-d4e4-a1df-3edd611c0000, accessed 31 March 2025.

10   Yaniv Kubovich and Nir Hasson, 'How could Israel's army abandon this kibbutz for seven hours on October 7?', *Haaretz*, 24 April 2024, https://www.haaretz.com/israel-news/2024-04-24/ty-article-magazine/.premium/how-could-israels-army-abandon-this-kibbutz-for-seven-hours-on-october-7/0000018f-0076-db42-a99f-adff41440000, accessed 31 March 2025. See also Bethan McKernan, '"Time stopped here on October 7": life in kibbutz that endured unimaginable loss one year ago', *The Guardian*, 4 October 2024, https://www.theguardian.com/world/2024/oct/04/time-stopped-here-on-7-october-life-in-kibbutz-that-endured-unimaginable-loss-one-year-ago, accessed 31 March 2025; Bob, 'October 7 probe'.

11   For more on the Abu Sitta family's history, see Salman Abu Sitta, *Mapping My Return: A Palestinian Memoir* (AUC Press, 2016).

12   Oded Lifshitz, 'Netanyahu is no "protector of Israel"', *Haaretz*, 20 February 2025, https://www.haaretz.com/opinion/2025-02-20/ty-article/.premium/netanyahu-is-no-protector-of-israel/00000195-243a-da01-abdd-243f88690000, accessed 31 March 2025 (originally published in Hebrew in 2019).

13   Kubovich and Hasson, 'How could Israel's army abandon this kibbutz for seven hours on October 7?'

14   The two Israeli citizens already in Gaza were Avera Mengistu and Hisham al-Sayed, both of whom suffered from serious mental health problems.

15   Jean-Pierre Filiu, *Gaza: A History*, 2nd ed. (Hurst, 2024), 443–4.

16   Jason Burke, 'Yahya Sinwar: the man who may hold key to release of Gaza hostages', *The Guardian*, 21 November 2023, https://www.theguardian.com/world/2023/nov/21/yahya-sinwar-the-man-who-may-hold-key-to-release-of-gaza-hostages, accessed 31 March 2025.

17   Summer Said and Rory Jones, 'Gaza Chief's Brutal Calculation: Civilian Bloodshed will help Hamas', *Wall Street Journal*, 10 July 2024, https://www.wsj.com/world/middle-east/gaza-chiefs-brutal-calculation-civilian-bloodshed-will-help-hamas-626720e7, accessed 2 April 2025.

18   Gideon Allon, '"No doubt" Netanyahu preventing hostage deal, charges ex-spokesman of Families Forum', *Times of Israel*, 26 April 2024, https://www.timesofisrael.com/no-doubt-netanyahu-preventing-hostage-deal-charges-ex-spokesman-of-families-forum/; Keir Simmons and Ken Dilanian, 'Hamas expresses willingness to release some captive women and children', NBC News, 18 October 2023, https://www.nbcnews.com/news/investigations/hamas-expresses-willingness-release-captive-women-children-rcna120776; both accessed 2 April 2025.

19 Human Rights Watch, 'Hamas, Islamic Jihad: Holding Hostages is a War Crime', 19 October 2023, https://www.hrw.org/news/2023/10/19/hamas-islamic-jihad-holding-hostages-war-crime, accessed 2 April 2025.

20 Figures sourced from B'Tselem.

21 Israeli journalist Amir Tibon survived the attack on his home in Nahal Oz. For his account of 7 October, see Yair Rosenberg, '"We're going to die here"', *The Atlantic*, 9 October 2023, https://www.theatlantic.com/ideas/archive/2023/10/amir-tibon-how-his-family-survived-hamas-massacre/675596/, accessed 31 March 2025.

22 Netanyahu's meeting with the Chief of Staff was reported on Ynet and is accessible via https://www.ynet.co.il/yedioth/article/yokra14303894, accessed 2 April 2025 [Hebrew].

23 'UNRWA Situation Report #3 on the situation in the Gaza Strip', UNRWA, 10 October 2023, https://www.unrwa.org/resources/reports/unrwa-situation-report-3-situation-gaza-strip, accessed 31 March 2025.

24 Emanuel Fabian, 'Defense minister announces "complete siege" of Gaza: No power, food or fuel', *Times of Israel*, 9 October 2023, https://www.timesofisrael.com/liveblog_entry/defense-minister-announces-complete-siege-of-gaza-no-power-food-or-fuel/, accessed 31 March 2025. For human rights condemnation, see 'Israel/OPT: Israel must lift illegal and inhumane blockade on Gaza as power plant runs out of fuel', Amnesty International, 12 October 2023, https://www.amnesty.org/en/latest/news/2023/10/israel-opt-israel-must-lift-illegal-and-inhumane-blockade-on-gaza-as-power-plant-runs-out-of-fuel/; 'Israel must stop using water as a weapon of war: UN expert', UN Office of the High Commissioner for Human Rights, 17 November 2023, https://www.ohchr.org/en/press-releases/2023/11/israel-must-stop-using-water-weapon-war-un-expert; both accessed 31 March 2025.

25 Gallant's words are recorded at https://www.youtube.com/watch?v=l9wx7e4u-xM, accessed 16 March 2025 [Hebrew].

26 Bethan McKernan and Quique Kierszenbaum, '"We're focused on maximum damage": ground offensive into Gaza seems imminent', *The Guardian*, 10 October 2023, https://www.theguardian.com/world/2023/oct/10/right-now-it-is-one-day-at-a-time-life-on-israels-frontline-with-gaza, accessed 31 March 2025.

27 For more on this rhetoric before 7 October, see Anne Irfan, 'Why Palestinians could be facing another Nakba', *The Nation*, 17 August 2023, https://www.thenation.com/article/world/palestine-second-nakba/, accessed 17 March 2025.

28 For a full list of genocidal statements by Israeli leaders, see 'Law for

Palestine releases database with 500+ instances of Israeli incitement to genocide – continuously updated', Law for Palestine, https://law4palestine.org/law-for-palestine-releases-database-with-500-instances-of-israeli-incitement-to-genocide-continuously-updated/; 'Statements by Israeli officials, soldiers and civil society on genocide', Al-Haq, 10 January 2024, https://www.alhaq.org/advocacy/22498.html; https://witnessing-the-gaza-war.com/1117-2/; both accessed 31 March 2025.

29 Eiland's op-ed was published in the print edition of *Yedioth Ahronoth*, 19 November 2023, under the headline 'Let's not be intimidated by the world' (in Hebrew).

30 David Ingram, 'Israeli government sparks outcry with X videos saying "there are no innocent civilians" in Gaza', NBC News, 14 June 2024, https://www.nbcnews.com/tech/social-media/israel-posts-video-saying-are-no-innocent-civilians-gaza-rcna157111, accessed 31 March 2025.

31 In January 2024, a group of prominent Israelis wrote to the attorney general calling for intervention to stop the normalisation of genocidal language in political and public discourse. See Emma Graham-Harrison and Quique Kierszenbaum, 'Israeli public figures accuse judiciary of ignoring incitement to genocide in Gaza', *The Guardian*, 3 January 2024, https://www.theguardian.com/world/2024/jan/03/israeli-public-figures-accuse-judiciary-of-ignoring-incitement-to-genocide-in-gaza, accessed 31 March 2025.

32 'Palestine (State of) 2023', Amnesty International, https://www.amnesty.org/en/location/middle-east-and-north-africa/middle-east/palestine-state-of/report-palestine-state-of/, accessed 17 March 2025.

33 Figures sourced from UN OCHA.

34 Arwa Mahdawi, 'We are witnessing the final stage of genocide in Gaza', *The Guardian*, 6 November 2024, https://www.theguardian.com/commentisfree/2024/nov/06/we-are-witnessing-the-final-stage-of-genocide-in-gaza, accessed 31 March 2025.

35 '10,000 people feared buried under rubble of Gaza', UN News, 2 May 2024, https://news.un.org/en/story/2024/05/1149256, accessed 31 March 2025.

36 Rasha Khatib, Martin McKee and Salim Yusuf, 'Counting the dead in Gaza: difficult but essential', *The Lancet* 404:10449 (2024), 237–8.

37 Figure sourced from remarks by Rosalia Bollen, UNICEF Communication Specialist, at UN Press Briefing in Geneva, 20 December 2024.

38 'RSF's 2024 Round-up: journalism suffers exorbitant human cost due to conflicts and repressive regimes', Reporters Without Borders

(RSF), https://rsf.org/en/rsf-s-2024-round-journalism-suffers-exorbitant-human-cost-due-conflicts-and-repressive-regimes, accessed 17 March 2025. See also '104 journalists killed this year, according to the IFJ', International Federation of Journalists, 11 December 2024, https://www.ifj.org/media-centre/news/detail/category/press-releases/article/104-journalists-killed-this-year-according-to-the-ifj, accessed 20 March 2025.

39 Nick Turse, *News Graveyards: How Dangers to War Reporters Endanger the World*, Watson Institute for International & Public Affairs, Brown University, 1 April 2025.

40 Mohamed Moawad (@moawady), 'Here is Ismail's tribute to himself and the dying humanity', X, 31 July 2024, https://x.com/moawady/status/1818669828841890088, accessed 17 March 2025.

41 Joint statement by Al-Haq, Al Mezan Center for Human Rights, Defense for Children International-Palestine, Palestinian Centre for Human Rights and the International Federation for Human Rights, 22nd session of the Assembly of Parties to the Rome Statute of the International Criminal Court, New York, 8 December 2023.

42 See for example 'Jewish survivors and descendants of survivors of Nazi genocide unequivocally condemn the massacre of Palestinians in Gaza', https://www.ictuni.org/sites/default/files/publications/full_page_b_tel_final_final.pdf, accessed 17 March 2025. See also 'Ten Holocaust survivors condemn Israel's Gaza genocide', *Mondoweiss*, 22 June 2024, https://mondoweiss.net/2024/06/ten-holocaust-survivors-condemn-israels-gaza-genocide/, accessed 31 March 2025. Human Rights Watch co-founder Aryeh Neier, himself a Holocaust survivor, has also accused Israel of committing genocide in Gaza; see Aryeh Neier, 'Is Israel committing genocide?', *New York Review of Books*, 6 June 2024, https://www.nybooks.com/articles/2024/06/06/is-israel-committing-genocide-aryeh-neier/, accessed 31 March 2025.

43 International Court of Justice, Order of 26 January 2024, Document 192-20240126-ORD-01-00-EN.

44 Report of the Special Rapporteur on the situation of human rights in the Palestinian territory occupied since 1967 to Human Rights Council, A/HRC/55/73, 24 March 2024.

45 Report of the Special Committee to Investigate Israeli Practices Affecting the Human Rights of the Palestinian People and Other Arabs of the Occupied Territories, A/79/363, 20 September 2024; '"You feel like you are subhuman": Israel's genocide against Palestinians in Gaza', Amnesty International, December 2024, https://www.amnesty.org/en/documents/mde15/8668/2024/en/, accessed 13 March 2025; Human Rights Watch, 'Extermination and acts of genocide: Israel deliberately depriving Palestinians in Gaza of

water', Human Rights Watch, 19 December 2024, http://hrw.org/
report/2024/12/19/extermination-and-acts-genocide/israel-
deliberately-depriving-palestinians-gaza, accessed 13 March 2025;
'Israel's unfolding crime of genocide of the Palestinian people & US
failure to prevent and complicity in genocide', Center for
Constitutional Rights, 18 October 2023, https://ccrjustice.org/
israel-s-unfolding-crime-genocide-palestinian-people-us-failure-
prevent-and-complicity-genocide, accessed 31 March 2025.

46 Although Sinwar and Haniyeh were included on the prosecutor's
original list, by the time the ICC issued the arrest warrants they
had both been assassinated. See Statement of ICC Prosecutor Karim
A. A. Khan KC: Applications for arrest warrants in the situation in
the State of Palestine, 24 May 2024; 'Situation in the State of
Palestine: ICC Pre-Trial Chamber I rejects the State of Israel's
challenges to jurisdiction and issues warrants of arrest for Benjamin
Netanyahu and Yoav Gallant', International Criminal Court, 21
November 2024, https://www.icc-cpi.int/news/situation-state-
palestine-icc-pre-trial-chamber-i-rejects-state-israels-challenges;
'Situation in the State of Palestine: ICC Pre-Trial Chamber I issues
warrant of arrest for Mohammad Diab Ibrahim al-Masri (Deif)',
International Criminal Court, 21 November 2024, https://www.
icc-cpi.int/news/situation-state-palestine-icc-pre-trial-chamber-i-
issues-warrant-arrest-mohammed-diab-ibrahim; both accessed 31
March 2025.

47 On the ethnic cleansing campaign in northern Gaza in late 2024,
see 'Zoom-in 3: the ethnic cleansing campaign in northern Gaza,
October–December 2024', 5 December 2024, https://witnessing-
the-gaza-war.com/zoom-in-3-the-ethnic-cleansing-campaign-in-
north-gaza-5-12-24/, accessed 17 March 2025.

48 On the Generals' Plan and its possible application in north Gaza,
see Samer Jaber, 'The Israeli "General's Plan" for northern Gaza is
unlikely to succeed', Al Jazeera, 16 October 2024, https://www.
aljazeera.com/opinions/2024/10/16/the-israeli-generals-plan-for-
northern-gaza-is-unlikely-to-succeed; Nadav Rapaport, 'What is
Israel's "Generals' Plan" and what does it mean for the war on
Gaza?', Middle East Eye, 15 October 2024, https://www.
middleeasteye.net/explainers/israel-gaza-palestine-what-generals-plan;
Bethan McKernan, '"Israel is trying to erase our presence":
Palestinians say "generals' plan" to clear north Gaza is under way',
The Guardian, 26 October 2024, https://www.theguardian.com/
world/2024/oct/26/israel-generals-plan-clear-north-gaza-palestinians;
all accessed 31 March 2025.

49 Eiland wrote about this in his aforementioned Yedioth Ahronoth op-ed.

50 Adam Makary and Nidal al-Mughrabi, 'Thousands trapped in Jabalia camp as Israel escalates deadly attacks in northern Gaza', Reuters, 13 October 2024, https://www.reuters.com/world/middle-east/thousands-said-trapped-jabalia-camp-israel-escalates-attacks-northern-gaza-2024-10-11/, accessed 31 March 2025.

51 Sarah Fowler, 'I went through hell, says elderly hostage released by Hamas', BBC News, 24 October 2023, https://www.bbc.co.uk/news/world-middle-east-67204479, accessed 31 March 2025, including a video of Lifshitz's release.

52 See reporting via https://www.ynet.co.il/news/article/ryoa9z1rr, 24 September 2024, accessed 16 April 2025 [Hebrew].

53 Bernard Avishai, 'Why Netanyahu won't cease fire', *New Yorker*, 8 October 2024, https://www.newyorker.com/news/the-lede/why-netanyahu-wont-cease-fire, accessed 31 March 2025.

54 Irfan, 'Why Palestinians could be facing another Nakba'.

55 Hanna Duggal and Marium Ali, 'Mapping 1,400 Israeli settler attacks in the West Bank over the past year', Al Jazeera, 10 October 2024, https://www.aljazeera.com/news/2024/10/10/mapping-1400-settler-attacks-in-the-occupied-west-bank-over-the-past-year, accessed 31 March 2025. See also 'How Israel is arming Israeli settlers', Visualizing Palestine, https://visualizingpalestine.org/visual/how-israel-is-arming-israeli-settlers/, accessed 17 March 2025.

56 Figures sourced from OCHA OPT.

57 Displacement figures: UNHCR; Norwegian Refugee Council. For death tolls, see 'Hezbollah says Israel "cannot impose conditions" for truce'; 'Israeli attack kills 3 more Lebanese soldiers as death toll passes 40'; Efrati; Fabian; Mroue and Lidman.

58 Hugo Bachega and Raffi Berg, 'Israeli troops stay inside south Lebanon after withdrawal deadline', BBC News, 18 February 2025, https://www.bbc.co.uk/news/articles/cn04lllp2zwo, accessed 31 March 2025.

59 UN Secretary-General, 'Note to correspondents: Syria', 12 December 2024, https://www.un.org/sg/en/content/sg/note-correspondents/2024-12-12/note-correspondents-syria, accessed 31 March 2025.

60 Lucas Lilieholm, Helen Regan, Sana Noor Haq, Caitlin Danaher, Tori B. Powell, Lauren Said-Moorhouse and Jack Forrest, 'January 15, 2025 Gaza ceasefire deal news', CNN, 16 January 2025, https://edition.cnn.com/world/live-news/israel-hamas-gaza-ceasefire-hostages-01-15-24/index.html, accessed 2 April 2025. Lorenzo Tondo and Sufian Taha, '"My arrest was unjustified:" released Palestinians decry their imprisonment', *The Guardian*, 20 January 2025, https://www.theguardian.com/world/2025/jan/20/my-arrest-

was-illogical-released-palestinians-decry-their-imprisonment, accessed
31 March 2025.

61 Rasha Jalal, '"They tried to break our morale in every possible
way": freed Palestinian women prisoners reveal torture in Israeli
jails', *New Arab*, 24 January 2025, https://www.newarab.com/
features/freed-palestinian-women-speak-torture-israeli-prisons,
accessed 31 March 2025. On the systemic mistreatment of
Palestinians in Israeli jails, see 'Welcome to hell: the Israeli prison
system as a network of torture camps', B'Tselem, August 2024,
https://www.btselem.org/sites/default/files/publications/202408_
welcome_to_hell_eng.pdf, accessed 31 March 2025.

62 'Four released Palestinians in critical condition, hospitalised in
Ramallah', Al Jazeera, 15 February 2025, https://www.aljazeera.
com/news/2025/2/15/it-was-hell-released-palestinian-prisoners-in-
poor-health-conditions, accessed 31 March 2025.

63 Israel has stated that the Bibas children were murdered by Hamas,
while Hamas has countered that they were victims of an Israeli
bombing. At the time of writing definitive evidence has not been
released into the public domain.

64 Danielle Greyman-Kennard, 'Red Cross demand Hamas give
hostages "dignified and private" release', *Jerusalem Post*, 8 February
2025, https://www.jpost.com/israel-news/article-841205, accessed
31 March 2025.

65 Gallant made this admission in an interview on the *Call Me Back*
podcast in February 2025, accessible via https://www.youtube.
com/watch?v=aPEPztvsJGQ, accessed 2 April 2025. See also
Muhammad Shehada, 'Is Israel weaponizing the tragic deaths of
the Bibas children?', Zeteo, 31 January 2025, https://zeteo.com/p/
is-israel-weaponizing-bibas-children-deaths, accessed
2 April 2025.

66 Jessica Steinberg, 'Family of freed hostage Yarden Bibas: He asks
about wife and sons, we have no answers', *Times of Israel*, 4
February 2025, https://www.timesofisrael.com/family-of-freed-
hostage-yarden-bibas-he-asks-about-wife-and-sons-we-have-no-
answers/#:~:text=Yarden%20asks%20about%20them%20and,save%20
his%20wife%20and%20sons, accessed 2 April 2025.

67 Sophie Tanno, Mick Krever and Mohammed Tawfeeq, 'Pale, gaunt
Israeli hostages freed from Gaza captivity as scores of Palestinian
prisoners released under hostage deal', CNN, 9 February 2025,
https://edition.cnn.com/2025/02/08/middleeast/hostages-release-
ifth-round-israel-hamas-ceasefire-intl-hnk/index.html, accessed 2 April
2025; Jacqueline Howard, 'Freed Israeli hostage's British family
concerned over gaunt appearance', BBC News, 8 February 2025,

https://www.bbc.co.uk/news/articles/c2l0yjnnd4go, accessed 2 April 2025; 'Cages, hunger, abuse: testimonies emerge from Israeli hostages freed Saturday from Hamas captivity', *Haaretz*, 1 February 2025, https://www.haaretz.com/israel-news/2025-02-01/ty-article-live/unrwa-chief-calls-claims-hostages-held-in-facilities-deeply-disturbing-shocking/00000194-bf47-dbd4-a9dc-bf4fc89d0000, accessed 31 March 2025.

68 Dalia Hatuqa, 'For Palestinians, this was never a ceasefire', *The Guardian*, 18 March 2025, https://www.theguardian.com/commentisfree/2025/mar/18/palestinians-ceasefire-israel-gaza, accessed 31 March 2025.

69 Emanuel Fabian, 'Israeli contractor mistakenly killed by IDF troops in Gaza, army says', *Times of Israel*, 28 January 2025, https://www.timesofisrael.com/israeli-contractor-mistakenly-killed-by-idf-troops-in-gaza-army-says/, accessed 31 March 2025.

70 See for example Amos Harel, 'Israel's renewed Gaza offensive exposes Netanyahu's real goal: political survival through endless war', *Haaretz*, 18 March 2025, https://www.haaretz.com/israel-news/2025-03-18/ty-article/.premium/israels-renewed-gaza-offensive-exposes-netanyahus-goal-political-survival-through-war/00000195-a83b-d922-af9d-be3f58640000; Emma Graham-Harrison, 'Netanyahu banks on political dividends as he restarts Gaza war', *The Guardian*, 18 March 2025, https://www.theguardian.com/world/2025/mar/18/netanyahu-banks-on-political-dividends-as-he-restarts-gaza-war-israel; both accessed 31 March 2025.

71 Statement by the UN Human Rights Office in the Occupied Palestinian Territory on the developments in Gaza, 21 March 2025.

72 Figure sourced from UNRWA. See UNRWA (@unrwa), '124,000 people in #Gaza have been displaced in just days', X, 24 March 2025, https://x.com/UNRWA/status/1904136670523396161, accessed 25 March 2025.

73 Figures sourced from OCHA OPT.

74 One account of life in Gaza since October 2023 is provided in Atef Abu Saif, *Don't Look Left: A Diary of Genocide* (Comma Press, 2024).

75 'Gaza Strip in maps: How a year of war has drastically changed life in the territory', BBC News, 7 October 2024.

76 Samer Sah, 'Infectious diseases are being allowed to run rampant in Gaza', *BMJ* 387:q2186 (2024), https://doi.org/10.1136/bmj.q2186.

77 Stephanie Hegarty, 'Born on 7 October: Gaza mum's fight to feed her baby', BBC News, 16 March 2024, https://www.bbc.co.uk/news/world-middle-east-68542331, accessed 31 March 2025.

78 '"Strong likelihood" of imminent famine in northern Gaza, food experts warn, as Israel continues siege', *The Guardian*, 9 November

2024, https://www.theguardian.com/world/2024/nov/09/strong-likelihood-of-imminent-famine-in-northern-gaza-food-experts-warn-as-israel-continues-siege, accessed 13 March 2025.

79 Aseel Mousa, "'I could no longer breastfeed": Gaza woman on two-month odyssey of displacement', *The Guardian*, 5 December 2023, https://www.theguardian.com/world/2023/dec/05/gaza-widow-mother-baby-israel-palestine, accessed 31 March 2025.

80 Julian Borger, 'Death feels imminent for 96% of children in Gaza, study finds', *The Guardian*, 11 December 2024, https://www.theguardian.com/world/2024/dec/11/death-feels-imminent-for-96-of-children-in-gaza-study-finds, accessed 31 March 2025.

81 'Gaza: Israeli war tactics condemned as aid still blocked from reaching north', UN News, 14 November 2024, https://news.un.org/en/story/2024/11/1156946, accessed 31 March 2025.

82 'Israel's siege now blocks 83% of food aid reaching Gaza, new data reveals', joint press release, 16 September 2024, available at https://www.nrc.no/news/2024/september/israels-siege-now-blocks-83-of-food-aid-reaching-gaza-new-data-reveals/, accessed 31 March 2025.

83 Statement by Principals of the Inter-Agency Standing Committee on the situation in the Occupied Palestinian Territory, 23 September 2024.

84 Annia Ciezadlo, 'The long and deadly war on humanitarian workers in Gaza', *New Republic*, 18 April 2024, https://newrepublic.com/article/180259/world-central-kitchen-unrwa-gaza-war-humanitarian-workers, accessed 31 March 2025.

85 Dan Sheehan, 'These are the poets and writers who have been killed in Gaza', *Literary Hub*, 21 December 2023, https://lithub.com/these-are-the-poets-and-writers-who-have-been-killed-in-gaza/, accessed 31 March 2025.

86 On the killing of Hind Rajab, her family and the PRCS paramedics, see Letter from the Special Rapporteur on extrajudicial, summary or arbitrary executions, the Chief-Rapporteur of the Working Group on Enforced or Involuntary Disappearances, the Special Rapporteur on the human rights of internally displaced persons, the Special Rapporteur on the promotion and protection of human rights and fundamental freedoms while countering terrorism, the Special Rapporteur on violence against women and girls, its causes and consequences and the Chief-Rapporteur of the Working Group on discrimination against women and girls, Ref. AL ISR 4/2024, 19 March 2024.

87 For these findings, see 'The killing of Hind Rajab', Forensic Architecture, 21 June 2024, https://forensic-architecture.org/investigation/the-killing-of-hind-rajab; Meg Kelly, Hajar Harb,

Louisa Loveluck, Miriam Berger and Cate Brown, 'Palestinian paramedics said Israel gave them safe passage to save a 6-year-old girl in Gaza. They were all killed', *Washington Post*, 16 April 2024, https://www.washingtonpost.com/world/interactive/2024/hind-rajab-israel-gaza-killing-timeline/; Stuart Ramsay, '"I'm so scared, please come": heartbreaking final moments of girl, 5, killed in Gaza', Sky News, 8 October 2024, https://news.sky.com/story/im-so-scared-please-come-heartbreaking-final-moments-of-girl-5-killed-in-gaza-13229813; all accessed 31 March 2025.

88   On the killing of Mohammad Bahr, see 'Israeli soldiers sicced a dog on a Gazan man with Down syndrome', *Democracy Now!*, 18 July 2024, https://www.democracynow.org/2024/7/18/headlines/israeli_soldiers_sicced_a_dog_on_a_gazan_man_with_down_syndrome; Fayha Shalash, 'Family remembers Muhammad, Gaza man with Down syndrome left to die by Israeli forces', *New Arab*, 22 July 2024, https://www.newarab.com/news/family-remembers-gaza-man-down-syndrome-killed-israel; Fergal Keane, 'Gaza man with Down's syndrome attacked by IDF dog and left to die, mother tells BBC', BBC News, 16 July 2024, https://www.bbc.co.uk/news/articles/cz9drj14e0lo; all accessed 31 March 2025.

89   On the killing of Sha'ban al-Dalou and his mother, see 'Shaban al-Dalou: the Palestinian teen burned to death in Israeli bombing', Al Jazeera, 15 October 2024, https://www.aljazeera.com/news/2024/10/15/shaban-al-dalou-the-palestinian-teen-burned-to-death-in-israeli-bombing; Abubaker Abed, 'Israel burnt Sha'ban al-Dalou alive. Palestine will rise from his ashes', *New Arab*, 28 October 2024, https://www.newarab.com/opinion/israel-burnt-shaban-al-dalou-alive-we-will-rise-his-ashes; Brett Wilkins, 'Palestinian seen burning alive in Israeli tent massacre identified', *Common Dreams*, 15 October 2024, https://www.commondreams.org/news/shaban-al-dalou; all accessed 31 March 2025.

90   See Hagar Shezaf and Michael Hauser Tov, 'Doctor at Israeli field hospital for detained Gazans: "we are all complicit in breaking the law"', *Haaretz*, 4 April 2024, https://www.haaretz.com/israel-news/2024-04-04/ty-article/.premium/doctor-at-idf-field-hospital-for-detained-gazans-we-are-all-complicit-in-breaking-law/0000018e-a59c-dfed-ad9f-afdfb5ce0000; 'Stripped down, blindfolded, held in diapers; Israeli whistleblowers detail abuse of Palestinians in shadowy detention center', CNN, 11 May 2024, https://edition.cnn.com/2024/05/10/middleeast/israel-sde-teiman-detention-whistleblowers-intl-cmd/index.html; Julia Frankel, '"They wanted to humiliate us." Palestinian women detained by Israel allege abuse in Israeli custody', AP News, https://apnews.com/article/israel-hamas-gaza-detainee-

palestinian-deaths-hospitals-51d4727a1365b9e06198579c3eb856f8, 2 March 2024; all accessed 2 April 2025.

91 'Israel's crimes against humanity in Gaza', Human Rights Watch, 14 November 2024, https://www.hrw.org/news/2024/11/14/israels-crimes-against-humanity-gaza, accessed 31 March 2025. See also 'Gaza: Possible atrocity crimes unfold, new UN report warns', UN News, 8 November 2024, https://news.un.org/en/story/2024/11/1156716; '"More than a human can bear": Israel's systematic use of sexual, reproductive and other forms of gender-based violence since October 2023', UN, 13 March 2025, https://www.un.org/unispal/document/report-of-commisison-of-inquiry-opt-13march2025/; both accessed 31 March 2025.

92 For a full database of Israeli war crimes in Gaza, see https://witnessing-the-gaza-war.com/

93 Laura Charney, 'It's time to stop ignoring the sexual violence happening in Gaza', *The Nation*, 7 May 2024, https://www.thenation.com/article/world/sexual-violence-gaza/, accessed 31 March 2025.

94 See Yaniv Kubovich and Michael Hauser Tov, 'Haaretz Investigation: Israeli army uses Palestinian civilians to inspect potentially booby-trapped tunnels in Gaza', *Haaretz*, 13 August 2024, https://www.haaretz.com/israel-news/2024-08-13/ty-article-magazine/.premium/idf-uses-gazan-civilians-as-human-shields-to-inspect-potentially-booby-trapped-tunnels/00000191-4c84-d7fd-a7f5-7db6b99e0000, accessed 31 March 2025; Mick Krever, Jeremy Diamond and Abeer Salman, 'The Israeli military has used Palestinians as human shields in Gaza, soldier and former detainees say', CNN, 24 October 2025, https://edition.cnn.com/2024/10/24/middleeast/palestinians-human-shields-israel-military-gaza-intl/index.html, accessed 2 April 2025; 'Palestinian in Gaza shot to death by Israeli commander while assisting IDF forces, report says', *Haaretz*, 7 January 2025, https://www.haaretz.com/israel-news/2025-01-07/ty-article/palestinian-in-gaza-shot-to-death-by-israeli-commander-while-assisting-idf-report-says/00000194-41c0-dfbb-a7bc-6ff647500000, accessed 2 April 2025; 'In Gaza, almost every IDF platoon keeps a human shield, a sub-army of Palestinian slaves', *Haaretz*, 30 March 2025, https://www.haaretz.com/opinion/2025-03-30/ty-article-opinion/.premium/in-gaza-almost-every-idf-platoon-keeps-a-human-shield-a-sub-army-of-palestinian-slaves/00000195-e627-deaf-a397-f6674e390000, accessed 2 April 2025. For video footage, see https://www.aljazeera.net/news/2024/6/30/%D8%B9%D8%A7%D8%AC%D9%84-%D8%A7%D9%84%D8%AC%D8%B2%D9%8A%D8%B1%D8%A9-%D8%AA%D8%AD%D8%B5%D9%84-%D8%B9%D9%84%D9%89-%D8%B5%D9%88%D8%B1-%D8%AA%D8%B8%D9%87%D8%B1-%D8%A7%D8%B3%D8%AA%

D8%AE%D8%AF%D8%A7%D9%85, accessed 17 March 2025
[Arabic].

95   Yuval Abraham, 'Expel all Palestinians from Gaza, recommends
Israeli gov't ministry', *+972*, 30 October 2023, https://
www.972mag.com/intelligence-ministry-gaza-population-transfer/,
accessed 31 March 2025. The original text of the white paper is
available at https://www.mekomit.co.il/%d7%94%d7%9e%d7%a1%d7
%9e%d7%9a-%d7%94%d7%9e%d7%9c%d7%90-%d7%a9%d7%9c-
%d7%9e%d7%a9%d7%a8%d7%93-%d7%94%d7%9e%d7%95%d7%93
%d7%99%d7%a2%d7%99%d7%9f-%d7%9b%d7%99%d7%91%d
7%95%d7%a9-%d7%a2%d7%96%d7%94-%d7%95/, accessed 25
March 2025 [Hebrew].

96   Danny Danon and Ram Ben-Barak, 'The West should welcome Gaza
refugees', *Wall Street Journal*, 13 November 2023, https://www.wsj.
com/opinion/the-west-should-welcome-gaza-refugees-asylum-seekers-
hamas-terrorism-displacement-5d2b5890, accessed 31 March 2025.

97   Jonathan Shamir, 'Israel's "humanitarian" expulsion', *Jewish Currents*,
12 December 2023, https://jewishcurrents.org/israels-humanitarian-
expulsion, accessed 31 March 2025. See also Ben Reiff, 'Israel's
return to war is a prelude to mass expulsion', *+972*, 18 March
2025, https://www.972mag.com/israel-trump-gaza-war-mass-
expulsion/, accessed 31 March 2025.

98   See for example 'Is Trump planning to help Israel "deport"
Palestinians in Gaza to Indonesia?', *New Arab*, 20 January 2025,
https://www.newarab.com/news/trump-planning-deport-
palestinians-gaza-indonesia; 'Trump envoy floats plan to relocate
Gaza civilians to Indonesia – report', *Jerusalem Post*, 20 January 2025,
https://www.jpost.com/israel-news/article-838293; Josef Federman,
Matthew Lee and Samy Magdy, 'US and Israel look to Africa for
moving Palestinians uprooted from Gaza', AP, 14 March 2025,
https://apnews.com/article/israel-palestinians-gaza-trump-
somaliland-sudan-somalia-575e03aaa0c487bae2fbadfdef8f5ca3; Jason
Burke and Mark Townsend, 'Sudan rejects US request to discuss
taking in Palestinians under Trump's Gaza plan', *The Guardian*, 14
March 2025, https://www.theguardian.com/us-news/2025/mar/14/
sudan-rejects-us-request-discuss-taking-palestinians-donald-trump-
gaza-plan; Anne Irfan and Jo Kelcey, 'Trump plans to "permanently
resettle" Palestinians outside Gaza – the very reason UNRWA was
originally created', *The Conversation*, 6 February 2025, https://
theconversation.com/trump-plans-to-permanently-resettle-
palestinians-outside-gaza-the-very-reason-unrwa-was-originally-
created-249185; all accessed 31 March 2025; Barak Ravid, 'Scoop:
Israeli Mossad asks African countries to take Palestinians from Gaza',

Axios, 28 March 2025, https://www.axios.com/2025/03/28/israel-move-palestinians-gaza-indonesia-somalia, accessed 2 April 2025.

99 On these protests, see Ruwaida Amer, '"We want to live:" Rage at Israel fuses with ire at Hamas as protests rock Gaza', +972, 27 March 2025, https://www.972mag.com/gaza-protests-war-israel-hamas/, accessed 2 April 2025.

100 Katz's statement is accessible via https://www.youtube.com/watch?v=JEGsu6RaryE. See also: Dahlia Scheindlin, 'Why don't Gazans rise up and oust Hamas? Dismantling a deeply dishonest claim', Haaretz, 20 March 2025, https://www.haaretz.com/israel-news/2025-03-20/ty-article-magazine/.premium/why-dont-gazans-rise-up-and-oust-hamas-dismantling-a-deeply-dishonest-claim/00000195-b429-d5aa-a3fd-bf2dd5e90000, accessed 2 April 2025.

101 Netanyahu's comments were first reported by journalist Jeremy Scahill, via https://x.com/jeremyscahill/status/1906336818917736599. Katz's statement is accessible via https://www.youtube.com/watch?v=JEGsu6RaryE. See also Dahlia Scheindlin, 'Why don't Gazans rise up and oust Hamas? Dismantling a deeply dishonest claim', Haaretz, 20 March 2025, https://www.haaretz.com/israel-news/2025-03-20/ty-article-magazine/.premium/why-dont-gazans-rise-up-and-oust-hamas-dismantling-a-deeply-dishonest-claim/00000195-b429-d5aa-a3fd-bf2dd5e90000; Lorenzo Tondo, 'Netanyahu repeats threat to seize territory in Gaza as anti-Hamas protests continue', The Guardian, 26 March 2025; both accessed 2 April 2025.

102 Quoted in Mahmoud Mushtaha, '"Gaza isn't for sale": Palestinians dismiss Trump's ethnic cleansing plan', +972, 5 February 2025, https://www.972mag.com/gaza-trump-ethnic-cleansing-refusal/, accessed 31 March 2025.

INDEX